The publisher and the University of California Press Foundation gratefully acknowledge the generous support of the Robert and Meryl Selig Endowment Fund in Film Studies, established in memory of Robert W. Selig.

The First True Hitchcock

Edward McKnight Kauffer (1890–1954): Poster design for *The Lodger*, 1926. Tempera on paper; 29¼ × 21¾ in. (74.3 × 55.2 cm). Museum of Modern Art, 389.1939. Gift of the artist. Digital image © 2021 Museum of Modern Art, New York/Scala, Florence. Original © Simon Rendall.

The First True Hitchcock

THE MAKING OF A FILMMAKER

Henry K. Miller

UNIVERSITY OF CALIFORNIA PRESS

University of California Press
Oakland, California

© 2022 by Henry K. Miller

Library of Congress Cataloging-in-Publication Data

Names: Miller, Henry K. (Editor), author.
Title: The first true Hitchcock : the making of a filmmaker / Henry K. Miller.
Description: Oakland, California : University of California Press, [2022] |
    Includes bibliographical references and index.
Identifiers: LCCN 2021033060 (print) | LCCN 2021033061 (ebook) |
    ISBN 9780520343559 (cloth) | ISBN 9780520343566 (paperback) |
    ISBN 9780520975033 (epub)
Subjects: LCSH: Hitchcock, Alfred, 1899–1980—Criticism and interpretation. |
    Lodger (Motion picture : 1927) | Motion pictures—Production and
    direction—United States—History. | BISAC: PERFORMING ARTS /
    Individual Director (see also BIOGRAPHY & AUTOBIOGRAPHY /
    Entertainment & Performing Arts) | PERFORMING ARTS / Film /
    Genres / Horror
Classification: LCC PN1997.L646 M55 2022 (print) | LCC PN1997.L646 (ebook) |
    DDC 791.4302/33092—dc23
LC record available at https://lccn.loc.gov/2021033060
LC ebook record available at https://lccn.loc.gov/2021033061

Manufactured in the United States of America

30 29 28 27 26 25 24 23 22
10 9 8 7 6 5 4 3 2 1

Contents

	Preface	vii
	Map of London, 1926–1927	xii
1.	The Embankment at Midnight	1
2.	The Reputation and the Myth	25
3.	No Old Masters	49
4.	The Autocrat of the Studio	78
5.	To Catch a Thief	102
6.	The First True Hitchcock	129
7.	Stories of the Days to Come	157
8.	Wilshire Palms	180
	Notes	203
	Bibliography	225
	Index	229

Preface

The story of the making of *The Lodger* has been told many times. Hitchcock used it as a model of suspense, and to illustrate the role of blind chance in his life. It goes like this: While the distributor C. M. Woolf watched the film unspool, forewarned by his underlings that it was no good, Hitchcock and his assistant director and fiancée Alma Reville tramped the streets of London in an agony that was not relieved when they returned to the studio to be told that *The Lodger* was being shelved. It was Hitchcock's third film, and his career was in the balance. But a few months later Woolf had a change of heart. *The Lodger* was shown to critics in September 1926 and acclaimed as the greatest British picture ever made. For Hitchcock himself it was "the first true Hitchcock movie."

Nevertheless, *The Lodger* is also a silent movie, not in pristine condition, and known largely as a handful of stills and a few clips. Such a film, from the land and the age of P. G. Wodehouse, might well have been put on the shelf in a fit of distemper, then taken off it on a whim. Film history is full of harmless apocrypha of this kind, but the story of *The Lodger* is the seed of something more substantial. On occasion Hitchcock admitted that one or two changes were made to the film before its belated unveiling, and the editor responsible for these improvements, Ivor Montagu, was happy to provide the fine-grained detail that Hitchcock's version of the story left out. Montagu's account has been highly influential on our understanding of Hitchcock's formation as a director.

In a pair of essays in his book *Paris Hollywood*, essays which led me to study this period, Peter Wollen made the particular story of Hitchcock's exposure to the influence of German and Russian films at the storied Film Society, of which Montagu was chairman, an integral part of a wider perspective on class and culture in Britain.

My doubts about Hitchcock's story, and Montagu's additions to it, began to be confirmed in a series of fragmentary discoveries in the British Library Newspapers facility at Colindale, North West London, and in the special collections department of the British Film Institute, in 2006–7. I saw correspondence from one of Montagu's friends about his dealings with "Miss Reville," flashes of professional envy, esoterica about release dates. All PhDs must have a thesis, and mine was that the role of the Film Society had been exaggerated in a variety of ways. *The Lodger* served as a paradigm, and my discoveries helped me to make an alternative case. Still, it was a somewhat negative case. If not under the tutelage of the Film Society, how *had* Hitchcock become Hitchcock?

Hitchcock himself tells us very little. All the accumulated interviews add up to not much, and without diaries or letters his inner life remains a blank. The solution devised by his best-known biographer Donald Spoto was to treat the films as "astonishingly personal documents." Hitchcock's outer, social life is almost as hard to make out, especially for the years before he joined the film business. The extent of his piety, as a Catholic in a more or less Protestant, increasingly irreligious country, is hard to gauge. He seems to have managed never to have expressed a political opinion. On the subject of films, and the books and plays that inspired them, he was more forthcoming, but even here the texture of his life as a filmgoer remains out of reach.

By the time he made *The Lodger*, in early 1926, Hitchcock was becoming a public figure, and he may be observed in the act of filming. But the first true Hitchcock was not brought to the screen by Hitchcock alone—nor indeed by Hitchcock and Montagu, or any other combination of individuals. What happened in the summer of 1926, between *The Lodger*'s shelving and unshelving, involves Harold Lloyd, the British government's deliberations on free trade, and a fortune in South African diamonds. Or, to move from the specific to the general, it involves Britain's place in the world after the catastrophe of the Great War, its fraying Empire, its relationship with the newly great power across the Atlantic.

"Only from about the year 1926 did the features of the post-war world begin clearly to emerge," wrote T. S. Eliot in 1939, "and not only in the sphere of politics. From about that date one began slowly to realize that the intellectual and artistic output of the previous seven years had been rather the last efforts of an old world, than the struggles of a new." Though it was probably not at the forefront of Eliot's mind, this was true of the sphere of cinema. A salient feature of the early postwar period, as seen from London, was the virtual supremacy of the American film. But in the year between the start of production on *The Lodger* and its general release in early 1927, that supremacy was made to become mere advantage. In this respect, and in others, the making of *The Lodger* straddled old and new worlds.

Hitchcock had served his apprenticeship in the old world, in the years of American supremacy. As Wollen wrote in his essay "Hitch: A Tale of Two Cities," Hitchcock's London "was closely connected to Los Angeles" from the start. He was a boy when the picture theaters began to be built before the war, a youth when Mary Pickford became the world's sweetheart, and barely of voting age when he got his first film job—at an American studio in London. Most of the films that he worked on in the early 1920s, as he rose through the ranks in a British film industry that was struggling to survive, had American stars, including the first two features he directed. Eventually, in the year Eliot made his pronouncement, Hitchcock went to Hollywood, a decision that now seems as natural as Hollywood's dominance over the world's screens, and of a piece with it. Shortly afterward he attempted to remake *The Lodger*, his "story of the London fog," as it was subtitled, in a city renowned for its sun.

In the narrative that follows I have tried to show Hollywood's dominance in a less familiar light, as it might have appeared to Hitchcock at its commencement. A discovery in the British Library's Newsroom in 2018 provided me with Hitchcock's account of his first visit to Los Angeles in 1938, including what amounts to his attempt to treat the unfamiliar city as if it were London. The distance between the studio where *The Lodger* was made and the cinema where it opened is about three and a half miles, and the scene of action is laid, for the most part, between these two points. If the disparate factors bearing on the film's production were global and extended well beyond the boundaries of the film business, their local manifestations were interwoven with the sites of the film's making in the fabric of the city Hitchcock grew up in.

Colindale, a great hangar full of old newspapers, is no more. This book began in the age of microfilm, but it could not have been completed without online access to digitized newspapers, not least because it was finished during the pandemic year 2020. Online research has its limits, however, and I have been more than usually reliant on the often invisible work of archivists and librarians, who have acted as Ingrid Bergman to my Cary Grant, going into the vaults and bookstacks while their buildings were closed to visitors.

About a week into the first British lockdown, I was given a Harry Ransom Center Research Fellowship in the Humanities, with a travel stipend from the Robert De Niro Endowed Fund, which would have flown me to Austin, Texas. This has proved impossible to take up, and I could not have completed the final chapter without the help of the Harry Ransom Center's film curator Steven L. Wilson. Also in the United States, I am indebted to Angela Maani of the California State Library, Patrick Kerwin of the Library of Congress, Kristine Krueger and Faye Thompson of the Margaret Herrick Library, and to Christina Lane. Closer to home, I would like to thank Louise North of the BBC archives in Caversham, Sue Crawford of the University of Reading, Lisa McDermott of Hackney Archives, Domniki Papadimitriou and Alison Zammer of Cambridge University Library, and Simon Rendall, who kindly gave permission for the use of his grandfather's design on the cover.

Within the academy thanks are due to Ian Christie and Laura Mulvey of Birkbeck College, where I wrote the thesis that this book grew of; to Charles Barr and Lawrence Napper, who examined it; and to Alison Butler, Sid Gottlieb, and Jan Olsson, who read the book in manuscript. In and around the British Film Institute I have to thank Rebecca Barden, Will Fowler, Bryony Dixon, James Bell, Pamela Hutchinson, Nathalie Morris, Jonny Davies, Victoria Bennett, and Storm Patterson. In pre-pandemic times I benefitted from travel grants from the Paul Mellon Centre for Studies in British Art, and the Bill Douglas Cinema Museum in Exeter. For getting the book onto the page, I would like to thank Kate Hoffman, Jon Dertien, and Gary J. Hamel.

Finally, I want to extend my gratitude to Raina Polivka and Madison Wetzell at University of California Press, and to my parents.

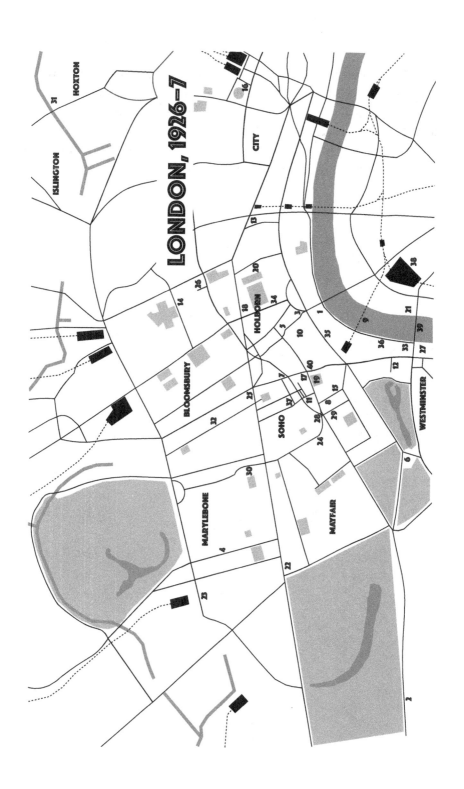

LONDON, 1926-7

ISLINGTON

HOXTON

31

CITY

13

MARYLEBONE

BLOOMSBURY

4

30

32

25

26

14

23

37

7

11

24

28

8

29

SOHO

15

HOLBORN

18

20

34

5

3

10

35

40

17

19

1

9

36

33

27

16

38

21

39

12

MAYFAR

6

WESTMINSTER

22

2

1. 2LO, Savoy Hill
2. Albert Hall
3. 11 Aldwych, home of Ivor Novello
4. Baker St.
5. Bow St. police court
6. Buckingham Palace
7. Cambridge Circus
8. Capitol, Haymarket
9. Charing Cross Bridge
10. Covent Garden
11. 6 Dansey Yard; Fifty-Fifty Club, 37 Wardour St.; Legrain's, 21 Gerrard St.
12. 10 Downing St.; Foreign Office
13. *Evening Standard* building, Shoe Lane
14. 14 Guilford St., home of Iris Barry
15. Haymarket Theatre
16. Henley's Telegraph Works, Blomfield St.
17. Hippodrome
18. Holborn Empire
19. Leicester Square
20. Lincoln's Inn, home of Ivor Montagu
21. London County Hall
22. Marble Arch Pavilion, Oxford St.
23. Marylebone Rd.
24. New Gallery, Regent St.
25. New Oxford Theatre, Oxford St.
26. Nonesuch Press, 16 Great James St.
27. Palace of Westminster
28. Piccadilly Circus
29. Plaza, Lower Regent St.
30. Polytechnic, Regent St.
31. Poole St.
32. Scala, Charlotte St.
33. Scotland Yard
34. Stoll Picture Theatre, Kingsway
35. Tivoli, the Strand
36. Victoria Embankment
37. W. & F. Film Service, Wardour St.
38. Waterloo Station
39. Westminster Bridge
40. Wyndham's Theatre

1 The Embankment at Midnight

Earth had fairer things to show than the view from Westminster Bridge on the night of 24 February 1926. Wordsworth, at the start of the nineteenth century, could imagine the city asleep at dawn as one of nature's spectacles, silent and still; twentieth-century London, even at midnight, was neither. The brightness in which the scene was steeped came not from any natural source, but from the beams of six massive arc lights, lined up along the parapet and directed toward the Victoria Embankment.

Down by the river's edge, a film journalist, on meeting a casting agent, "severely criticised the unconvincing appearance of the large crowd that had assembled, but was told that they were not professional but the real thing."[1] A. Jympson Harman, film critic of the *Evening News*, reported that police "were specially detailed, from midnight until six in the morning, to 'keep a ring' for the camera, and they even held up the trams while the cables were manipulated" for the lights.[2] Inside the ring was another crowd, this one of professional extras, and in the middle were actors: one playing a policeman, and one a reporter; one playing a witness, and another a corpse. The fog in which they were all enveloped, at the heart of a city synonymous with the stuff, had to be simulated.

FILM DRAMA ACTED ON THE EMBANKMENT.

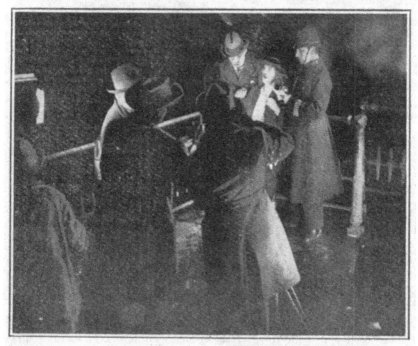

Dramatic scenes were enacted on the Embankment in the night for a film by Gainsborough Pictures. This shows the great thrill—the rescue of a woman from the Thames.

Daily Graphic, 26 February 1926. Reproduced by kind permission of the Syndics of Cambridge University Library.

"No one could have believed there was such a number of people with nothing to do at 2 a.m.," wrote Walter Mycroft in the following weekend's *Sunday Herald*, "but the director, Mr. Alfred Hitchcock, who is expected to do big things, was imperturbable—tactful and commanding by turns amid the unexpected crowd."[3] It was the first day of production on the first film Hitchcock would make in England. Later he would recall that "the thing I wanted above all else was to do a night scene in London, preferably on the Embankment. I wanted to silhouette the mass of Charing Cross Bridge against the sky. I wanted to get away from the (at that time) inevitable shot of Piccadilly Circus with hand-painted lights."[4] As Iris Barry reported in the *Daily Mail* on the morning of the shoot, he had been "out daily with his camera man in search of coffee-stalls, bits of the Embankment, and street corners for the exterior scenes of this new London murder mystery," *The Lodger*.[5]

Also behind the camera that night, though unmentioned in the press, was Hitchcock's assistant director, Alma Reville, recently profiled in *Picturegoer* magazine as a "super-woman, whose eye is sharper than an eagle's," and the occupant of a "unique position in European films."[6] The article ended with "two deadly secrets," one cryptic—"she possesses (but never wears) a pair of horn-rimmed glasses"—and one less so—"she has never had time to get married!" Around Christmas 1925, shortly after the article was published, during a rough crossing from Germany, where the pair of them had made two films almost back to back, and side by side, Hitchcock had proposed to her, and she, too seasick to speak, had made "an affirmative gesture."[7]

Neither of the two German films, *The Pleasure Garden* and *The Mountain Eagle*, had been released when the couple began work on *The Lodger*, but the first of them had been shown privately to the film critic of the *Express* newspapers, G. A. Atkinson. "The technical skill revealed in this film is superior, I think, to that shown in any film yet made by a British producer," he had written earlier in February.[8] "It is improbable that Mr. Hitchcock chose this hectic story of his own accord," Atkinson went on, "but the point is that he has produced it with remarkable power and imaginative resource."

About the same time, Hitchcock was made the subject of his own *Picturegoer* profile, three months after his fiancée, in which "the world's youngest film director"—he was twenty-six—was presented as "the man who starts on the bottom rung and achieves his aim purely by his own industry and enterprise."[9] At fifteen, wrote Cedric Belfrage, a studio publicist, "his education at an Art school was suddenly interrupted by the death of his father, and he was left alone—practically penniless." The adolescent Hitchcock had joined an advertising firm as a clerk, Belfrage continued, his hard work ensuring that he was soon "laying out and writing copy." Having gained a degree of financial security, he "began to take up the old dreams where they had been cut short years before—the old dreams of his old love, the kinema." At twenty, he won a job writing and designing title-cards in the editorial department of what Belfrage simply called "Famous."

Product of the merger in 1916 of the Jesse L. Lasky Feature Play Company and Adolph Zukor's Famous Players, "Famous" was Famous Players-Lasky, led by Zukor and increasingly known by the name and logo of its distribution arm, Paramount. By either name it was not merely a film studio, but a trust or combine, vertically integrated from where the cameras rolled to where the projectors whirred. Ten years after the merger, in the midst of a great scramble for possession of cinema chains, Paramount and a handful of rivals, chief among them Metro-Goldwyn-Mayer, dominated the screens of the United States, and their ambitions did not end at the three-mile limit.

Famous Players-Lasky had opened a studio at Poole Street, on the border of Hoxton and Islington, in 1920, partly to be close, as Lasky said at the time, to "famous British authors" and "famous British players" from the West End stage, and to film British stories "in their original settings."[10] Less conveniently, the studio was also, as one British trade paper pointed out, "not only well within the London fog-belt, but on the very banks of a canal."[11] Hitchcock would describe himself as American trained, and Belfrage pictured him seizing the opportunity "to stay down at the studio often for hours after his own work was finished for the day, to make himself familiar with the essentials of scenario writing and art direction," but the apprenticeship was brief. In February 1922, just months after perfecting the plant's fog-suppression apparatus, the Americans shipped out. Behind their decision was the realization that a film studio need not be anywhere in particular. In 1913, when Lasky's "director-general" Cecil B. DeMille arrived in Hollywood, still "bowered in orange and pepper trees," to shoot the longest film yet made there, he worked in the open air.[12] But in the month FP-L's London unit came home, less than a decade later, Lasky could write that "Los Angeles' sunshine is no longer a necessity; indeed many of our pictures in Hollywood are made entirely inside the Lasky studio by artificial light."[13]

Los Angeles had become the center of world film production in the interim, and if its sunshine was no longer a necessity, it was certainly no deterrent. The novice screenwriter Herman Mankiewicz, in California for the first time in February 1926, wrote to his wife, Sara, that it was "delight-ful beyond belief with its tropical vegetation and its mad, colored, pretty bungalows."[14] London—or Roman, or Russian—landmarks could be rec-reated on the Lasky lot, which by 1926 was spread over two city blocks bordered by Sunset Boulevard and Vine Street, now major thoroughfares in a Hollywood that had lost the scent of citrus. Writers more famous than Mankiewicz were prepared to come to it. Famous players, whether from the West End or Broadway, could be brought out too, but nor were they strictly a necessity. Rudolph Valentino, whose latest film *The Eagle* was playing all over London on the night of 24 February, had no such pedigree. And Hollywood was already attracting established talent from Europe—Ernst Lubitsch at Warner Brothers, Mauritz Stiller and Victor Sjöström at MGM. February 1926 saw the premiere of the first American film of their compatriot Greta Garbo, *Torrent*.

Though Paramount had abandoned its London studio, it had not abandoned London. On the morning of the 24th, journalists were shown around its new West End "shop window," the two-thousand-seat Plaza cin-ema, within sight of Piccadilly Circus on Lower Regent Street. At the press lunch afterward, held in the Kit-Cat Club beneath the Capitol cinema, in nearby Haymarket, J. C. Graham, Paramount's London chief, tried to impress upon his audience the venue's Britishness. But as part of a chain that ran, in the evocative phrase of Paramount's historian, "from Vienna to San Francisco," the Plaza was inescapably an emblem of the American cinema's global supremacy.[15] Its foyer, reported the *Star* that evening, was filled with "handsome antique Italian furniture," while its ceiling conjured up "memories of decorations in the Palace of Versailles and the Louvre."[16] The construction of this ostentatious gallimaufry had been overseen by Al Kaufman, Zukor's brother-in-law and fixer since their days in the Chicago fur trade. Twenty years earlier, in the mid-1900s, Kaufman had managed Zukor's first nickelodeon on Union Square, in the middle of immigrant Manhattan, and was on good terms with the neighborhood's gangsters. Now he aimed to entice the carriage trade.

It was a development that Hitchcock regarded with ambivalence. When François Truffaut, in their famous interview, made his notorious remark on the "incompatibility between the terms 'cinema' and 'Britain,'" Hitchcock's reply went into the question of cinema's changing status in the 1920s.[17] Whereas films had once been "held in contempt by the intellectuals," and "No well-bred English person would be seen going into a cinema," he recalled, in the mid-1920s the tide began to turn.[18] The Plaza provided his example. "The management set up four rows of seats in the mezzanine which were very expensive, and they called that section 'Millionaires' Row.'" Indeed, as the *Star* reported, its 7s, 6d seats were "so spaciously arranged that the wearer of a crinoline skirt could move comfortably between the rows." Readers of the *New Yorker* learned that "the most stirring event of the month is the appearance in *The Times* of an editorial on the opening of London's new movie cathedral, the Plaza. What the editorial said is beside the point."[19]

Poole Street, Britain's best-equipped studio, had not lain fallow in the four years since the Americans' departure, but had been leased, along with its complement of American-trained technicians, to a variety of British producers, most consistently Michael Balcon, who had been quick to notice Hitchcock's promise and ambition. At twenty-three, as Belfrage recounted, Hitchcock was "scenarist, art director and general assistant" to Balcon's chief director Graham Cutts, with Reville as second assistant and editor. Gainsborough Pictures, as their company was known from 1924, had done well to survive. British production was at a low ebb: of the 283 films offered for distribution—"trade-shown"—in the first half of 1926, 226 were American, 20 German, and 19 British; and those 19 had a slim chance of being seen widely or in the better and more profitable cinemas.[20] Many firms had gone under or were dormant.

Gainsborough, however, was flush with the success of Cutts's *The Rat*, which had opened in London in December 1925, then nationally in February 1926, and was still playing on the 24th. Its star and coauthor was Ivor Novello, a player who had become famous as a songwriter during the Great War, and was supposedly drawn into the film world after the director Louis Mercanton saw his photograph. Having tried and failed to establish a serious stage career, Novello and his friend Constance Collier—later to appear in *Rope*—had come up with *The Rat*, a "good old-fashioned melodrama," in his words, of the Parisian underworld.[21] Heedless of the critics' chortles, an audience of predominantly female film fans had flooded into theatreland to see it. Cutts's adaptation had needed the insurance policy of an American costar, Mae Marsh.

At the end of January 1926, Iris Barry reported in the *Daily Mail* that although "tempting offers of film work have recently been made to this actor by American film companies, in whose eyes he is the 'Latin Lover' type so popular on the screen," Novello had instead signed a contract with Gainsborough, the first fruit of which would be *The Lodger*.[22] It would not occupy all his energies. On the night of 24 February, a West End theater-goer could have chosen between two future Hitchcock films, *The Farmer's Wife* at the Court or Sean O'Casey's *Juno and the Paycock* at the Royalty, a small theater in Soho; or gone to see Noel Coward's *Hay Fever*, Tallulah Bankhead in *Scotch Mist*, a revival of J. M. Barrie's *Mary Rose* at the Haymarket—or Ivor Novello in *The Firebrand*, at Wyndham's. It would continue through most of the *Lodger* shoot.

Novello also had nighttime duties as part-owner of a Soho nightclub, the Fifty-Fifty, occupying the upper floors of 37 Wardour Street. Decorated with "life-size caricatures of famous contemporary stars," it had opened on Armistice Night 1924, "which in those crazy 'twenties," recalled Novello's business partner Henry Kendall, later to star in Hitchcock's *Rich and Strange*, "was an occasion for celebration."[23] Though it was intended to provide cheap meals for stage folk, the club had instantly been taken up by fashionable society. It had also attracted the less welcome attention of the police; "officers in plain clothes, with female companions" visited three times in the weeks before the *Lodger* shoot, as a prelude to a raid, which would come on the night of Saturday 27 February.[24]

Novello's costar, known simply as June—her surname, Tripp, had been excised by the impresario Charles B. Cochran on the grounds that it "sounds a bit comical for a dancer"—had been a fixture of the West End stage since childhood, and of the gossip columns more recently.[25] In January 1926, while performing nightly at the Hippodrome in *Mercenary Mary*, a musical comedy imported from Broadway, and rehearsing daily for another, *Kid Boots*, destined for the Winter Garden, she had collapsed on stage, suffering from appendicitis, an event that made the front page of the *Daily Express*. Two weeks later, the paper's theater columnist, Hannen Swaffer, wrote that she "will not be able to dance for six months" following her appendectomy, and that "her representatives are trying to find for her a straight play suitable to her unobtrusive charm."[26] June did not leave her nursing-home until early February—this too was widely reported—and then went to recuperate in the countryside. On the 17th, just seven days before Hitchcock set up his lights on Westminster Bridge, Swaffer reported that June was in Brighton—and that she "leaves in a few days for the Riviera."[27] It was there, by her own account, that she received a telegram from Novello with an offer of work. "No dancing required. You will act beautifully and we shall have fun."[28] With Novello and June in the lead roles, *The Lodger* was the first Gainsborough film without an American star.

Novello's apparently carefree attitude belied a need for respect. In the days between the Fifty-Fifty raid and his arrival, reportedly delayed by a bout of bronchitis, at Poole Street, he published an article in the *Daily Sketch* titled "Why I Loathe My Looks," ironically phrased but sincerely meant.

> Having always experienced a deep, though kindly, contempt for those mummers, pedestalled and aloof, known as "Matinée Idols," it is not without disgust and anger that I find myself having to struggle against what I might almost call a plot to cover me with the same inglorious treacle and impale my repute as an artist on a profile for which I am in no way responsible.[29]

Having claimed that he "lives for the theatre," and without bothering to mention his imminent employment in the cinema, Novello went on to declare that his "great ambition is to create Raskolnikov in 'Crime and Punishment.'"

A film adaptation of Dostoyevsky's novel, made in Berlin by Robert Wiene in the Expressionist style of his earlier film *The Cabinet of Dr. Caligari*, with players from Stanislavsky's Moscow Art Theatre, had recently been shown in London, and Novello is highly likely to have seen it. Its single screening, on 20 December 1925, at the New Gallery cinema in Regent Street, had been arranged by the Film Society, a new organization whose membership also included Hitchcock and Reville. Its principal object, according to a prospectus published that autumn, was to present films that the trade would not touch, or that the censor forbade, "to the most actively-minded people both inside and outside the film-world."[30] Founder members included H. G. Wells, George Bernard Shaw, and John Maynard Keynes. Hitchcock described it to Truffaut, in the course of the same exchange in which he discussed the Plaza, and with the same ambivalence, as "something for the intellectuals to do on Sunday afternoon."[31]

The Film Society's organizers included the critics Iris Barry and Walter Mycroft—both of them friends of Hitchcock and Reville's—and a number of other figures who would take part in the production of *The Lodger*. Novello was named in the weekly *Sphere* as one of the "inevitable celebrities" who attended its first performance in October 1925.[32] *Crime and Punishment* had been the centerpiece of its third. On that occasion the *Daily Graphic*'s correspondent described an audience composed of "men in brown jumpers, brown shirts, brown boots, and brown hats, and women in black jumpers, black bow ties, black boots and sloppy black hats," with a leavening of aristocrats.[33] "A feature of the performance," reported the *Westminster Gazette*'s society columnist, "was the absence of music, and the extraordinary number of people afflicted with coughs."[34]

Marie Belloc Lowndes's *The Lodger*, published as a short story in 1911 and as a novel in 1913, was not *Crime and Punishment*. Nor, however, was it a penny dreadful, though Lowndes feared it would be regarded as one.[35] Indeed, there were points of contact between the two books apart from their being about misanthropic lodging-house killers. What would become the most resonant image in Hitchcock's film appears in both. On the very first page of the short story, published in the American magazine *McClure's*, the landlady Mrs. Bunting hears or imagines hearing "her lodger's quick, singularly quiet—'stealthy,' she called it to herself—progress through the dark, fog-filled hall and up the staircase," and the same scene, which Lowndes recounted as having been the germ of her story, taken from life, occurs more than once in the book.[36] Meanwhile Raskolnikov, on the first page of Dostoyevsky's novel, is heard to "creep down the stairs like a cat and slip out unseen," and does the same again, "cautiously, noiselessly," when setting out with murderous intent later on. It was Hitchcock who chose to film the scene from above, with only the Lodger's hand visible on the banister. In January 1955, on his first substantial encounter with Truffaut and Chabrol, when asked whether he accepted the common perception of "le vrai Hitchcock," meaning a mixture of comedy and suspense, he said "I would be more interested in filming Dostoyevsky, *Crime and Punishment*, for example; that would be very easy for me."[37]

Lowndes's *The Lodger* was and continues to be known as a "Jack the Ripper" story, but almost all of it unfolds inside a house on Marylebone Road, on the northwestern fringe of the West End, and the murders—in the novel, though not in the short story—take place in roughly the same area. Jack the Ripper, however, was distinctly a creature of the East. The murders of 1888 were committed in or near Whitechapel, and the mass-produced and mass-disseminated image of the Ripper, from the first newspaper reports onward, exploited what was already popularly believed of the East End—teeming with immigrants, ridden with vice, its women-folk preyed upon by slumming aristocrats—and intensified it. Thus in D. W. Griffith's *Broken Blossoms*, from 1919, Limehouse, where Hitchcock had spent part of his childhood, was introduced in a subtitle as the place "where the Orient squats at the portals of the West."

The first murder in Hitchcock's *The Lodger*, by contrast, is discovered not at the portals but at the very center of the Empire on which the sun never set. The Victoria Embankment was itself, in the words of the historian G. M. Young, a "visible symbol" of "the conversion of the vast and shapeless city which Dickens knew—fog-bound and fever-haunted, brooding over its dark, mysterious river—into the imperial capital."[38] Dickens had died a few weeks before its opening, by Victoria's son, the future Edward VII, in 1870. Built on land reclaimed from the water, and displacing what had been a Dickensian mess of wharfs and warehouses downriver, to the great new docks past Limehouse, the Embankment was also an invisible sym-bol of London's modernity, containing a branch of the underground rail-way and electricity, water, and gas mains, while decorously concealing the city's main sewage pipe.

Rising above the tree-lined roadway, as inevitable an image of Lon-don as Piccadilly Circus, was Big Ben, more pedantically the clock tower of the Palace of Westminster, completed in 1859. The neo-Gothic palace itself contains the Houses of Parliament; the new Westminster Bridge, completed in 1862, replacing the one Wordsworth had crossed sixty years earlier, was expressly designed to complement it. As befitting the seat of a maritime empire in the electrical age, Big Ben was synchronized by telegraph signal with the Royal Observatory at Greenwich, since 1884 the source of standard time around the world. In Conrad's novel *The Secret Agent*, which Hitchcock would adapt as *Sabotage*, the titular agent's con-troller proposes an attack on the observatory, rather than a conventional political target, because it would strike at the "sacrosanct fetish" of the bourgeoisie—at "the source of their material prosperity." Since 1924 the chimes of Big Ben had been broadcast daily over the BBC's 2LO station, itself based just back from the Embankment at Savoy Hill. Westminster's dominion extended even over the fourth dimension and the ether.

The same stretch of the Embankment housed an authority more local in its operations: the Metropolitan Police. Norman Shaw's New Scotland Yard, under construction at the time of the Whitechapel murders and completed in 1890, was as characteristic a building of the late Victorian era as the Palace of Westminster was of the middle part. As well as the office of the Commissioner and the headquarters of the Criminal Investigation Department, the building in its lower depths contained what a writer in 1926 called "a depository of relics of remarkable crimes and their detection," history narrated "in blood-rusted razors, revolvers and a whole arsenal of other implements of violence"—the Black Museum, originally intended for the training of detectives, but accessible to a select few outsiders.[39] Arthur Conan Doyle had visited in 1892, early in the career of Sherlock Holmes, and read the original letter signed "Jack the Ripper." Lowndes almost certainly visited too; one of the few scenes in *The Lodger* to take place outside the lodging-house is set there. Hitchcock would follow them.

The view down the Embankment framed in *The Lodger*'s first shots was a visual distillation of the self-confident nation Hitchcock had been born into in August 1899, on the eve of the Second Boer War, a conflict that began, as the historian Jan Morris put it, with "the British at the apogee of their imperial advance," but that by its end in 1902 "had cracked the British mirror."[40] It was in the foreground of this panorama of power, amid the Embankment's enormous masonry, almost under the shadow of Big Ben, the most famous emblem of national, imperial, and temporal authority, within hailing distance of Scotland Yard, "that great organism which fights the forces of civilised crime," as Lowndes called it in her novel—it was here that Hitchcock chose to stage *The Lodger*'s first murder. The choice marked the real beginning of a film career in which appearances deceive, identities divide, and authorities are undermined.

Hitchcock's river prospect was not Wordsworth's but G. K. Chesterton's. He began his film on or near the spot where Gabriel Syme, the titular Man Who Was Thursday of Chesterton's 1908 novel, "walked on the embankment once under a dark red sunset" and was recruited by a pass-ing policeman for undercover detective work among the philosophical anarchists, having been persuaded that "the most dangerous criminal now is the entirely lawless modern philosopher." In the course of Ches-terton's story, in which all but one of the anarchists turn out to be fel-low detectives, Syme finds himself in disarray "recalling the dizziness of a cinematograph"—vertigo, perhaps—and confronting "that final scepticism which can find no floor to the universe." At the first night of a theatrical adaptation of his novel, in January 1926, Chesterton told the audience at the Hampstead Everyman that he had written it "during a period of youthful and turbulent doubt."[41] Hitchcock's cinema would be a cinema of profound doubt, forged in an age of ceaseless turbulence.

The view down the Embankment had changed hardly at all in the years since Hitchcock's birth, but beneath the surface all had changed utterly. The international order to which its monuments belonged had been shattered by the Great War. There was, wrote H. G. Wells in his best-selling *Outline of History*, published in 1919–20, "a universal desire for the lost safety and liberty and prosperity of pre-war times, without any power of will to achieve and secure these things."[42] The facade was nonetheless impressive. Indeed, in the autumn of their preeminence, the British could be encouraged to believe that the world as they imagined it to have been in the high summer of 1914 had after all been restored, or even improved upon.

Doubting intellectuals were starting to discover a terminology for the postwar condition in the writings of Sigmund Freud, whose notion of the sovereign individual as a fiction, imperfectly masking the effects of con-flicting unconscious drives, was itself the distinctive product of another disintegrating empire—Austria-Hungary, riven beneath its well-ordered surface by irreconcilable forces, even before they engulfed the rest of the continent. Looking back, Freud's countryman Arnold Hauser saw in his work "the same anxiety, the same loss of confidence in the meaning of culture, the same concern at being surrounded by unknown, unfathom-able and indefinable dangers" as was characteristic of fin-de-siècle art.[43] Had Chesterton known of Freud in 1908, he may well have included him in the "purely intellectual conspiracy" that Syme was recruited to coun-ter. Freud's work, translated, glossed, and popularized, came into wide circulation at the start of the 1920s; how much of it Hitchcock absorbed is unknown, but many of his heroes and villains, beset by inhibitions and perversions, belong to the Freudian casebook. One complex of particular significance for his films, repetition-compulsion, "*a tendency innate in living organic matter impelling it towards the reinstatement of an earlier condition*, one which it had to abandon under the influence of external disturbing forces," could also be discerned in the comportment of the nation in which he was raised.[44]

One manifestation was the expectation at the war's end, enforced by government, trade unions, and the press, that the one-and-a-half million women who had taken up traditionally male occupations would simply return to hearth and home. Iris Barry, who was one of them, and had largely enjoyed herself, recalled realizing, during the Armistice celebrations, that "the quite excellent jobs which any fairly proficient girl could get for the asking would be less plentiful. Indeed most of the jobs would cease to exist."[45]

Another was the return to the gold standard at the prewar exchange rate with the dollar, announced by Winston Churchill, as chancellor, in April 1925, and described by Keynes as the application of an economic theory "which was worked out on the hypotheses of laissez-faire and free competition," pillars of British prosperity before the Great War, "to a society which is rapidly abandoning these hypotheses."[46]

The British Empire had actually expanded since the war, albeit in the form of "mandates" assigned by the League of Nations to the victors. The most prominent recent addition to the view down the Embankment was the Royal Air Force Memorial, unveiled in 1923, when the RAF's primary role was policing one such mandate, Iraq, from the skies. The first shots of *The Lodger* were taken at the monument's base. The acquisition of another mandate, formerly German Tanganyika, made possible for the first time the fulfilment of Cecil Rhodes's dream of a Cape-to-Cairo railway over British-controlled land. On 17 February 1926, the aviator Alan Cobham landed his de Havilland at Cape Town after a well-publicized eight-thousand-mile flight along what would have been its path. Though the wilder schemes of the Empire's late Victorian heyday had lost whatever hold over the British electorate they had once had, and though Ireland, which had been an integral part of the United Kingdom, had been partitioned in 1921–22 after a dirty civil war, the trappings of Imperialism were not easily shed.

The League of Nations itself was the cornerstone of a new international order that would, it was hoped and even believed, restore Europe to a lasting peace. The American journalist Vincent Sheean, in the book that Hitchcock would adapt as *Foreign Correspondent*, wrote of it from direct observation of its inner workings at Geneva as "the best dream of middle-class idealism in its dying years—the perfect dream-flower of a culture that had always preferred to disguise ugly reality with pleasant appearance."[47] This idealism was in full flood after the Locarno conference of October 1925, at which the major League powers, France and Britain, cleared the way for Germany to join them on its governing council, and Germany consented to recognize its western borders, with Britain and Italy as guarantors. Germany did not consent to recognize its eastern borders with the new states of Poland and Czechoslovakia, nor did Britain want to guarantee these remoter borders; this, according to the *Nation and Athenaeum*, house journal of the Bloomsbury intelligentsia, was a "purely Eastern quarrel."[48] When the various foreign ministers came to London to sign the Locarno treaties at the Foreign Office, on 1 December 1925, the normally hardheaded *Spectator* perceived "the beginning of a new age of more friendly, because more rational, relations throughout Europe."[49]

One of the few voices raised against this consensus was G. K. Chesterton's paper *G. K.'s Weekly*. Out of a mixture of Catholic fellow feeling and anti-Prussianism—which it combined with anti-Semitism—the paper had early pointed out that "since the Pact has not certainly determined the position between Germany and Poland, there is still a risk of war."[50] A few days before the signing ceremony, Hilaire Belloc, Marie's brother and Chesterton's brother in arms, had provided a parodic history lesson for children on the "Locarno spirit," the catchword of the moment, which he mockingly defined as "one of goodwill to all human beings and of sympathy with all nations," which entailed "making friends with our late enemies, and not exactly enemies of our late friends, but anyhow showing less partiality for them."[51]

In February 1926, as it happened, the Polish question became the cause of a rift among the Locarno signatories when the French attempted to make Poland a member of the League's council on equal terms with

Germany. Locarno had outraged the Pan-German right, under the sway of the press baron and politician Alfred Hugenberg, and further concessions were impossible. On the morning of the 24th it was reported that the German government was prepared to withdraw its application to join the League in response. During the afternoon and early evening, perhaps even as Hitchcock and his crew arrived on the Embankment, both Houses of Parliament discussed the crisis—the weight of opinion being against the French and the Poles. But this wrinkle was soon smoothed out and soon forgotten, and continental amity was soon restored.

The League's unreality derived in part from the fact that the United States was not a member. Woodrow Wilson, having led his country into the Great War, and having insisted on the League's creation as part of the settlement reached at the Paris Peace Conference in 1919, was then kept out of it by his own Senate. His successor, Warren Harding, offered a return to "normalcy," including extraction from the muddled affairs of the Old World, and Harding's successor, Calvin Coolidge, continued in the same direction. Having done so much to shape the European political landscape, the United States abruptly departed from it; and yet "Americanization" became the specter that haunted Europe in the 1920s. For all that the League of Nations represented the prolongation of European influence, financial power in the world had moved decisively from the City of London to Wall Street, and American economic penetration of European markets was relentless. Nowhere was this more sheerly visible than in the cinema.

British film producers in the years immediately after the Great War, during which European film production had slumped, hoped that the ground lost to the burgeoning American industry could be recovered; but American films had come to prevail even before 1914, and there was no recovery. Through the policy of block and blind booking, the Americans dominated the British market not by direct ownership of cinema chains, as was increasingly the case back home, but by offering their sure-fire star vehicles only as parts of blocks containing other, less desirable films, "programmers," often before they had been shown or even made. American films, having recouped their costs in the United States, could be rented to British exhibitors at lower rates than British producers, whose films were practically excluded from the American market, could afford to offer.

The British government had begun to interest itself seriously in the plight of British films in mid-1925. The ruling Conservative Party, though its leadership was broadly committed to laissez-faire and free competition, contained a significant faction in favor of "Imperial Preference," a protectionist tariff barrier behind which the Empire would be more closely bound together; and it was this faction, in the person of Sir Philip Cunliffe-Lister, president of the Board of Trade, that took the lead in seeking a solution. More than cinema was at stake. On the first day of the *Lodger* shoot, the *Daily Mail* ran an article by the deputy director of the Federation of British Industries, which had taken up the cause, arguing that a revived industry "would be a credit to British prestige throughout the world and act as the pioneer of British culture and commerce."[52] It had been hoped that the three branches of the trade—production, distribution, and exhibition— would be able to agree on a voluntary scheme to promote the production of British films and make sure they were shown, so that legislation, which was offensive to laissez-faire orthodoxy, could be avoided. But in late 1925, just such a scheme, the centerpiece of which was a quota requiring distributors and exhibitors to offer and show a fixed percentage of British films, was rejected by a majority of exhibitors. Writing from his head office at the New Gallery, Lord Ashfield, president of Provincial Cinematograph Theatres, the country's largest chain, put the exhibitors' side of the case thus: "Had British producers been able to provide satisfactory films they would have found a ready market for their goods, but with a few exceptions their films have not found favour with the public."[53] On 24 February there was yet another meeting of the deadlocked trade committee at the Queen's Hotel in Leicester Square. On 12 March, Sir Philip would give the trade one year in which to devise a voluntary quota, failing which the government would devise a compulsory one.[54]

As G. A. Atkinson had observed in the *Daily Express* in December 1925, protectionist legislation had not saved the German film industry from American influence. In that month, Sidney Kent of Paramount, Leopold Friedman of MGM, and Carl Laemmle, Universal's president, had raced one another from New York to Berlin by liner and airplane, in what Atkinson called "a heartrending drama of international finance," the outcome of which was that the Americans together provided Ufa, Europe's biggest film combine, with a rescue loan in return for privileged access to its cinema chain.[55] Ufa's difficulties were blamed on the enormous budget allocated to Fritz Lang's spectacular *Metropolis*, which had been in production at Neubabelsberg, outside Berlin, since May 1925. Walter Mycroft, having been shown extracts, had called it "an expression of modern life, a thrilling picture-poem of machinery," but there was still no sign of a release date.[56] In the last week of February 1926, Erich Pommer, the production chief held responsible for the overrun, having left Ufa and traveled to New York to entertain offers, signed a contract with Paramount that would eventually take him to Hollywood; other illustrious names with whom he had been associated would follow.

Gainsborough, which had stayed afloat by striking deals with American and German companies, including Ufa, largely kept its distance from the quota controversy. *The Rat*, one of Lord Ashfield's "few exceptions," had opened at the New Gallery. In January 1926, Cedric Belfrage had written an article knocking the quota's partisans as "the monstrous regiment of incompetents formerly engaged in film production," and alluding to a firm—clearly his own—which "neither expects nor relies upon any form of Government assistance."[57] On the morning of 24 February, Balcon was quoted in the *Westminster Gazette*, which had earlier alleged that the American distributors were evading tax, as saying "it would be well worth the Government's while thoroughly to investigate the whole problem," but he was generally on good terms with the Americans.[58] The very next day, on the morning after the night shoot, it was announced in the *Daily Graphic* that Paramount had sold Poole Street to Gainsborough outright, "after considerable competition."[59] In his autobiography Balcon claimed that J. C. Graham, having asked for £100,000, accepted £14,000 in installments, less than the reported cost of the Plaza's Wurlitzer organ.[60]

The international Hollywood system that the Plaza symbolized, and in which Hitchcock had been apprenticed, made a certain kind of film, telling a certain kind of story, hundreds of times a year. "Nobody seems to want a story that might be termed a tragedy, believing that the public want the customary clinch and the inevitable happy ending," complained Ernst Lubitsch, in the *New York World*, in March 1926.[61] To its critics in London and New York, Hollywood cinema was defined by its optimism. "Almost every American photoplay that I have ever seen," said

Robert E. Sherwood, film critic of *Life* magazine and a member, like Herman Mankiewicz, of the Algonquin "Round Table," "has carried the message that right will triumph over wrong, that the lovers will ultimately be united in holy matrimony and that the United States Cavalry will never fail to arrive on time."[62] Iris Barry, in her book *Let's Go to the Pictures*, published in the autumn of 1926, identified a strain of belief "that the movies are going to do what President Wilson and the Quakers and the League of Nations and two thousand years of a kind of Christianity have failed to do—that is, to bring universal understanding, tolerance and peace."[63] In the view of Gilbert Seldes, the American critic whose book *The Seven Lively Arts*, published in 1924, was much admired by the Film Society cognoscenti—and would be mentioned by name in *Rope*—the rot had set in when Hollywood, in its bid to attract a middle-class audience, decided that it "had to be dignified and artistic; it had to have literature and actors and ideals," with the result that "nearly every picture made recently has borrowed something, usually in the interest of dignity, gentility, refinement—and the picture side, the part depending on action before the camera, has gone steadily down."[64]

What was missing, aesthetically and psychologically, was brought into relief by the German industry that Lubitsch had left behind, and upon which the American combines were now encroaching. In her book, Barry wrote that whereas American directors "show you everything except the plain faces of some of their stars, which they always photograph charitably through gauze," their German counterparts "pick out from darkness, that is, what they wish to be seen."[65] She and her confederates in the Film Society were the German films' main standard-bearers. At the start of February 1926 they had opened an exhibition of work by the director and set designer Paul Leni at the Mayor Gallery in Sackville Street, close by the New Gallery, "the first thing of its kind to be shown in England" according to another of Hitchcock's critic friends, C. A. Lejeune of the *Manchester Guardian*.[66] The *Evening Standard*'s reviewer wrote that Leni was known to "make brilliant drawings for all the principal scenes before they are photographed."[67] The exhibition, which closed on the 25th, included sketches Leni had executed for his film *Waxworks*, shown in the Film Society's first program, alongside stills from the completed production. These included an Expressionist treatment of the Jack the Ripper story.

Iris Barry, as depicted in the *Graphic*, 20 February 1926. © Illustrated London News Ltd/Mary Evans.

The German films had earlier prompted Barry to a remarkable meditation on the viewing experience. In an article of 1924, she wrote of picturegoers as voyeurs, resembling "the solitary creatures who sit at home behind a veil of window-curtains, peeping out at passers-by," but more consistently satisfied, since "besides the spectacle of moving creatures they are constantly drawn out of themselves by a vicarious participation in the action of the play."[68] The most satisfying films of all, from this vantage, were the German films whose makers "have been the first to appreciate how much more than mere spectators a cinema audience can be moved to become."[69] Evoking her first encounter with *The Cabinet of Dr. Caligari*, she wrote that "I suddenly doubt the evidence of my senses, which I had thoughtlessly accepted as testimony on the appearance of the world: it is good and important that I should doubt that evidence."[70] Hitchcock, who shared Barry's admiration for the German films, would become a master of picking out, of not showing everything, by designing every shot in advance of shooting; it was part of what distinguished his films from the mainstream of Hollywood film style.

The critics of Hitchcock's day perceived the "picture side" of this style only fitfully and without precision. It fell to later generations to provide it with a definition. The most influential of them was the *Cahiers du cinéma* critic André Bazin, who in an essay of 1952, parts of which were included in his book *What Is Cinema?*, set "the classical American cinema" in historical perspective.[71] Rising to a peak of "classical perfection" in the late 1930s, he wrote, Hollywood filmmaking was characterized by its "perfectly clear and intelligible style, photography and montage."[72] Hollywood montage, meaning the division of scenes into shots, was "'invisible,'" seamless, simply intended to tell the story. Having described the typical breakdown of a typical scene, Bazin claimed that "acted on the stage and viewed from the stalls this scene would have exactly the same meaning," and that editing added nothing but clarification and emphasis—for example, through the use of close-ups.[73] "In 1938 all films in all countries, with the single exception of Jean Renoir's work (and perhaps Alfred Hitchcock's)," he continued, "were actually based on the same principles."

Bazin's sympathies were with Renoir. He distinguished between "the trend followed by film-directors who believed in the 'picture' and that followed by those who believed in reality," and Renoir was among the latter.[74] Bazin argued that the cinema was reborn when it had relearned how to "express events in their real time relation, to show them in their real time setting, whereas classical montage had insidiously substituted an intellectual and abstract time."[75] Yet he did not discourage Truffaut, his protégé at *Cahiers du cinéma*, from taking up the alternative case.

Hitchcock believed in the picture. "The only thing that matters is whether the installation of the camera at a given angle is going to give the scene its maximum impact," he told Truffaut.[76] "The beauty of the image and movement, the rhythm and the effects—everything must be subordinated to the purpose." And he believed in abstract time. "The ability to shorten or lengthen time is a primary requirement in film-making," he went on.[77] "As you know, there's no relation whatever between real time and filmic time." Montage was his tool, for purposes beyond emphasis and clarification. These were not convictions lately arrived at. Hitchcock had said much the same thing in 1938, the crucial year for Bazin, the year Hitchcock made his penultimate British film, *The Lady Vanishes*, and the year he visited Los Angeles for the first time. "The best films have their material *created* for the camera," he told BBC listeners in January.[78] "That's the difference between the film that is a stage play and a film that is a motion-picture." Nor indeed did these ideas belong to the 1930s; they were in circulation when he made *The Lodger*.

Only in *Caligari*, wrote Seldes in *The Seven Lively Arts*, had the cinema succeeded in "giving us the highest degree of pleasure, that of escaping actuality and entering into a created world, built on its own inherent logic, keeping time in its own rhythm—where we feel ourselves at once strangers and at home."[79] C. A. Lejeune, similarly, had written in 1925 that the cinema "must think of herself no longer as a play pictorial, a volume visualised, a sort of poor relation of the drama and the novel."[80] The art-form's peculiar power lay instead in "complete illusion of the eye, complete illusion of time and space." Hitchcock's difference from the mainstream of Hollywood style was not absolute, just as Bazin suggested, but it was considerable. His films would have the clarity of classical American cinema, but he did not offer a stable view from the stalls. Through the stories he chose to tell, and through his manipulation of point of view in their telling, his choice of what to show and what to hide, he would make his audiences doubt the evidence of their senses, especially—and appropriately—their sense of sight.

In particular, he would excite, frustrate, and make palpable what Freud had called, in publications that were known among Hitchcock's circle in London in the 1920s, scopophilia, or "the sexual 'lust of the eye'" as one of Freud's translators had it.[81] The theory was already being applied to art forms adjacent to the cinema. In November 1924 two British Freudians, M. D. Eder and John Rickman, had presented papers to the British Psycho-Analytical Society on "A Camera as a Phallic Symbol" and "Photography as a Pseudo-Perversion." In the latter, Rickman described a case in which "the processes of taking a photograph were substitutes for the sexual act"; in another "the sitting [*sic*] and object was a matter of indifference (so long as the picture was of a girl); the patient found gratification in the thought that he had 'got her,' had 'snapped her.'"[82] Though it is improbable that Hitchcock was directly aware of these developments, some of his friends may have been—Iris Barry, whose husband Alan Porter was closely interested in psychoanalysis, foremost among them.

"The covering of the body, which keeps abreast of [i.e., goes along in step with] civilization," Freud had written in *Three Contributions to the Theory of Sex*, "serves to arouse sexual inquisitiveness, which always strives to restore for itself the sexual object by uncovering the hidden parts. This can be turned into the artistic ('sublimation') if the interest is turned from the genitals to the form of the body."[83] Knowingly or otherwise, this was something like Hitchcock's view of things. "Sex on the screen should be suspenseful, I feel," he told Truffaut.[84] "If sex is too blatant or obvious, there's no suspense." In the dynamic play of concealment and exposure, showing all and picking out, in which the scopophilic drive threatened to overwhelm or derange the eye's ordinary purpose of "sensorial perception," not only the integrity of the ego but the continuity of civilization, both dependent on the drive's successful repression, were at stake.[85] Hitchcock's characters are put in danger by their inquisitiveness; they see what their unconscious urges them to believe, and are regarded as mad for doing so; others are made to conform with what the desiring eye demands to see; and his audiences are no mere spectators, but are intensely involved. All this began with *The Lodger*.

"Hitchcock's professional pleasure in the malign is now a matter of some 15 or 20 years' record," wrote a profiler for *Life* soon after Hitchcock began his Hollywood career in 1939.[86] In *The Lodger* he was said to have "displayed a cynicism astonishing in a profession that is compounded largely of sweetness, light and holocausts in which only the bad people are ever fatally wounded." Hitchcock had won his American reputation in 1935, with *The Man Who Knew Too Much* and *The 39 Steps*, two timely spy thrillers. The latter of them had had its world premiere at the New Gallery in the week Hitler's Germany tore up the Locarno settlement. In one scene Hitchcock's hero, pursued both by British police and by agents of "a certain foreign power," improvises a speech that parodies the by then evaporated Locarno spirit, a forlorn plea for "all those who love their fellow men to set themselves resolutely to make this world a happier place to live in, a world where no nation plots against nation."

His move to Los Angeles came at the height of the Hollywood studio system, and at the height of the classical Hollywood style. The town was by then thoroughly "organized, methodical, businesslike, and regulated," as the playwright and occasional screenwriter Maxwell Anderson complained in 1937.[87] "Nobody succeeds alone or fails alone in that rainless picnic ground." It was a place still remote from the affairs of Europe, and the films it produced and sent around the world still tended to end with a clinch and the triumph of right over wrong. Hitchcock brought with him all the doubt and anxiety of the turbulent continent he had left behind. With his first Hollywood film, *Rebecca*, he helped usher in the darker mood that came over Hollywood in the 1940s, just as the world slid back into war. He did not succeed alone, and enlisted writers like Robert Sherwood and Maxwell Anderson to help him, but his was nonetheless a singular career.

In the early 1950s, after the US government finally succeeded in breaking up the film combines, he would secure an extraordinary degree of creative control at a changed Paramount, the studio he had first joined while moonlighting from his job in a cable manufacturing company. He would reach his apotheosis with his first film there, *Rear Window*, a story about one of "the solitary creatures who sit at home behind a veil of window-curtains, peeping out at passers-by," told with the most rigorous control of cinematic point of view. It would have its London opening at the Plaza in 1954. *Rear Window* was made entirely within the confines of a Paramount sound stage, and this was not untypical of Hitchcock's American films. "I wasn't in the least interested in Hollywood as a place," he told Truffaut.[88] "The only thing I cared about was to get into a studio to work."

All of this lay a long way in the future as he took his first shots on *The Lodger*, far outside the studio, in the middle of the night. "At 5 a.m. the scene of operations was transferred to the County Hall," Walter Mycroft reported, the headquarters of London County Council being directly across the Thames from Scotland Yard.[89] Hitchcock himself recalled the night rather ruefully. As he wrote in 1937, "finally, we shot the big scene. The sun-arcs turned night to day. The artists did their stuff. The bridge stood out clear and sharp. The camera turned. The number of this scene was 45. It should have been 13."[90] The cameraman had failed to put a lens in the camera, and the take was lost. Hitchcock reflected that "these accidents always happen not in the studio, where everything can be put right with a re-take, but when a couple of thousand people have been specially engaged, when we are shooting something we can never shoot again, when the mistake costs thousands."

It would be almost a full year before *The Lodger* was seen by the public, and by then the film industry had been transformed, both in Britain and the United States. Though the film anticipated all of the films of Hitchcock's maturity, it was made in very different circumstances even from his 1930s thrillers. If it lacked the polish of the films he made only a few years later in London, let alone those of his contemporaries in Hollywood, Hitchcock himself never doubted that "*The Lodger* was the first true 'Hitchcock movie.'"[91]

2 The Reputation and the Myth

It was a necessarily retrospective characterization, dependent on the subsequent course of Hitchcock's career, but a familiar one by the time Truffaut flew to Los Angeles to hear it in 1962. Five years earlier, Truffaut's confrères Eric Rohmer and Claude Chabrol had written that "most of what was latterly known as the famous 'Hitchcock touch' is already present in this well-made variation on the Jack the Ripper theme."[1] *The Lodger*'s reputation was formed even earlier, however, among British critics and curators in the 1930s and '40s, when the film was at its least visible. That reputation has endured through the years, even as the culture that sustains it, and the media on which the film itself can be seen, have changed out of recognition; and around it has been erected an equally enduring myth.

The Film Society's forty-fifth performance took place at the Tivoli, a giant cinema on the Strand, on 8 February 1931. The Film Society's purpose, and its audience, was much as it had been five years earlier, though it was by now proverbially associated with Soviet cinema, "Russian cutting," montage. The 1930–31 season had begun with Dovzhenko's *Earth*, and the forty-fourth performance, in January, had included Dziga-Vertov's *Man with a Movie Camera.* The Film Society also sought to keep alive a past that was now cordoned off as silent. The middle part of the forty-fifth performance carried on, as the notes put it, "the series of technical studies in this season's programmes, in order to compare the technique of silent and sound film production by the same English director."[2] The director in question, though he himself was absent, recovering from an attack of pleurisy, was Alfred Hitchcock, and the comparison was between the auction scene from his new film, *The Skin Game*, as yet unseen in its entirety, and the first reel of *The Lodger*.[3]

The critics, against the intentions of the Film Society's inner circle, preferred the latter. "I well remember that afternoon rather over four years ago when 'The Lodger' was first shown at the London Hippodrome—," wrote Charles Davy in the *Yorkshire Post*, "the excitement of that opening reel which revealed Mr. Hitchcock as the master of that cross-patter technique which Russian films had not yet made familiar to us."[4] Whereas Davy's first sight of *The Lodger* had been "like a breath of new life, pulsating and vivid," *The Skin Game*, adapted from John Galsworthy's play, found Hitchcock "tied down to a remorseless current of speech from which there can be no escape." C. A. Lejeune, now at the *Observer*, likewise saw that *The Lodger* "has its own montage, shaped by Hitchcock for his purpose before montage became a fashionable term."[5] Anticipating Rohmer and Chabrol, she wrote that "'The Skin Game' and 'Murder,' and 'Blackmail,' as well as 'The Ring,' are implicit in this early piece of Hitchcock's work."

The program had been arranged by Thorold Dickinson, a young film editor, who used his pulpit to win over "the sophisticated conservatives dedicated to the dying art of the silent film," in this instance without success.[6] The Film Society was then, he would recall, "our only means of studying cinema as a means of expression," lynchpin of the cluster of institutions that Ernest Lindgren, another central figure within it, later called the "film art movement."[7] Even the critics, Dickinson continued, "could only live from film to film," and "you could accommodate the whole literature of cinema on a bookshelf three feet long."[8] A few inches were taken up by Paul Rotha's *The Film Till Now*, published in London in 1930 and destined to be highly influential within the film art movement. Rotha identified "the fundamental basis of film creation in the work of Kuleshov and the Soviet directors," decried "the Hollywood atmosphere of dollars and unintelligence," and regarded the dialogue film as "illegitimate"; more distinctively, he anathematized the cinema of his own land.[9]

Attributing its inferiority to "the scarcity of intelligent directors, and the unsuitable type of people of which the executives in British studios were composed," Rotha refused to treat British cinema "in the same way as has been done with that of other countries."[10] Grudgingly, however, it had to be conceded that the "accredited pre-eminent director of the British school is, I suppose, Alfred Hitchcock," and that "Hitchcock's most sincere work was seen in *The Lodger*."[11] The more generous judgments of newspaper critics were, by nature, transient; Rotha's were preserved between hard covers, and the idea of *The Lodger* as a rose in the desert of British cinema would persist within the film art movement for decades to come.

As Rotha's remarks suggest, the early film art movement's relationship with the film trade was marked by class differences. Its protagonists tended to belong to the tiny educated elite—Dickinson had been at Oxford, Davy at Glasgow, Lejeune at Manchester, Lindgren at Birkbeck College, Rotha at the Slade School of Fine Art; and the cultural forms it adopted—the little magazine, the private society—were those of the intelligentsia. Correspondingly, albeit paradoxically, its outlook was often that of an intelligentsia that felt its authority being undermined, and its very existence threatened, by the brash commercial civilization of which the cinema was a conspicuous manifestation. At its most optimistic, the film art movement hoped, in the words of the Film Society's founding chairman Ivor Montagu, in 1925, that "though we shall retain our incorruptible independence, the Trade will begin to look on us and use us as a sort of research station for trying out the experimental and studying the past."[12]

"Five and a half years is a long time," wrote the *Guardian* critic Robert Herring, looking back at *The Lodger* on the appearance of Maurice Elvey's remake—again starring Ivor Novello—in 1932; "we have all lost money and most of us have lost hope, and Mr. Hitchcock himself has just made *Number 17*," his professional nadir.[13] Unmentioned by Herring, Elvey's script had been written by Rotha and Miles Mander, an associate of Hitchcock's and Reville's. "There is cause here for retrospect," Herring went on, since "it is something that the old *Lodger* should still haunt the memory when a new tenant arrives." For Herring, the old *Lodger* also overshadowed the new Hitchcock, who "replaces his earlier use of light and shade with cobwebs."

The sense that Hitchcock's path was laid down by *The Lodger*, and that he had strayed from it, was implicit in the critical response to *The Man Who Knew Too Much* and *The 39 Steps*. "Because he was famous, he was put on to do things to which he was not suited," wrote John Betjeman, then film critic of the *Evening Standard*, but *The Man Who Knew Too Much* was "an honest-to-God thriller."[14] Lejeune confessed to "a certain amount of self-congratulation" on seeing her friend succeed, having kept faith with him during the rocky early 1930s.[15] When the Film Society revived *The Lodger* she wrote that "I do not believe that we shall get the best work out of our best commercial director until he can free himself of all the years between 'The Skin Game' and 'The Lodger,' cutting himself clear of Galsworthy and O'Casey and the men of words."[16] *The Man Who Knew Too Much* and *The 39 Steps* did just that.

The film art movement grew in size and scope through the 1930s, with the establishment of specialized cinemas in London and the proliferation of film societies in the provinces. The first director's "season" to be mounted by the Hampstead Everyman, shortly after its conversion into a repertory cinema, was an "Alfred Hitchcock Week" consisting of two films, *Murder* and *The Skin Game*, in February 1934. Meanwhile, *The Lodger* was made available on 16 mm film to the small audience equipped to project it, through the GeBescope and Kodascope libraries. The most consequential event for film preservation in Britain in these years was the establishment of the National Film Library, a branch of the British Film Institute, in 1935. Though the BFI, founded in 1933–34, was initially confused in its objectives and dysfunctional in its governance, it provided a forum for the film art movement in its quarterly magazine *Sight and Sound*, and became an integral part of the movement through the influence of Olwen Vaughan, organizer of the London Film Institute Society, an adjunct of the BFI that put on screenings of films old and new, and Ernest Lindgren, the National Film Library's curator.

Alistair Cooke, who served as *Sight and Sound*'s principal critic in the mid-1930s and claimed to reject "the current snobberies, that Hollywood is commercial and therefore cannot be art, or that films showing up at Hampstead are a Bloomsbury fad," was not among Hitchcock's most

THE REPUTATION AND THE MYTH 29

ardent admirers.[17] Nor for that matter was Lindgren. Nonetheless, it was through the National Film Library that *The Lodger*—or at least its opening reel, once again—was first projected as part of a historical survey, on the afternoon of 16 October 1938, during a special Sunday screening at Charles B. Cochran's Palace Theatre, a vast variety hall on Cambridge Circus. Hitchcock's latest film, *The Lady Vanishes*, had opened at the Empire, in nearby Leicester Square, a few weeks earlier.

The Palace program was divided in two, the first half being a chronicle of the cinema from the Lumières and Méliès via *The Great Train Robbery* to Chaplin, represented by extracts from ten films; the second a celebration of British cinema since the Great War, with *The Lodger* as the penultimate item before "the first British talking film," *Blackmail*.[18] The selection was made with advice from Thorold Dickinson, himself now a film director. It was not an isolated event, but part of an intensified study of the past within the film art movement. Six months earlier, *Sight and Sound* had published the concluding part of the first scholarly history of British cinema, covering the 1920s; its author, Marie Seton, had written that Hitchcock's "early films, *The Lodger* and *Downhill*, stamped him not only as England's most remarkable director with an innate feeling for real national characteristics, but also as a director of international importance."[19]

Nor was interest in the cinema's past confined to the film art movement proper; popular repertory cinemas were beginning to spread across the country, and the Palace event itself took place during the run of Cochran's *Flashbacks: The Evolution of the Movies*, a historical pageant running from the magic lantern down to that day's news—which was for much of the show's duration consumed by the Sudetenland crisis. Another sign of popular interest in film history, and of Hitchcock's place within it, was the republication in the same autumn of 1938 of Charles Davy's anthology *Footnotes to the Film*, first published the previous year at the high price of 18s, now issued in a Readers' Union edition, with a still of Garbo on the cover, at 2s, 6d. Hitchcock's chapter, "Direction," the most revealing exposition of his method up to that time, earlier excerpted in *Sight and Sound*'s Summer 1937 issue, was the first in the book.

The Lodger was acquired by the National Film Library in May 1939.[20] No negative survived, but the existence of a print put it in the minority of

British silent films; most had not survived in any form. It came from the basement vaults of F. R. A. Arton, a veteran dealer who had got his start in showmanship exhibiting slides of the Boer War around 1900, before becoming a touring film projectionist.[21] Unlike others, he had kept hold of his films, and by the late 1930s his collection had at last attracted the attention of archivists like Lindgren—a new breed, quite different in sensibility from the dealers with whom they dealt. In the 1939 *Kinematograph Year Book*, Arton's firm advertised itself as "Film Junk Buyers"—but they were sellers too.[22]

Hitchcock had by then departed for the United States. It was not simply that his reputation had preceded him there, through the success of his films and the publicity surrounding his two visits in 1937 and 1938; rather, the ballyhoo on both continents grew in volume by being echoed between them. Alistair Cooke, in *Garbo and the Night Watchmen*, his anthology of transatlantic film criticism, published in London in 1937, took care to include a paean to Hitchcock by his best American critic, Otis Ferguson of the *New Republic*.

The Lodger was not much more than a title on a publicity sheet in the United States. In July 1940, Ferguson wrote that the Fifth Avenue Playhouse "has been running a program of all the Alfred Hitchcock films—that is, the films starting with 'The Man Who Knew Too Much' and going up to the time our blessed fat man fell into 'Rebecca.'"[23] Nevertheless, the *Brooklyn Daily Eagle*'s Janet White, who interviewed Hitchcock on his first visit in 1937, referred to his having made "a cheerful little thing about Jack the Ripper,"[24] while the *New York Times*'s B. R. Crisler, who covered Hitchcock's second visit in 1938, related that "in an early thriller on 'Jack the Ripper' he began with an unprecedentedly daring shot: a close-up of the face of a woman screaming."[25] Katharine Roberts, profiling him for *Collier's* during the preparation of *Rebecca* in 1939, wrote that *The Lodger* "had in it what is now recognized as a typical Hitchcock shot—a dark house, with the camera pointing down the black well of a stairway, following an eerie white hand as it moved down the bannisters," and that this was the "forerunner of the technique used in Thirty-nine Steps, Secret Agent and others."[26]

The bookshelf had expanded beyond three feet, and successful talkies could expect to live on in repertory, but by the 1940s the silent past was largely unknowable except through memory. The arrival in 1944 of Twentieth Century-Fox's period adaptation of *The Lodger*, with Laird Cregar, Merle Oberon, and George Sanders, provided an opportunity for comparison that could not be taken. "Few among present-day audiences will have seen the silent version," reflected the *News Chronicle*'s Richard Winnington, one of the few critics who could recall "how it pierced through the murk of British screen production."[27] The absence of comparison is all the more striking in light of the fact that the remake opened almost simultaneously with Hitchcock's *Lifeboat*, a film that prompted reflection on his place in Hollywood as a resident, no longer a guest. For Manny Farber, film critic of the *New Republic* since Otis Ferguson's death in action, it contained "less of the original Hitchcock quality," meaning the quality of the 1930s thrillers, "than any of the American films Hitchcock has made since."[28]

Two years later, in April 1946, Dilys Powell, occupant of the most prestigious berth in British film criticism, at the *Sunday Times*—she had called *Lifeboat*, "after 'Rebecca,' his most elaborate floperoo"—used her column to discuss the career of Fritz Lang.[29] Lang, whose early American film *You Only Live Once*, from 1937, had recently been revived at the London Pavilion, she wrote, was fortunate in having his work kept in circulation.

> Others with a claim to critical consideration have not been so lucky. Hitchcock, for example; though the latest Hitchcock piece is always sure of a large audience, though the last Hitchcock but one or two is probably to be tracked down in the repertory cinemas, the early Hitchcock has almost vanished, and you can whistle for a sight of "The Lodger."[30]

Powell had not mentioned Hitchcock in her review of the remake, but hers was by no means an idle comment. She was on the selection committee of the National Film Library, and so theoretically well placed to do more than just whistle for *The Lodger*: the National Film Library acquired its second print of the film in the same year. Powell was also well placed to show it, as one of the organizers of the New London Film Society, which had been established in December 1945 "to replace the London Film Institute Society, which had carried on throughout the war, and the old Film Society, which had been compelled to stop its work when war broke out."[31] Run by Olwen Vaughan from her drinking club near Piccadilly, and using

the Scala Theatre on Charlotte Street—a thoroughfare recreated in Hollywood for *Foreign Correspondent*—its council also included the playwright
Rodney Ackland, who had performed as an extra in *The Skin Game*'s auction scene before helping Hitchcock and Reville write *Number 17*. The
NLFS's fourth program, in January 1946, had included Lang's *Destiny*,
from 1921, "his first important film" in Powell's view.[32]

But *The Lodger* was not yet on the cards. Vaughan had indeed kept the
London Film Institute Society going through the war, moving from venue
to venue, since the BFI had none of its own, before ending up at the Academy Cinema on Oxford Street, where in September 1944 she had shown
the first reel of *Blackmail*—presumably the same reel shown at the Palace
in 1938—on a bill with Lang's first sound film, *M*. But at the end of the war
Vaughan had left the BFI in frustration. As she explained to Iris Barry in
a letter written in the summer of 1945, "Lindgren does a fine job collecting
material but he has the sort of 'preservation' mind quite unique. As long
as he knows the films are in a tin in his vaults he doesn't want anyone to
ever see them."[33] Barry, since 1935 the director of the Museum of Modern
Art Film Library, was Vaughan's (and Lindgren's) nearest equivalent in
New York, but with far greater resources, including a permanent cinema.
The New London Film Society found that the thirty-five hundred miles
from Barry's vault in New York were more easily traversed than the thirty
miles from Lindgren's vault in rural Aston Clinton; but Barry did not have
a print of *The Lodger*.

Changes were afoot at the BFI, however. At the end of 1947, Powell was
appointed to a government committee of inquiry into its future, the result
of which was its reconstitution as a body more adequately funded from the
exchequer, and committed, in the words of its new director, Denis Forman,
to "raise the standard of filmgoing from the level of a habit to something
more like serious critical appreciation."[34] One step in this direction, in the
summer of 1949, was the appointment as head of publications, including
Sight and Sound, of the twenty-five-year-old Gavin Lambert, author of a
number of short stories in little literary magazines like *Windmill* and *New
Writing*, and coeditor of the little film magazine *Sequence*. First published
in 1947, *Sequence* had instantly been recognized by Powell—one of the few
critics it showed any respect—as being "devoted to the almost lost cause of
formal beauty on the screen."[35] Started at Oxford, it had been taken over

by Lindsay Anderson, Peter Ericsson, and Penelope Houston; then moved, with Anderson and Ericsson, to Lambert's flat facing Regent's Park, from which setting it established its international reputation.

The main feature in the magazine's ninth issue, published in the autumn of 1949, was Lindsay Anderson's study of Alfred Hitchcock; it remains an acknowledged landmark in film criticism. Anderson's preference for Hitchcock's 1930s thrillers as "his most memorable and enjoyable contribution to the cinema," only matched since his departure by *Shadow of a Doubt*, was nothing but the critical consensus, but Anderson, over the course of eleven pages and a filmography, could go into far more detail than was possible for the newspaper critics, had space to quote Hitchcock's "famous article on his methods of direction, published in 'Footnotes on the Film,'" and, most importantly, was able to draw upon the resources of the National Film Library in order to see silent works that had not been shown in full for more than twenty years.[36] It was on a Moviola at Aston Clinton that Anderson was able to see *The Lodger*, and it was thus that he had the authority to write of its "rapid, ingenious style of narration" as well as "the conscientious realism of its locales and characters," and to remark: "This inventiveness and visual dexterity was to form the basis of Hitchcock's style; they are the characteristics of a born story-teller, of one who delights to surprise and confound expectation, to build up suspense to a climax of violence and excitement."[37]

Anderson's article appeared a few weeks before the first issue of *Sight and Sound* under Lambert's editorship. Hitherto produced for the BFI's members, and reflecting the BFI's somewhat divergent purposes, the magazine now sought to address a broader public, while retaining *Sequence*'s sharp critical edge. Lambert's first issue adverted to "a repertory season of films, silent and sound, designed to illustrate the historical progress of the cinema," arranged by the BFI and including "some rarely seen, important films from the Preservation Section of the National Film Library."[38] The same month's issue of the BFI's *Monthly Film Bulletin*, also edited by Lambert, gave details of the venue, the Institut Français in South Kensington, and of the films, which included *The Lodger*.[39] The screening, the third in the series, took place on 2 February 1950, with music arranged by Lambert, and program notes written by Anderson, expanding on his treatment of the film in *Sequence*:

Its realistic settings, its lower-middle class locale (presented without any false glamour) are those which were to form the background to Hitchcock's famous series of melodramas in the thirties. Most, indeed, of the later films' ingredients are here; the ingenious visual touches, the acute and sometimes caustic observation, the imaginative, economical style, the long build-up of suspense, the climactic violence. In all these THE LODGER pointed forward to its director's great future.[40]

The Institut Français series was followed by a second repertory season in 1950–51, given at the BFI's own tiny screening room in its offices at Great Russell Street, and again including *The Lodger* over two nights in February 1951. The film's first screenings at the BFI's National Film Theatre, which opened in October 1952, near its present location on the South Bank—opposite the Victoria Embankment—came in September 1953. It has been part of the repertory ever since.

Anderson's overview appears near the start of most Hitchcock bibliographies, but it was not the first of its kind. He was preceded by Julian Maclaren-Ross, whose article "The World of Alfred Hitchcock" appeared in the September 1946 issue of the Hogarth Press miscellany *New Writing and Daylight*. Maclaren-Ross had begun publishing short stories early in the Second World War; after his discharge from the army in 1943, at which time he was writing what he described as a "Hitchcockian melodrama," sometimes titled *Conspiracy of Silence*, never completed, he became a fixture of the literary bohemia around Fitzrovia, or North Soho, a West End district with Charlotte Street at its center.[41] He and Lambert frequented the same pubs, and Maclaren-Ross's essay actually shared the same pages as a Lambert short story, but there is no evidence of communication between them. Maclaren-Ross was for a time engaged to write propaganda films for the Ministry of Information, and it is probably in this connection that he once had a telephone conversation with Hitchcock, who made two films for the MOI in England in early 1944. According to his biographer Paul Willetts, had Maclaren-Ross "lived to complete *Memoirs of the Forties*, his notes indicate that the conversation would've featured in the finished book."[42]

Maclaren-Ross's ambition to discuss Hitchcock's whole career down to *Lifeboat* exceeded his ability, without any possibility of seeing the

older films, to do so. Thus he wrote as "one who has admiringly followed Mr. Hitchcock's progress as a film-director since the days when
The Lodger, wearing a silk white scarf and the face of Mr. Ivor Novello,
climbed from carpet to linoleum," but as he also confessed in the same
passage: "I don't remember it; it's some time ago since I was fifteen; at the
time I didn't even know that the director's name was Alfred Hitchcock:
the film when I saw it in France was called *Les Cheveux d'Or*."[43] Nonetheless, Maclaren-Ross identified it as the first true Hitchcock, writing that
"here, for the first time, is the stated theme: the impact of the abnormal on
the normal—the figure of the psychopath stepping from out of the fog into
the world of kippers and aspidistras," a theme, he said, that was reprised in
Shadow of a Doubt.[44] Complementing this theme was the recurring figure
of "the bewildered, frightened man"—often, as his own examples showed,
a woman—"shouting out the truth of the conspiracy which no one will
believe"; a figure with whom Maclaren-Ross, who was not infrequently
gripped by drug-induced paranoia, may have found himself in sympathy.

Anderson's article was immediately followed, in the pages of *Sequence*, by
a contribution by Ruth Partington on the Cinémathèque Française, newly
located at 7 Avenue de Messine. Partington first described the Musée Permanent du Cinéma, a treasure trove assembled by Henri Langlois and
Lotte Eisner, most of it from the cinema's prehistory and earliest years,
then the venue's fifty-seat screening room. "There is never time to explore
it all; and at night a small theatre shows film classics, a hundred chosen from half a century of films. For the moment the Cinémathèque has
become the birthplace of the cinema."[45] It was an unwittingly ironic judgment, since the small theater in the Avenue de Messine would come to be
seen, within the mythology of film culture, as the incubator of the cinema's
rebirth through the *nouvelle vague*; and an unwittingly prescient juxtaposition of articles, since within that same mythology the Cinémathèque
would come to be seen as the fulcrum of a revolution in taste—a revolution in which Hitchcock's reputation would be the decisive factor.

The ailing *Sequence*, essentially superseded by *Sight and Sound*, caught
wind of this revolution early, again without knowing where it would lead.
Its penultimate issue, published for New Year 1951, welcomed the arrival
of two little magazines from across the Channel, *Gazette du cinéma* and

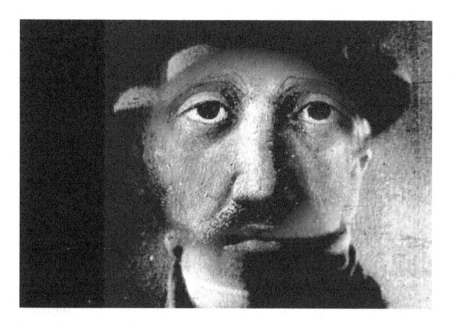

The Lodger, as seen in Godard's *Histoire(s) du Cinéma*.

Raccords; but *Sequence*'s anonymous reviewer, writing about the former, was "disconcerted to find, amongst some good, detailed analyses, rhapsodies on films like *Rope* and *Under Capricorn*."[46] The offending articles were written by, respectively, Eric Rohmer and Jacques Rivette. A fuller examination was promised in a later issue, but it never came. Soon both *Sequence* and *La Gazette du cinéma* were gone, the latter to be succeeded, in April 1951, by *Cahiers du cinéma*.

It is here that the familiar story begins, leading via the publication of Truffaut's *Le Cinéma selon Hitchcock* in November 1966 to the explosion of Hitchcockiana in the more than half-century since. The principal account of Hitchcock's transformation "from popular entertainer to distinguished auteur," achieved "in response to encouragement from European artists" such as the *Cahiers du cinéma* critics became, is given in Robert E. Kapsis's *Hitchcock: The Making of a Reputation*, published in 1992, in which it is argued that "American reviewers, because they were more inclined to embrace auteurism than their British counterparts, came to view Hitchcock less as a thriller director and more as a serious artist whose work, they believed, often transcended the thriller form."[47] Influential though the *Cahiers* critics' rhapsodies were, however, few of their specific judgments, such as Truffaut's assertion in *Cahiers*'s first Hitchcock special, in October 1954, that "it is in *Under Capricorn* and *I Confess* that what I dare to call, without laughing, Hitchcock's message, finds its purest and noblest expression," were to survive this process.[48] The exception to this rule was a preference, then rare among critics, for the American Hitchcock over the British.

In the foreword to their book, Rohmer and Chabrol wrote that they had considered excluding the British films from their survey, only to decide to "let the reader profit from the chance we had to see them recently at the Cinémathèque," which had mounted a retrospective of "la période anglaise" at its new home in the Rue d'Ulm in the summer of 1956.[49] In most respects, Rohmer and Chabrol's treatment of *The Lodger* did not differ from Anderson's: his "inventiveness and visual dexterity" became their "virtuosity and remarkable visual sense."[50] But for them, as for Truffaut, *Rebecca* was a kind of second debut for Hitchcock, "the first manifestation of a mature talent," and his move to Hollywood "acted as a catalyst."[51] Just as Kapsis says, young American—and British—critics of the early 1960s were only too pleased to embrace this revaluation of American Hitchcock, but the transformation of his reputation since then cannot be explained solely with reference to little magazines like *Movie* and *Film Culture*, which published the Anglophone auteurists, or institutions like the Museum of Modern Art, which mounted a full Hitchcock retrospective in 1963.

It is better understood as part of a transformation of the cultural environment beyond the film art movement, one that is touched upon by Kapsis's notion of "a growing cultural eclecticism in American life as the old cultural categories—'high' versus 'low'—have lost their meaning for many artists and critics"; but this loss of meaning throws into doubt his own categories of "popular entertainer" and "serious artist," and, in turn, the hierarchy of cultural institutions on which such categories depend.[52] The advent of television and the expansion of higher education and of film studies within it—phenomena seemingly at opposite ends of the old cultural spectrum but in practice interacting—constituted a transformation in kind of the arena within which Hitchcock's films could be seen and

The Lodger, as seen in Truffaut's *Hitchcock*, as seen in De Palma's *Greetings*.

appraised, and it was in this postmodern space that he took on the reputation he has today. Television broadcasts of the films themselves naturally favored the sound era in general and the American period in particular; but the silent films, *The Lodger* especially, became topics of discussion in the interviews Hitchcock gave on the same medium in the 1960s and '70s, and they were shown in extract in television documentaries like Richard Schickel's *The Men Who Made the Movies*, made for PBS in 1973. Meanwhile the British period inevitably attracted the attention of academic researchers seeking to understand Hitchcock's place in film history.

It was within this transformed cultural space, even as *The Lodger* was being defined for the hundreds of thousands who read Truffaut's book as "the first true Hitchcock," that a myth was propagated about how it came to be so, one that has lasted to this day, with profound implications for our understanding of his art. The first half of the myth was retailed by Hitchcock himself in the Truffaut interview and others from around the same time, but it had been part of his repertoire of anecdotes for decades, and versions of it had appeared within months of the film's release. The bare bones of it had reached *Variety* by August 1927, months before the film's US debut. "The distributors saw it and threw up their hands," wrote the paper's London correspondent, but subsequently "the wise ones" were persuaded to show it—"and the press went crazy over it."[53] Two years later, Iris Barry told her *Daily Mail* readers that while Hitchcock "has no time for the quadrisyllabic labels which intellectual people want to attach to his work," almost all his films have "reduced his employers to excesses of despair. 'The Lodger,' for example, was said by all the experts to be an impossible film. Yet 'The Lodger' was one of the few British successes of its year."[54]

In April 1939 the episode came up in the first interview Hitchcock gave after his arrival in Los Angeles. Running through Hitchcock's career, *Los Angeles Times* columnist Philip K. Scheuer wrote that *The Lodger* "was shelved but afterward released—a hit despite its horror."[55] More detail was forthcoming after Hitchcock had established himself. In April 1943, Hedda Hopper, in her famous column for the same paper, wrote that Hitchcock was meeting studio opposition over *Lifeboat*. "Well, Hitchy's used to that kind of criticism. Years ago he made 'The Lodger' in London. Moguls got a look-see, threw it on the shelf. The Hitchcocks walked the streets of London looking for consolation. Two months afterward picture was sneaked into a theater and later hailed as the greatest British picture."[56] This was the short version of the story that Hitchcock would tell for the rest of his life, though in his own idiom.

Hitchcock was rarely able to explain the wise ones' change of heart. He came closest in the Truffaut book, which reproduced the story, by now well-rehearsed, almost verbatim from the tape:

> When it was first shown, they sent—the distributors sent the head of their publicity department, a woman, and one of their high officials. They looked at the film, and went back to report to the big boss in the film centre, Wardour Street it's called. . . . Anyway, they said "impossible to show. Too bad, the film is terrible. Terrible film." Two days later, the big boss comes down to the studio to look at it. He arrived at 2.30 pm. Mrs. Hitchcock and I were not married then, but we were going to be married in about three or four months' time. We couldn't bear to wait in the studio, to know the result, and we walked the streets of London—wandering, wondering, what's happening? And finally we walked for about one hour and a half or more, and I said it must be over by now, we'll get a cab, taxi and go back. We got back, and I went in, looking at the faces of the people in the studio. He agrees, it's terrible. There wasn't a happy ending to the walk—we were hoping we'd go

back and they'd say "oh, it's wonderful." No. So they put the film on the shelf. They stopped booking it—because they were booking it on Novello's name, you see. And about, oh some, couple of months later they decided to take another look at it. And they wanted some changes made—I can't remember what they were. I agreed to make about two. And finally the picture was shown. And it was acclaimed as the greatest British picture ever made.[57]

Other renderings—including Mrs. Hitchcock's—omitted to mention these changes; but it is this second half of the story that forms the myth's core. Most of it appeared in Anderson's 1949 article, which noted the involvement of Ivor Montagu, "who was called in by the distributors when they found themselves dissatisfied with the first copy of the film. After specifying certain re-takes, which Hitchcock shot, Montagu re-edited the film, and produced a version which the distributors accepted with delight."[58] Anderson's source, quoted directly in his program note for *The Lodger*'s revival in 1950, was Peter Noble's *Index to the Work of Alfred Hitchcock*, published in a series of "Special Supplements to *Sight and Sound*," before its takeover by Gavin Lambert, in May 1949.

Noble was himself a prolific author, editor, and publisher, responsible for among other short-lived magazines a *Film Quarterly*, whose Winter 1946–47 issue included a substantial study by Harry Wilson titled "Hitchcock in Hollywood: An Interim Report: 1939–46."[59] Noble and Wilson remain obscure figures, subject to an unspoken stratification of film publications, even though Wilson also contributed a notable article on what came to be known as film noir to *Sequence*. As of 1947, he was embarked on a biography of Hitchcock; none materialized, but Noble extended him special thanks in his *Index*, presumably for information gleaned from his research.[60] Noble also had access to Hitchcock himself, as well as Alma Reville, Michael Balcon, Ivor Novello—whose biography he went on to write—and perhaps most importantly Ivor Montagu, from whom he took this:

When *The Lodger* was cut and finished it was taken to Ivor Montagu, who was then running a company in association with Adrian Brunel. Montagu was asked to re-edit the film as C. M. Woolf of W. and F. Distributors was not particularly pleased with it. He re-cut some sequences, ordered some re-takes (which Hitchcock shot), wrote a new set of titles, reducing them to a sparse minimum, and commissioned McKnight Kauffer, the famous commercial designer, to design the titles and backgrounds. *The Lodger* was then released by W. and F., and was one of the biggest successes of the year. It established Hitchcock.[61]

It was in the 1970s and after that the implications of this story were teased out, eventually beyond plausibility, partly because the story confirmed what had been the film art movement's attitude toward British cinema—and its idea of itself—since its inception. Paul Rotha's awkwardly phrased view that Britain had produced "no school of thought for the furtherance of filmic theory" was not contradicted for many years.[62] When *The Film Till Now* was republished in 1949, largely unrevised, though supplemented by what amounted to a whole new book by Richard Griffith, Barry's assistant at the Museum of Modern Art, Rotha's original was warmly praised by the *Sequence* writers, in three separate reviews, despite their vaunted differences with the senior generation of critics. The *Movie* critics of the early 1960s, though they resented the fact that "verdicts pronounced by Rotha when *The Film Till Now* was first published thirty years ago are still being pressed into service," as V. F. Perkins put it, nonetheless endorsed Rotha's verdict on British cinema.[63]

The classic expression of the "film art movement" perspective on British cinema was provided by Rachael Low, a contemporary of the *Sequence* critics, in the fourth volume of her *History of the British Film*, published in 1971. Here, as well as giving Noble's account of *The Lodger*, Low provided a historical framework within which it could be understood. In the 1920s, the "intellectual life of Europe had been in a state of creative ferment for some time. Great Britain was only on the fringe of these movements," she wrote.[64] "Until the later twenties, with the foundation of the Film Society and *Close Up* and the appearance of intellectual young film makers and critics, there were few who showed any conscious interest in developments of film technique abroad."[65] There was, as Rotha had said, no native school of thought. Low herself, being closer to the events and their participants, had a shrewd sense of Hitchcock's character and his relationship with the intellectuals, but over time this perspective on British cinema was combined with Montagu's detailed memories of *The Lodger* to produce the extended myth.

Montagu gave his account directly on a number of occasions, an early instance being his autobiography *The Youngest Son*, published in 1970.

In this version it was not only that W. & F. was displeased with *The Lodger*:

> But the situation was even worse than this. It was not Hitchcock's first, but third. He had made two others, *The Pleasure Garden* and *The Mountain Eagle* . . . and W. and F. liked neither of these, either. So Mick [Balcon] had been holding them up because he had thought it important that Hitch's first picture should be a winner. . . . An investment not only in one but in three pictures and in a man's career was in jeopardy.[66]

Hitchcock accepted Montagu's advice and carried out some retakes, while Montagu himself cut the titles "down to eighty instead of the usual from three hundred and fifty to five or six hundred."[67] Hitchcock and Balcon were pleased; W. & F. was satisfied; and on that memorable afternoon at the Hippodrome the press "went gooey-eyed over *The Lodger* and Mick's gamble paid off. The log-jam broke, the two earlier films could now come out." In a later rendition Montagu made more of it: *The Lodger*'s success "opened the door to the two delayed predecessors waiting in the wings, and from then on Hitch was unstoppable."[68] Montagu's recollections have gone on to inform the three main biographies of Hitchcock—John Russell Taylor's in 1978, Donald Spoto's in 1983, Patrick McGilligan's in 2003—and sundry other accounts of Hitchcock's life and work, in print, over the airwaves, and on screen. As a consequence, the Film Society has been given an altogether more significant role in Hitchcock's early life than "something for the intellectuals to do on Sunday afternoon." Spoto called Balcon's decision to hire Montagu "an idea that made history."[69]

The Film Society connection received its most compelling treatment in two essays by Peter Wollen, who had interviewed Montagu at length for *Screen* in 1972. In "The Last New Wave," a brilliant reworking of the history of British cinema, first published in 1993, Wollen gave to Low's narrative the flavor of the *New Left Review*, another influential journal with which he was associated. Briefly, just as Britain had never experienced a thorough bourgeois revolution, having had its Civil War early, and therefore never developed either a mass socialist movement or an independent socialist cadre, so did it fail—again as a result of its premature political and industrial revolutions—to produce a true modernist movement, since these tended to flourish in countries where the shock of the new was that much more shocking. "Modernism, in its pure form," Wollen argued, had often come to Britain through expatriates like T. S. Eliot, and was all too smoothly assimilated, with "a bloodless transfer of power to the Bloomsbury group." It "first impinged on British film culture during the silent period with the London Film Society and the journal *Close Up*," and was quickly diluted by the loss of Iris Barry to New York in 1930, among other factors.[70] "The Film Society's most significant outcome," Wollen went on to say, "was its impact on Alfred Hitchcock, a habitual and doubtless punctual attender at screenings. There Hitchcock not only mingled with the cultural elite but also absorbed modernist aesthetic ideas, which he later attempted to nurture within narrative film."[71]

A decade later, in "Hitch: A Tale of Two Cities," Wollen expanded on this vision of "the more sophisticated world whose values he envied, the world of Ivor Montagu and Adrian Brunel," making a sharp distinction between the "staunchly middle-brow" tastes that were Hitchcock's native inheritance, and "another side of England, the artistic sophistication that Hitchcock acquired through his social superiors at the London Film Society, which stimulated his abiding interest in experiment, and led him towards the dream sequences in *Spellbound* and *Vertigo*, the rolling camera in *Rope*, the virtuoso montage in *Psycho*, the use of the Kuleshov Effect in *Rear Window*," and so on.[72]

The most complete synthesis, the definitive version of the myth, is Richard Allen's article "*The Lodger* and the Origins of Hitchcock's Aesthetic," published over forty pages in the *Hitchcock Annual* for 2001-2. This affirmed the idea that by the time he made *The Lodger*, "Hitchcock was familiar with German expressionism not only from screenings of German films at the London Film Society but also through his practical exposure to Weimar film-making during his residence in Berlin" in 1924.[73] But Allen went further, discerning the "influence of Soviet montage and in particular, Eisenstein," through the same connection.[74] He was not the first to claim this. Tom Ryall, for example, in his book *Alfred Hitchcock and the British Cinema*, published in 1986, had written that the chess sequence in *The Lodger* "seems to draw on the editing techniques of the Soviet cinema."[75] Allen, however, gave supporting evidence, and was careful to record that it was "highly unlikely" that Hitchcock himself had seen any of the Russian films when he made *The Lodger*.[76] Instead, he claimed, Montagu had not only seen *Battleship Potemkin* in Berlin, where it had opened—after much difficulty—on 29 April 1926, while *The Lodger* was still in production, but that in his capacity as a *Times* correspondent he "met up with Eisenstein, Alexandrov, and Tisse during their European tour." So it was that "the Eisensteinian influence that seems so evident in the film derives in part from Montagu, fresh from his firsthand experiences with Eisenstein and a viewing of *Potemkin*."

By the time Allen's article appeared, *The Lodger* and Hitchcock's other silent films were more visible than at any time since the 1920s. Hitchcock's centenary in 1999 saw the publication of *English Hitchcock* by Charles Barr, a *Movie* critic of the 1960s who had gone on to become a leading academic historian of British cinema. In Barr's chapter on *The Lodger*, anticipating Allen's article, Montagu "was already associated with the dynamic new Soviet film-makers" when he stepped in.[77] The BBC's two-part documentary *Hitch*, first broadcast in May 1999, meanwhile told its viewers about "the lessons of Soviet cinema" over shots from *The Lodger*, and repeated Montagu's story about Hitchcock's first three films being shelved. The centennial year also saw the restoration of *The Lodger* by the BFI, followed by its release on VHS tape—though more dubious editions had preceded it in the United States. The same restoration would be put on DVD in the 2000s, before it was superseded by a new one in 2012, released as a Criterion Blu-ray disc in 2017. These too sustained the myth, through commentaries and booklet essays.

Most of this myth—the role of the Film Society in introducing German films to British screens, the "log-jam" of releases and Hitchcock's "jeopardy," the Eisensteinian influence on *The Lodger*—is just that, and the rest has been inflated out of proportion. Its perverse result has been to present Hitchcock, the original *auteur*, as a vector of ideas introduced by others, so that what is thought distinctive in him is that which was grafted on, in a delirium of influence-seeking that all but occludes the culture he was formed in. Barr himself has explored some of these byways in the years since *English Hitchcock*, and Wollen's "Hitch: A Tale of Two Cities" had the salutary aim of breaking down "the national compartmentalization of Hitchcock into 'English' and 'American,'" but the myth has yet to be comprehensively overturned.[78]

The background for the specific scene of the Hon. Ivor Montagu, not long down from Cambridge, back from his European travels, the Odessa steps in his head, toiling with scissors and cement in a Soho editing room—the background that gave this scene credibility and luster, the background of sharp divisions between modernist and middlebrow, entertainer and artist—was a projection, an exaggerated image of stable values and stiff hierarchies and unbridgeable schisms, thrown back across the decades. This background was made to loom most large during the epoch of what Kapsis called "cultural eclecticism," the information explosion of the 1960s, not least through paperback publication of the most severe and schismatic critics from the preceding generation, in the British context Eliot and the Leavises, characteristically described by Wollen as "the most powerful and effective protagonists of modern literature."[79] They did not appear as powerful to many of their contemporaries, and would not have done so to Hitchcock; rather, they consciously addressed a minority even within the intelligentsia, believing that theirs were voices being drowned out in a vortex of values, including a kind of cultural eclecticism, that they experienced just as intensely as later generations would do, perhaps more so, since they had far less influence within the academy of the 1920s— smaller then in any case—than they would enjoy later.

That apart, the modernist assault on the literary giants of Hitchcock's childhood was only beginning at the time of *The Lodger*'s making, most consistently in the pages of the *Calendar of Modern Letters*, a little magazine published between 1925 and 1927—and, significantly, reprinted in 1966. The authors it subjected to piercing "Scrutinies"—the rubric that would give the Leavises' journal its name—included some Hitchcock revered, adapted, wanted to adapt, or was proud to have met, including J. M. Barrie (March 1925), George Bernard Shaw (September 1925), H. G. Wells (July 1927), John Galsworthy (in the book *Scrutinies*, published in March 1928), and G. K. Chesterton (ditto). "To you, it may seem that it wasn't sticking one's neck out to criticise Barrie, but really it was so in those days," the *Calendar*'s editor Edgell Rickword reflected fifty years later. "He was still rather a deity; and even if some people admitted that he was a bit soppy, they still thought him a charming man, so witty and lovely, and 'Have you been to *Mary Rose*?' The tears! People actually wept."[80] As Charles Barr has shown, Hitchcock's memories of *Mary Rose*, first performed at the Haymarket in 1920, were "a consistent and explicit reference point as late as 1957 in constructing the dream-like narrative of *Vertigo*," and he planned to film it.[81]

The young Hitchcock seems to have been unaware of the finer literary distinctions that later critics have assumed were in place, particularly in relation to the thriller. It came as a shock, registered only after his arrival in the United States, that while "that form of writing is highly respected in England," as he told Truffaut and other interviewers, "in America it's definitely regarded as second-rate literature."[82] In his most illuminating comment on the topic, given in 1973, Hitchcock told Arthur Knight:

> You can go back to Conan Doyle, you know, or Wilkie Collins. Go as far back as you like, right up to the present day, crime has always interested the English litterateurs. They write books on the most recent *cause célèbre* and it's always taken seriously. Whether you take John Buchan or Mrs. Belloc-Lowndes, Galsworthy's *Escape*, or a playwright like Clemence Dane, G. K. Chesterton's *Father Brown*, all of these serious writers have at one time or another contributed to the literature of crime. I follow in that tradition.[83]

Two years later, as if in confirmation, Gavin Lambert, who had left London for Los Angeles in 1956, published a book, *The Dangerous Edge*, which chronicled precisely this tradition of "crime-artists," from Collins via Conan Doyle, Chesterton, Buchan, Ambler, Simenon, and Chandler, to—Hitchcock.

As is now well known, T. S. Eliot was among the litterateurs of the 1920s who took an interest in crime fiction; even he was not free from cultural eclecticism. This eclecticism, in the form of Parisian auteurism, came to seem novel in the 1960s in part because of the paradox that the sterner pronouncements of literary critics like Eliot, despite their hostility toward film, had influenced the film art movement's sense of itself as a realm apart from the commercial cinema. As its livelier spirits quite frequently acknowledged, however, this was always a fiction. In the final issue of *Sequence*, published for New Year 1952, Lambert wrote of growing up as a film fan in the 1930s—"one had scarcely heard of *Close Up*"—with celluloid in his veins, "a wonderfully rich and intoxicating compound, with a few droppings of Joan Crawford, Charlie Chan and *Boots of Destiny* in it as well as Bunuel, Flaherty and the rest."[84] He knew enough to know of "the permitted relaxations of the 20's, Pearl White, Laurel and Hardy, westerns," but in truth the film art movement was only in its infancy then, the lines even less sharply drawn.

The critic who best understood Hitchcock's outlook was Julian Maclaren-Ross. It was in the mid-1950s, when Maclaren-Ross was occasionally engaged as a screenwriter, that he came to devise a genealogy of the thriller from Robert Louis Stevenson to Hitchcock and beyond. Like other books of his, it exists only in fragments, some composed of articles published anonymously in the *Times Literary Supplement*. In a signed review of Richard Usborne's *Clubland Heroes*, published in 1954, he argued that behind much of the serious literature of the day lay the disavowed influence of John Buchan, whom he credited with having introduced a "swifter pace and colloquial style" to the thriller.[85] In a subsequent *TLS* article he wrote that Buchan had "adapted the sense of helpless terror conveyed in the first part of *Treasure Island* to a metropolitan setting and surroundings even more prosaic than those described in *The Suicide Club*," also by Stevenson.[86] (Usborne's book, important in itself, is a study of Buchan, Dornford Yates, and "Sapper," author of the Bulldog Drummond stories that were the seed of *The Man Who Knew Too Much*.)

In the same article, Maclaren-Ross wrote that Hitchcock had "carried the Buchan formula a step farther," and that in so doing he "had evidently learnt from the silent films produced in France and Germany during the post-1914–18 War years." What Maclaren-Ross called "Lang's melodramas," including *Dr. Mabuse: The Gambler*, he went on, "had a strange allegorical Kafkan-nightmare quality and, by an ironic juxtaposition of background and situation, prefigured," together with "the Louis Feuillade serials," the Hitchcock thriller. In a further *TLS* article, published in 1956, he wrote that Buchan's *The Three Hostages* had amplified "a method initiated by Stevenson in *The New Arabian Nights* and since adapted, cinematically, by Mr. Fritz Lang, Mr. Alfred Hitchcock and Sir Carol Reed"—the method of "imbuing realistic settings with a sense of menace and stealthy terror."[87] Maclaren-Ross concluded with a citation from *The Three Hostages*, published in August 1924, uncannily suggestive of the first shots of *The Lodger*, taken eighteen months later. "The West End of London at night always affected me with a sense of the immense solidity of our civilization," Buchan's hero Richard Hannay muses; but "Might not terror and mystery lurk behind that barricade as well as in tent and slum? I suddenly had a picture of a plump face all screwed up with fright muffled beneath the bed clothes."

Though he wrote for some of its most prestigious organs, Maclaren-Ross did not belong to the settled literary intelligentsia; nor was he part of the film art movement, and thus his essays, despite their place of publication, are unknown within academic film studies. Yet it was this same estrangement that enabled him to clear the way for a perspective on Hitchcock's formation as a sophisticated artist in a popular medium, outside the narrow confines of the film art movement, exposed to seminal influences as he found them, mixed together and without elite supervision, during his adolescence and early adulthood.

3 No Old Masters

Around the start of December 1915, a poster appeared on the hoardings and in the tube stations of London, showing a face in a slouch hat and scarf, with only his eyes visible, and below it just the words "Who is he?" Soon it was revealed that *Who Is He?* was the title of a new play, adapted by the prolific Horace Annesley Vachell from a novel by Marie Belloc Lowndes; but the secret "as to which novel Mr. Vachell has taken is a well-guarded one, and all a 'Star' man can say," reported that newspaper, "is that Mr. Vachell's remodelling of the principal character in Mrs. Lowndes' novel will considerably surprise and amuse the readers of the book."[1]

Produced by Frederick Harrison, it opened at the Haymarket on the 9th, replacing Vachell's *Quinneys*, a sentimental comedy with the same star, Henry Ainley. On his first appearance as Mr. Parker, in the costume familiar from the posters, Ainley "was greeted with applause as an old friend," wrote E. A. Baughan of the *Daily News*, and not for a moment as a potential murderer, because "a leading actor never could be cast as a murderer."[2] Moreover, the play was written as a farce and received as one; "light and clever and wholesome," said the *Pall Mall Gazette*, "and just the thing for wartime."[3]

The Haymarket, with the colonnaded theater on the right, c. 1912. SOURCE: Historic England Archive.

The streets of London were all but blacked out, the way to the once gaily lit theaters now marked by a few blue-shaded lamps. Bombs had exploded near the Lyceum and the Strand during a Zeppelin raid on the night of 13 October, and in the immediate aftermath some theaters, including the Haymarket, had restricted themselves to matinées. The damage did not come close to the horrors prophesied in such prewar novels as H. G. Wells's *The War in the Air*, but the Zeppelins happened to cross Hitchcock's path more than once. Leytonstone, the northeastern suburb where he was born, and where he and his mother had returned after his father's death in December 1914, was bombed in the first raid on London, in May 1915, and more extensively in August, as Hitchcock would recall. On 8 September, during a Zeppelin raid on the City, a bus was hit in Blomfield Street, where Hitchcock toiled by day as a clerk for W. T. Henley's Telegraph Works, leaving three dead.

Hitchcock ventured into the gloom undeterred, though two decades later the image of a bus blown apart in a London street would find its way into *Sabotage*. "I remember seeing Mrs. Belloc Lowndes's 'Who is He?' at the Haymarket and making up my mind there and then that there was a good film in it," he wrote in 1928. Already, by the age of sixteen, he "had formed the habit of thinking in the terms of the film wherever I went. I never saw a play in a theatre without automatically visualising the play as a film." *The Lodger*, he claimed, was by now familiar to "millions of cinema-goers. As a boy I saw possibilities in the play for the screen. As a man in my twenties I directed it—which was something the boy certainly did not dream of."[4]

The "terms of the film" in 1915 were not what they would be in 1928, however. There were already thousands of cinemas in Britain, serving millions of cinemagoers, but this was a new phenomenon that had arisen only in the half decade before the war, and in important respects the terms of the film were in the process of being invented. Vital questions of how films were made, sold, and shown—and by whom—were still open. For the past few years, the fault line dividing the industry, on both sides of the Atlantic, lay between two conceptions of what a visit to the cinema might mean: a program of shorts of one or two reels apiece, changed twice a week, as had become the custom; or a program centered on a single, multireel film approximating the length of a stage play.

In November 1915, for example, Jack Graham-Cutts, Hitchcock's future mentor, then manager of the Scala Theatre in Birmingham, had written an article for the trade paper *Cinema News* arguing that the future was "one screen one play one performance," three times a day, appealing to "better educated people."[5] Many of his peers remained wedded to the short films still being turned out by older American companies like Vitagraph, Kalem, Selig, and Essanay, former members of the Motion Picture Patents Company or "Edison trust," and by the trust's "independent" rivals, above all Universal. These were rented from distributors without limitation and shown without fixed start times. As Cutts admitted, the "necessary productions," the longer and more expensive films that could be sold as "exclusives," barring rival cinemas from showing them, were still in the minority. The new companies that specialized in making them, household names of the future, had only recently begun to establish branches in Britain.

The major cinemas of the West End, built during the second half of the prewar cinema construction boom, in 1912–14, tended to show the long films, and their programs for the night of 9 December 1915 provide a partial freeze-frame of the terms of the film as Hitchcock would have understood them. The New Gallery, which had opened to some fanfare in January 1913, was showing *The Unafraid*, whose star Rita Jolivet had survived the sinking of the *Lusitania* earlier in the year. *The Unafraid* was exactly what Cutts meant by necessary: a four-reel exclusive from the Lasky company, which had established itself in Wardour Street—soon to become a synecdoche for the film trade in general—only in the autumn of 1914, sharing an office and a release program with Famous Players two years before their merger. Also on the bill was a film that did not need to be named: its star, Charlie Chaplin, was advertisement enough, and his unparalleled success in 1915 was proof that the day of the short film was not yet done.

The West End Cinema, on Coventry Street, between Leicester Square and Piccadilly Circus, was showing *She Stoops to Conquer*, a staple of the West End stage, first performed in 1773, done in three reels. It starred Henry Ainley, who was, by day, a leading light of the London Film Company, the most promising British film studio—albeit heavily American staffed—of the prewar period. The film had debuted at the same venue in April 1914. Despite its promise, the LFC had recently announced losses, blamed on the war, and was beginning to break up. Nevertheless, it was still hiring. It was in 1915–16 that sixteen-year-old Alma Reville, a "film mad" aspiring actress, found a job in the cutting room of the company's studio near the Reville family home in the southwestern suburb of Twickenham.[6] During 1916 the LFC would cast Ainley in an adaptation of Hall Caine's *The Manxman*, readapted by Hitchcock in 1929.

The Marble Arch Pavilion, on the corner of Oxford Street and Park Lane, had opened in May 1914, less than a month before the assassination of Franz Ferdinand, making it the last of the great prewar cinemas. Seating eighteen hundred, it was the biggest cinema in the West End at the time, "beautifully decorated in bronze gold and pink, a semi-Egyptian style being followed throughout."[7] The structure was the work of Frank Verity, who would become the most celebrated British cinema architect of his generation and go on to design the Plaza. Its creation was the crowning achievement of Israel Davis, scion of an East End building family, "who became a cinema proprietor as the result of the building slump in

1909," as Iris Barry would later write.[8] He had given his chain of Pavilions to his wife, Minnie, initially "to run as a hobby."

On 9 December 1915, the Marble Arch Pavilion was showing the Italian epic *Cabiria*, a recent transfer from the West End Cinema, where it had played for more than two months. *Cabiria* was typical of the films that had helped raise the cinema's social standing in the years before the war, and which the cinemas of the West End had been built to show; but it was already eighteen months old, and it belonged to a lost world. Italy had entered the war in May 1915, and its film industry would suffer as badly as any in Europe. The Marble Arch Pavilion's program also included a more recent film of American origin—the latest installment of Pathé's serial *The Exploits of Elaine*, the first of which had been released in October, and which was being shown in at least nine hundred British cinemas.

The fault line was more visible in the four cinemas of Leytonstone, two of them, the 800-seat Academy (opened in March 1913) and 450-seat Gaiety (January 1913), tending toward short films, the others, the vast 1,500-seat Rink (June 1911) and the 850-seat Premier (June 1910), longer exclusives. Typical suburban cinemas, all four showed mostly American films. In early December 1915 the Academy was showing installments from two American serials, Universal's *The Black Box*, and Thanhouser's *The Zudora Mystery*.[9] The Premier, meanwhile, had an example of the new "necessary productions," *The Heart of a Painted Woman*, a five-reeler from a new firm, Metro, that had come into being only in March 1915 and launched itself in London in August.[10] On the 9th the top-liner at the Gaiety was a two-reeler, *A Fateful Test*, from the French company Gaumont.[11] (On the 10th, Gaumont's British branch would open its new studio at Shepherd's Bush in West London.) The Rink's offerings are imperfectly documented, but later in December it had another Metro release, *The Second in Command*.[12]

Also on the 9th, in the adjacent district of Leyton, the King's Hall was showing a similarly scaled production, *The Wishing Ring*, a four-reeler from another of the new American companies specializing in exclusives, World, which had opened for business in London not long before Metro, in June 1915. The two companies had begun releasing films in Britain in July and November respectively. Like Famous Players and Lasky, they offered long films in a volume and with a regularity that no British company could match. World would not sustain its early pace, but these four companies pointed the way ahead. Fox Films would join them in London in early 1916.

While the preponderance of American films on British screens was plain for all to see, the industry behind them was visible to British observers only in flashes. One of the brightest came with the opening of the expanded Universal City, north of Hollywood, in March 1915, photographs of which appeared in the British trade press. In August, *Pictures and the Picture-goer* reprinted a glimpse from the American *Moving Picture World* "of the Bohemian existence which adds charm to the life of the picture-people on the Californian Coast," and of the "town of motor-cars" they inhabited; but Hitchcock professed not to have read fan magazines.[13]

Nor were the leading personalities of the American industry as prominent as they would become. A rare exception came in the summer of 1915 when W. G. Faulkner of the *Evening News*, one of the few British newspapers to run regular film coverage, determined "that the British people should realise what the complete capture of the British picture theatre by Americans means to this country."[14] To this end he mounted a campaign against American firms led by "presidents whose German names no man could mistake," an incendiary remark in wartime, and probably anti-Semitic in intent.[15] Prompting righteous criticism from the trade press, Faulkner named and provided photographs of, among others, Adolph Zukor, Carl Laemmle, and the managing director of World, Lewis J. Selznick.

A close reader of the trade press—such as the adolescent Hitchcock—would have known that the ambitions of the "Film Kings," as Faulkner called them, went beyond capturing British screens. The nineteenth installment of the Famous Players-Lasky bulletin "Films Weekly," dated 29 April 1915, which was included in each of the British trade papers, announced that "After the war Jesse L. Lasky will open a studio in London. Now, pretty would-be actresses who haunt Wardour Street, don't crush."[16] A few months later, Zukor, too, was quoted as saying that the end of hostilities would see "the erection of an elaborate studio in London for the purpose of producing pretentious transcontinental subjects."[17]

The directors of the exclusives that the Film Kings were sending across by the week were obscure figures. Rarely if ever was it mentioned that

The Wishing Ring was the work of Maurice Tourneur, or *The Heart of a Painted Woman* that of Alice Guy-Blaché. The director of *The Unafraid* was a slightly different case. On the day of its release in August 1915 it was the thirteenth film directed by Cecil B. DeMille to have come to Britain in a year, and by 9 December three more had appeared. DeMille's name only came up in reviews from time to time, and was rarely used in advertising, but as Richard Koszarski, the pioneer historian of this period, was to demonstrate, DeMille was on the verge of a breakthrough at the end of 1915. *The Cheat*, shown to the trade in London in early 1916, was treated as the work of an *auteur*.[18] Even before then, however, DeMille's words had been quoted in ways that might have captured the young Hitchcock's imagination.

In an interview published in *Cinema News* in September 1915, DeMille, whose father and brother were Broadway playwrights, looked forward to "when the seemingly inexhaustible supply of material for the photo-play from the legitimate stage and written literature will be no more."[19] That supply was central to the new American companies' strategy. Lasky had the rights to the David Belasco catalog; Famous Players was associated with Daniel Frohman; World with Lee Shubert—all leading Broadway producers. Yet, for DeMille, "the medium of transmitting emotion and feeling is through the eye, not through the ear, as on the legitimate stage"—and films also required "a different technique than the novel." These would become commonplaces; Hitchcock began the article in which he recalled *Who Is He?* by declaring that the "most important development of the film will be its entire severance from both the stage and the novel, and the command of a medium of its own."[20] In October 1915, DeMille was quoted as saying that he preferred the new medium because "there are no old masters. We are just as apt to be the old masters as anybody else."[21]

Questions of this kind were also being discussed by British filmmakers. In July 1915, for example, a debate in *Cinema News* over the division of tasks between writer and director included a contribution from a scenario editor employed by British and Colonial, whose studio was near Hitchcock's home, on the border of Leyton and Walthamstow. Eliot Stannard, who had recently adapted his mother's novel *Grip* for the director Maurice Elvey—shown at the Leytonstone Rink in November 1915—wrote that the ideal director, apart from his or her general education, must "acquire

a technical knowledge of cinematography, including camera work, lighting, densities of colours, and a perfect understanding of the cutting up of
negatives."[22] The significance of cutting would become an axiom of the
1930s, under Russian influence; in 1915 it was seldom remarked upon. A
few weeks earlier, in the *Kinematograph Weekly*, Stannard had reflected
on the fate of films by even the best-known directors—"gone like a sunset."[23] His examples included the one name that overshadowed them all,
D. W. Griffith.

The Birth of a Nation did not open in one of the West End cinemas,
nor were its twelve reels destined to unspool in any cinema at all for the
next few years. It opened instead at the Scala, a theater, albeit one that
had been largely given over to film shows since before the war, being too
remote from theatreland proper. Griffith's epic was still there on 9 December, playing twice a day, more than two months after its heavily advertised debut on 27 September, which had attracted notices in publications
that rarely covered goings-on in the film world. Program notes were provided by Cecil Chesterton, editor of the *New Witness*, whose contributors included his brother G. K., Marie Belloc Lowndes, and her brother
Hilaire. Chesterton had seen the film in the United States earlier in the
year, and become an avowed sympathizer of the Ku Klux Klan as a result.
In March 1916 *The Birth of a Nation* transferred to the historic Theatre
Royal, Drury Lane, where it lasted a further two months; by that time
Who Is He? had gone.

On the evening of 30 March 1939, the day before he and his family
began the last leg of their move to Los Angeles, Hitchcock gave a talk
at the Museum of Modern Art, then in temporary accommodation at
Rockefeller Center, as part of an extension course organized for Columbia University by Iris Barry and MoMA's director, her second husband,
John Abbott. Having discussed his reservations about using dialogue as a
means of delineating character, Hitchcock came to his preferred method.
Since the days of Griffith, he told his audience, there had developed "two
types of suspense."[24] There was the "objective suspense" of the "race to
the scaffold" type that Griffith employed in *Orphans of the Storm*, from
1921, and "subjective suspense, which is letting the audience experience it
through the mind or eyes of one of the characters." Instead of "cutting to

the galloping feet of the horse and then going to the scaffold—instead of showing both sides, I like to show only one side," he said. The film he was about to make, *Rebecca*, would indeed be told from one side, through the eyes of one character.

Hitchcock later explained how he had arrived at this distinctive approach. Asked to name his favorite chase sequence, he mentioned a number by Griffith, including the climax of *Orphans of the Storm*, which he knowingly or otherwise misnamed *A Tale of Two Cities*, and the earlier "ride of the hooded men" in *The Birth of a Nation*.[25] "Griffith's chase was fairly elementary," said Hitchcock. "It didn't include any mental action, any characterization." Hitchcock had "derived more from novelists like John Buchan, J. B. Priestley, John Galsworthy, and Mrs. Belloc Lowndes than from the movies. I like them because they use multiple chases and a lot of psychology." Hitchcock's chases—his subjective suspense—combined "what I got from these novelists with what I got from Griffith." Thus in *The Lodger*, the chase "was in the mind of the onlooker seeing the picture, you might say." Priestley, who contributed dialogue to *Jamaica Inn*, did not begin publishing novels until after *The Lodger*'s release. Galsworthy is not renowned for his chase sequences. But Lowndes's influence entered Hitchcock's life at about the same time as Griffith's—and the same may be true of Buchan.

A former colonial administrator who had served in South Africa in the aftermath of the Boer War, Buchan was mostly occupied during 1915 as one of the war's instant historians—his friend and intellectual sparring partner Belloc was another—publishing a regular *History of the War* that was approaching its ninth volume by December. He presented *The Thirty-Nine Steps* as a side project, product of a bout of illness spent reading thrillers. It came out in book form in October, a few weeks after the London opening of *A Birth of a Nation*, having debuted as a serial in *Blackwood's Magazine*, under a pseudonym, earlier in the year.

In *English Hitchcock*, Charles Barr identified a "Buchan/Belloc Lowndes dialectic" in Hitchcock's work, with Buchan "the novelist of action and adventure," Lowndes "the novelist of interior drama"; but although *The Thirty-Nine Steps* is a novel of action and adventure for most of its length, the climax constitutes an interior drama.[26] The whole story is told in the first person by Richard Hannay, a Scotsman who has made his "pile" in the mines of Rhodesia and feels cast adrift in prewar London, and this final chapter is an exercise in subjective suspense, shown from one side. Hannay suspects that an enemy spy will be exfiltrated by yacht from the Kentish coast, but, with the clock ticking, he begins to doubt himself when surveilling the "horribly English" inhabitants of the villa where he has been led to believe the villains are holed up; and the reader has no perspective but his. Buchan draws out the uncertainty for as long as possible, and the real climax when it comes is a flash of perception, not action, a "little thing, lasting only a second."

There was another author Hitchcock encountered during the second year of the war whose influence on his method would be considerable. In an article published in 1960 in the French weekly *Arts*, a magazine Truffaut had written for before becoming a director, Hitchcock wrote that he had discovered Poe at sixteen, having read, "par hasard," his biography, and would come home from the office and rush to his bedroom to read a cheap edition of Poe's *Histoires Extraordinaires*.[27] It is improbable that Hitchcock read Poe in French, though he was aware that the French translation was by Baudelaire, whose introduction, translated in turn, had been included in Chatto and Windus's collection of Poe's *Choice Works*, first published in 1902. At 3s, 6d., however, this was not cheap. At 7d., Nelson's collection *Tales of Mystery and Imagination*, published in 1911, was the price of a cinema ticket; moreover it was introduced by John Buchan.

Poe, wrote Hitchcock, provided the model of "a perfectly incredible story told with a logic so hallucinatory that one has the impression that this same story could happen to you tomorrow." Buchan, half a century before, had credited Poe with having "in the highest degree the constructive imagination which can reproduce a realm of fancy with the minute realism of everyday life," and found that "in all his tales there is a clear sequence of cause and effect which gives them an imaginative coherence and verisimilitude."[28] The affinities between Poe's stories and Hitchcock's films are legion, but the most significant recurring link is the figure of the damaged hero obsessed by a dead woman—central to *Rebecca*, reaching its apex in *Vertigo*, but also present in *The Lodger*. Poe was also a practitioner of subjective suspense, notably in *The Tell-Tale Heart*.

Narrated by a maniac who seeks to explain, with perfect logic, that he killed an old man he had befriended because of his "Evil Eye," passing off his madness as "over acuteness of the senses," the suspense begins halfway through when—the madman having hidden the body—police arrive to investigate a neighbor's report of a shriek in the night. The madman, having convinced them that nothing is untoward, begins to hallucinate the sound of the dead man's heartbeat, and to believe that the police can hear it too, and finally confesses his crime, without the police having heard a thing.

It is conceivable that Hitchcock was led to Poe by Griffith. In August 1915, before the arrival of *The Birth of a Nation*, Griffith's bowdlerization of "The Tell-Tale Heart," titled *The Avenging Conscience*, was shown at the West End Cinema for a four-week run. It was reviewed in the *Weekly Dispatch* as "a commonplace story enough, but told in an inimitable way by a great imaginative artist. In America they say there are only two kinds of film plays—those that are produced by Griffith and . . . the others."[29] Its most striking sequence, toward the end, conforms with the climax of Poe's story, in which the culprit is questioned by a detective. Here Griffith incorporates close-ups and detail shots into an editing pattern, timed for suspense, that has no rival in the rest of the film. Unlike *The Birth of a Nation*, *The Avenging Conscience* was given a general release, and was still playing in parts of London on 9 December. "Hardly any filmgoer of to-day has ever heard of 'The Avenging Conscience,'" wrote Hitchcock in 1931, "but that picture made in the first year of the War, was the forerunner and inspiration of most of the modern German films, to which we owe so much artistically."[30]

Hitchcock's withdrawal to his bedroom to read the writer celebrated by Baudelaire as "a being created to breathe in a purer world" was scarcely in keeping with the martial ethos of the times.[31] Also in August 1915, the month he turned sixteen, a register was drawn up of all men between fifteen and sixty-five as a prelude to conscription, which was introduced— after a steady drumbeat of semi-compulsion—six months later.

Famous Players-Lasky's announcement that it would build a studio in London was one element within a concerted bid for supremacy. The news appeared in the American press on 16 May 1919, the same day that

FP-L announced it had acquired control of two of the three principal cinemas of Times Square, the Rialto and the Rivoli, both built in 1916–17.[32] In the same month FP-L was listed on the New York Stock Exchange; until now Wall Street had had relatively little to do with the parvenu movie business. The two moves together were the prelude to its expansion into exhibition; hitherto Famous Players-Lasky, like most of its competitors, had only made and distributed films. Through June and July, reports appeared of FP-L's purchase of stock in cinema chains across the United States, and in November its bankers arranged a $20 million share issue to finance further acquisitions. As Zukor explained in his autobiography, the first move had become necessary when the Strand, first of the Times Square cinemas, came under the control of a formidable new rival, First National Exhibitors Circuit.[33]

This had come into being in 1917, in direct response to FP-L's commanding position in the industry. With the most popular stars under contract, Zukor was able to impose terms on cinema owners, namely block booking. The cinema owners had therefore banded together as First National. Comprising circuits covering most of the United States and Canada and including many of the "first-run" sites—the large and well-situated cinemas access to which was vital for success—it had the financial heft to commission productions on its own account. The idea was largely that of J. D. Williams, a West Virginian described by his obituarist as an "entrepreneur and adventurer" rather than a mogul.[34] He had been a touring showman before the nickelodeon era; in the early 1910s he had established one of the major cinema circuits in Australia, where he had met his English wife; and after leaving First National he would play a part in the drama of *The Lodger*.

Soon after First National was founded, "Jaydee" had signed lucrative contracts with Chaplin and Zukor's brightest star, Mary Pickford, and although they had both departed by May 1919, along with Douglas Fairbanks and D. W. Griffith, to form United Artists, the rivalry between First National and Famous Players-Lasky propelled the American cinema into the era of vertical integration and high finance. Later in the year Zukor's friend and former associate Marcus Loew, furrier turned nickelodeon and vaudeville magnate, would borrow $5 million on Wall Street and acquire Metro, to keep his screens supplied.

Expansion overseas suited the moment. When Al Kaufman left to establish the FP-L studio in London on 30 June 1919, two days after the signing of the Treaty of Versailles, the American trade press relayed "the belief of officials of Famous Players-Lasky that motion pictures can take the leadership in bringing about closer and more friendly relations between the nations of the earth," and claimed that "the motion picture camera is expected to be the gun which will hold sway over the hundreds of millions who will be guided by the League of Nations."[35] Less Wilsonian language was used to describe the mission of William Fox—himself at the helm of a vertically integrated operation—to establish distribution exchanges across France and Italy and that of the Atlantic Cinema Corporation, one of whose executives was posted in Copenhagen, "completing the shipping arrangements for the placing of the American product across the borders of Germany as soon as the country is opened up."[36]

By now the long film had prevailed. It had entailed a new way of making films, though not an entire severance from the stage and novel, which together continued to provide much of the source material. The result was Bazin's "classical American cinema." Rodney Ackland wrote in 1943 that "the days when cinema did indeed become an art" were "the one thing that not even a bare handful of earnest cinemagoers and film critics remember."[37] Defining and tracing the roots of the classical style was a formidable task that only became possible once film had become an object of academic study, and it was accomplished preeminently by David Bordwell, Janet Staiger, and Kristin Thompson in their book *The Classical Hollywood Cinema*, published in 1985. These scholars and their peers identified the decisive period as the mid-to-late 1910s; it was then that the filmmakers of Los Angeles and Fort Lee, New Jersey, developed a system of narrative filmmaking, made up of such devices as cross-cutting, flashbacks, and insert shots, that constituted the language Hitchcock had to master.

In 1915 it was far from unusual for a scene to be covered in a single shot; by 1919 scenes were much more likely to be divided into multiple shots, and with greater fluency than before. This crucial development required techniques to render the scene's division—just as Bazin said—invisible, seamless. Continuity editing, as it became known, concealed the cut from shot to shot: scenes appear to take place in continuous time; and made the fragmented result easily comprehensible: scenes appear to play out in continuous space. The central device within this system was the reverse angle, typically the cut from one character talking to another listening, or one looking and the other being looked at; in either case, the sequence will only make sense if the rules governing the direction of the actors' eyelines and the placement of the camera are observed. One application of the reverse angle was of particular importance for Hitchcock. To Truffaut he explained that the "cinematic motif" of *Rear Window* was three shots: "the immobile man *seeing*," followed by what he sees, followed by his reaction.[38] According to Hitchcock, placing a characteristic emphasis on point-of-view, "the three pieces of film represent what we know as the purest expression of cinematic idea."

His attitude toward the more conventional use of reverse angles was still distinctive. In conversation scenes it was often expected that the actor talking and the actor listening would both be on set, even though only one would be visible on screen—but not by Hitchcock. In the autumn of 1939, during the production of *Rebecca*, David O. Selznick wrote him a memo complaining that it was "awfully unfair, and damaging to performances as well, for the principals not to stand in and read the off-scene lines in important close-ups instead of having the script girl read these lines."[39] Such was Hitchcock's insistence on severance from stage technique, and on using "material *created* for the camera."

Hitchcock had been one of Ackland's "bare handful." Whether he apprehended the classical style as it came into being, as a cinemagoer in London, can only be speculated upon, but at Poole Street he would have been taught it by some of its progenitors, seasoned filmmakers of the 1910s.

The most pleasing version of how Hitchcock entered the film business is the *Movie* critic Paul Mayersberg's recounting of "Hitchcock's tale of how he was cycling past a movie studio in England one day in the early twenties when he noticed a sign outside which read: *Writers Wanted: Apply Within*."[40] He told Truffaut that he had seen news of the coming of Famous Players-Lasky to London in the trade papers, which is more likely, but the story was picked up by the daily press, which was beginning to devote quantities of newsprint to the cinema by 1919. The news that FP-L's first British production would be *The Sorrows of Satan*, from Marie Corelli's bestseller

Poole Street. SOURCE: Hackney Archives.

of 1895, was announced by Al Kaufman on his arrival on 7 July 1919, and printed in the next day's *Daily Mail*.[41] The second film, said Kaufman, was to be an adaptation of Arthur Wing Pinero's *His House in Order*, a play of 1906 that Hitchcock saw as the inspiration for *Rebecca*.[42]

"Now why, if I wanted to do illustrated titles," Hitchcock asked Truffaut, "why didn't I offer them to a British company?"[43] There were British firms to do them for. By 1919, Alma Reville was working as an assistant to Maurice Elvey, chief director at the new Stoll Film Company, the most prominent British studio of the day. "There seemed to be no urge," Hitchcock went on. "But the moment I read an American company is going to open up, I said 'I want to do their titles.'" The advent of Famous Players-Lasky British Producers, its full name, was controversial, partly because FP-L had announced plans to build a chain of cinemas in Britain, but if this concerned Hitchcock, he never showed it. He read *The Sorrows of Satan* and devised a set of illustrated title-cards on spec. Evidently he was seeking creative outlets. He had published his first Poe-esque short story in June 1919, in the magazine of the Henley's Telegraph Works social club.

While working at Henley's, where he had become a layout man, designing advertisements, Hitchcock took night classes in a host of subjects including art. Evidence for Hitchcock's claims about these classes, which must have been in addition to his cinema- and theatergoing and his dance classes, has never materialized, but John Russell Taylor's biography names Hitchcock's teacher as E. J. Sullivan, a book designer who taught at Goldsmiths' College in South East London. Hitchcock would "sit in Waterloo Station and sketch attitudes," a significant choice of location, since Waterloo, during the war years, was a spectacle—of weeping families, wounded soldiers, loitering prostitutes.[44] He described himself as "veering into, shall we call it, the 'mechanical-visual,'" away from the freedom of "paint and brush," suggesting an affinity with modernist painters like C. R. W. Nevinson.[45]

In the account Hitchcock gave Peter Bogdanovich, "they hadn't even finished building the studio" when he presented his unsolicited work to FP-L, only to be told that *The Sorrows of Satan* had been abandoned.[46] Construction at Poole Street, formerly a power station for the Metropolitan Railway, began in the autumn of 1919, and the company's intention to make *The Sorrows of Satan* was still being publicized when the studio opened in the spring of 1920. Whenever it happened, Hitchcock made an impression, and so began a period of moonlighting. Then, as he told Truffaut, "I enter the American studio. Now all that I used to read about in the trade papers—American directors, American stars and writers—here they are, all alive, and I am among them."[47]

What he had read had appeared in *Kinematograph Weekly* under the rubric "Pars from the Pacific," by Elsie Codd. One July 1919 installment told of DeMille's location work on Santa Cruz Island for his adaptation of J. M. Barrie's *The Admirable Crichton*, starring his discovery Gloria Swanson.[48] Another described how Hugh Ford, one of the directors Hitchcock would serve at Poole Street, was responsible for the "first London fog to be produced in motion pictures" for his adaptation of Hall Caine's *The Woman Thou Gavest Me*, produced at the ever-growing Lasky plant.[49] In November 1919 Codd devoted an article to Thomas Ince's new studio in Culver City, a new development six miles southwest of Hollywood, illustrated with a photograph of Ince's administration building, modeled on George Washington's house at Mount Vernon.[50] Two decades later, once it had become the home of Selznick International Pictures, it would be the first American studio that Hitchcock worked in. Codd noted its twelve-strong subtitling department, and in January 1920 wrote a defense of "The Art of the Sub-Title": "the handiwork of a group of experts," no longer that of an "emotional stenographer."[51]

By mid-1921, Codd had been engaged as Poole Street's publicist and became one of Hitchcock's supporters inside the studio. In July that year, shortly after going full-time there, he published his first film article—on the art of the subtitle. "Titles—Artistic and Otherwise," published in *Motion Picture Studio*, a spin-off of *Kinematograph Weekly* intended for filmmakers, covered the practicalities of fonts and spacing, and the folly of illustrating dialogue titles.[52]

Alma Reville had arrived at Poole Street some months earlier, as an assistant to Donald Crisp, the British-born actor-director who had played the villain in Griffith's *Broken Blossoms*. Her double role encompassed the shooting and editing phases of production. On set she was a floor secretary, or second assistant director, paying attention to problems of continuity that she knew would confront her once in the cutting room. Crisp and his screenwriter Margaret Turnbull, also British, had arrived in September 1920, reportedly to make a film based either on Shaw or on Barrie.[53]

In the event they made neither, but FP-L had recently acquired the rights to more of Barrie's plays, and these became the focus of the London branch's efforts. It was in order to confer with Barrie on a film of *Peter Pan* that the director John S. Robertson and his screenwriter and wife Josephine Lovett came to London in May 1921, though only after Barrie had approved their new adaptation of his novel *Sentimental Tommy*. Hitchcock would work on both of the two films they made in London—neither of them by Barrie—and of the list of "Ten Favorite Pictures" which he submitted to the *New York Sun*, "over champagne cocktails and beefsteak at Twenty-One," in March 1939, two were from the Robertson-Lovett team.[54] As well as *Sentimental Tommy*, the oldest film on the list, trade-shown in Britain in October 1921 and released a year later, he chose their Pinero adaptation *The Enchanted Cottage*, trade-shown and released in mid-1924.

The American combines' control of the rights to the major West End playwrights may well have been a factor in Hitchcock's urge to work for FP-L. He regarded Pinero and Barrie as "masters of the modern stage," a judgment that becomes more intriguing in light of his choice of authorized biographer.[55] John Russell Taylor was given the role at least partly on the strength of his book *The Rise and Fall of the Well-Made Play*, yet Taylor presented Pinero as the chief exponent of a genre that had peaked before Hitchcock's birth. *His House in Order* was "his last considerable play," out of fashion even on its first production, while *The Enchanted Cottage* was dismissed as "faintly Barrie-esque."[56] Meanwhile Galsworthy, with his focus on "clear, logical continuity" was "a dyed-in-the-wool conservative" for whom a play "meant a play as the 1890s had understood it."[57] Hitchcock's severance from the stage was never "entire"; in matters of construction, he drew on the lessons these playwrights provided, as well as the specialized training he received at Poole Street.

The most famous FP-L couple, DeMille and Jeanie Macpherson, responsible for two more of Hitchcock's "Ten," *Forbidden Fruit* and *Saturday Night*, both released in Britain in 1922, visited Poole Street but did not make films there. Indeed, DeMille's visit, at the end of 1921, was followed almost instantly by the company's decision to close it down. As if commenting on its demise, Myron Selznick, who had been in London to organize distribution for his family's latest venture, declared in January 1922 that "I wouldn't try to make pictures in England under any circumstances. . . . In the first place the climate is all against it, and in the second place there are no locations or scenes which lend themselves particularly to the making of pictures."[58] *Peter Pan* would be made in Hollywood.

In February 1922, shortly before the studio's closure was announced, Hitchcock was mentioned in a special "Cinema" number of *The Times* as head of "a special art title department," one of just two members of the Famous Players-Lasky staff to be named; but he had done much else besides titling.[59] Fifty years later he told Richard Schickel that

> there was a period when I was learning to write scripts—I fought terribly hard, [but] I could not understand how the various cuts went together. It seemed almost like a blank wall to me. Then one day, all of a sudden, I discovered it. And then I learned cutting. And out of that, of course, learned the pure cinema.[60]

.   .   .   .   .

It was probably in the immediate aftermath of Famous Players-Lasky's departure, in the spring of 1922, that Hitchcock started but did not finish his first film as director, *Number Thirteen*, a comic fantasy, and the biggest mystery of his career. He told Bogdanovich that he had been "talked into it" by Codd, who also wrote it; earlier, in an autobiographical article published in 1936, he said that "relatives, carried away by my enthusiasm, put up the money," but the film left no trace in the trade press.[61] Since Codd's name was left out of the published version of Bogdanovich's interview, her involvement became known only in 2015, when unearthed by Charles Barr and Alain Kerzoncuf.[62] The cast included Clare Greet, a character actor who had been in *Who Is He?*—and, more recently, the British FP-L film *Three Live Ghosts*—and Ernest Thesiger. It is possibly significant that Greet and Thesiger appeared together on stage, at the Court Theatre, in a production of Galsworthy's *Windows*, between late April and late May 1922—a new play coming after a series of Galsworthy revivals at the same venue, all produced by Leon M. Lion. FP-L's assistant art director Norman Arnold served as assistant director; his brother Wilfred would serve as art director on *The Lodger*.

It was only when Poole Street was rented out to independent producers, with Hitchcock—though not Reville—retained on the studio staff, that he became enmeshed in the British film industry proper. His employers were newcomers to the production side of the business, with transatlantic ambitions. The pattern was set by Graham Cutts, as he was now styled, and Herbert Wilcox, the latter a provincial distributor turned producer, who brought over Mae Marsh, best known for her work with Griffith, to make two films at Poole Street in the second half of 1922, first *Flames of Passion*, then *Paddy-the-Next-Best-Thing*, adapted by Eliot Stannard. It is not certain that Hitchcock worked on either; when reminiscing, he passed over this period to the arrival at Poole Street of a second pair of novice producers in early 1923, Michael Balcon and Victor Saville.

Friends since childhood, Balcon and Saville had worked together in distribution, both in London and their native Birmingham, but in November 1922, as if to announce their move into production, they had trade-shown a number of promotional films that they had made under the banner Cinema Publicity Service, at the West End Cinema. Some of them, made for Anglo-American Oil, the British branch of Standard Oil, had brought them into association with Sidney Bernstein. Born in Ilford, not far from Leytonstone, Bernstein had recently inherited his late father's small chain of cinemas, built—like the Davises'—before the war; one of them, the West Ham Empire, was just south of Leytonstone. He would become Hitchcock's close ally and, much later, his producer.

Balcon and Saville were brought to Poole Street by Cutts, who, having parted company with Wilcox, approached them with his plans to adapt a recent play, *Woman to Woman*, by Michael Morton. Saville was dispatched to Hollywood to enlist Betty Compson as lead actress for two films, most of the capital for which came from W. & F., a distributor whose profits derived from Harold Lloyd's comedies. Saville was married to the niece of C. M. Woolf, a City fur trader, who provided the W., while the father of Balcon and Saville's business partner Jack Freedman provided the F. The company had got going in 1919 with the franchise for Metro in London and southern England—many American studios of the time distributed through British middlemen—and although by 1923 W. & F. had lost Metro, they had gained Lloyd.

Hitchcock again worked on spec to impress his new masters, turning in a scenario based on an I. A. R. Wylie story, probably *The Inheritors*; thus was the novice screenwriter entrusted with *Woman to Woman*. Norman Arnold having stayed with Wilcox, Hitchcock also became art director; and, as assistant director—a third role—was empowered to hire the film's editor. He approached Alma Reville, who had recently written an article for *Motion Picture Studio* on her area of expertise, "Cutting and Continuity." "The art of cutting is Art indeed, with a capital A," she wrote, and "it is most necessary for any producer to have a continuity writer, who has an experienced knowledge of cutting, working continually with him whilst on production."[63] In 1923 British filmmakers still had to be told "what a vast difference smooth continuity of action—good matches, small technical details too numerous to mention—makes," and needed spelling out "the art of switching [i.e., cutting] on your new camera angles, until it is impossible to detect the change."

Half a century later, Balcon looked back on "the 'Pack' which assembled at the Legrain coffee shop in Brewer Street, Soho, on the days we were not working (which were all too frequent). Among those present from time to time were Graham Cutts, Alfred Hitchcock, Victor Saville, Adrian Brunel, Ivor Montagu, Eliot Stannard, Edwin Greenwood and myself. We talked about films in those days and not about deals."[64] With Reville as a glaring omission, these characters were Hitchcock's closest associates in the industry. Not all of them were present in the early 1920s, and the Legrain coffee shop was actually at 21 Gerrard Street, near Balcon's offices opposite the Hippodrome, in sight of the Fifty-Fifty Club on Wardour Street—and even closer to Adrian Brunel's rooms at 6 Dansey Yard, which it practically backed onto. Ten years Hitchcock's senior, Brunel had had a mostly bohemian upbringing in Brighton, interrupted by a spell at Harrow. After a number of not quite successful filmmaking ventures, in 1922 he had managed to obtain finance to make a feature with Ivor Novello, *The Man without Desire*, shot partly in Germany. His day-to-day business at Dansey Yard was that of a film surgeon, where the art of cutting was practiced on films badly in need of it.

In addition to his other roles, Brunel was a staunch advocate of the German films, against which British exhibitors had maintained a boycott until the end of 1922, when Lubitsch's *Passion*, as *Madame DuBarry* was titled in Britain, opened at the Scala. A few months earlier, he had written in *Motion Picture Studio* that "when we have mastered the German methods and the American methods, we will start in earnest and beat the world."[65] The arrival of the German films over the next three years coincided with Hitchcock's rise from writer to director, and it occurred well before the formation of the Film Society in 1925. Commercially released in the ordinary way, they became the great cause of the newspaper critics Hitchcock befriended around this time, none more so than Walter Mycroft, who became critic of the *Evening Standard* and *Illustrated Sunday Herald* in

1923. His father was "a sporting journalist, known to Conan Doyle," who had borrowed the family name for Sherlock Holmes's brother.[66] Mycroft recalled Hitchcock as

> the first I had met to be endowed with a completely cinematic mind, to see films as a flow of moving images which must always be significant. They did not have to stay objective, but could be used subjectively as well.
>
> He reduced life to "shots." He had the advantage of being able to illustrate his ideas by making little sketches on anything that came to hand. His podgy fist would close round a pencil, lines would appear and suddenly an arresting picture presented itself.[67]

Mycroft was truly "converted to the cinema" by Lubitsch's *The Loves of the Pharaoh*, shown at the Scala in February 1923.[68] "While so many producers strive to emphasise the stark realism of the camera, using floods of 'sunlight' to pick out every detail," he wrote in the *Evening Standard* at the time, "the producer in this case has aimed at bending it to purely imaginative effects."[69] Mycroft and Hitchcock had similar tastes, and for the next few years, in his two newspapers, he would act as Hitchcock's Boswell.

C. A. Lejeune, who had become the *Manchester Guardian*'s critic in the first week of 1922, met Hitchcock when he was "a chubby, rosy-cheeked young man with eyes like bright boot-buttons."[70] In March 1923, shortly after Reville's "Cutting and Continuity" article appeared, she had written an article on the same theme, quite probably in response. "Nobody," she wrote, "has really mastered the art of film-cutting as yet. For an art it is, and needs a touch as sure and an instinct as swift as that demanded—but rarely won, alas!—from the producer himself."[71] Her "first intimation of the German riches," she wrote in her autobiography, was *Dr. Mabuse*.[72] On its arrival she greeted it as the lineal descendent of the serials, now out of favor. "But the curious part of the business is that every episode and every catastrophe is the logical result of character development, not a mere accident from the blue."[73] The first part of Fritz Lang's thriller epic, tidings from a Germany in crisis, opened at the New Gallery in May 1923, even as the Ruhr was under French occupation, with inflation surging, and revolutionaries plotting.

By then *Woman to Woman* was in production. It made its British debut six months later, on 12 November 1923, beginning a two-week run at the

Marble Arch Pavilion, now managed by the Davises' son Alfred. As Hitchcock would recall, G. A. Atkinson hailed it as "the best American picture ever made in England."[74] It was already promised an American release. In September Balcon had gone to New York, staying at the Algonquin, in order to find an American distributor, and within a few weeks he had signed an agreement with the Selznick organization.

The film had already been endorsed by Metro's star director Rex Ingram, who saw it while passing through London in October 1923, before its debut, and reportedly said that *"he himself could not produce a better picture with all the wonderful light in Los Angeles."*[75] He subsequently hired Claude McDonnell, who had shot *Woman to Woman*, for his own crew. Ingram's words would have meant something to Hitchcock, whose "Ten Favorite Pictures" included Ingram's French Revolution melodrama *Scaramouche*, which opened at Metro's new Tivoli cinema, the first big West End cinema built since the war, in December. (Another of the "Ten," Tourneur's *Isle of Lost Ships*, opened in London in the same month.)

Woman to Woman's British release came on 4 February 1924, the first day of the "British Film Weeks," a "Buy British" campaign, forerunner of the campaign for a quota, that had won the support of the Prince of Wales, the future Edward VIII. The luncheon that launched it, in November 1923, was attended by senior politicians, and writers and artists including Marie Belloc Lowndes and John Buchan, as well as members of the film trade; but despite the timing of *Woman to Woman*'s release, the Balcon "Pack" had little or nothing to do with the campaign or the British National Film League that had organized it. Hitchcock told Truffaut that "when I first started to direct, up to that point the English films had been very mediocre, kind of a rustic type of film; they were made mostly for local consumption."[76] This echoed another critic who entered the profession in early 1920s, Iris Barry, who wrote of the "sheep and water school" of British cinema.[77] The outspoken Lejeune dismissed the British Film Weeks as "a harmless pastime of a number of well-meaning people who show little real appreciation of the mentality of their fellow-countrymen."[78]

Of more interest to Hitchcock and his circle in February 1924 was the London opening of one of the few "modern German films" he ever mentioned by name, Lang's *Destiny*, at the Polytechnic on Regent Street. Barry, writing in the *Spectator*, numbered it among "the few pictures which rank as complete expressions and raise cinematography to the level of good romantic poetry or symbolical sculpture."[79] Lejeune reviewed it together with one of the few British films exempted from her strictures, Brunel's *The Man without Desire*, "worth all the British Film Weeks put together" and "directly modeled on German methods of production."[80] Brunel's film was shown for a week at the Tivoli, whose owners had provided its budget. Shortly after making it, while in the United States playing opposite Mae Marsh in Griffith's *The White Rose*, Novello had devised the idea of *The Rat* for Brunel to direct, and the project had been announced in June 1923.[81] Finance, however, was not forthcoming, and while Novello and Constance Collier turned the idea into a play, Brunel started making short comic films, called "burlesques."

February 1924 also saw the establishment of Gainsborough Pictures, consisting at this stage of Balcon and Cutts, Saville having left their company and Freedman having died. In place of W. & F., which had been unimpressed by Cutts's second film with Compson, *The White Shadow*, its distributor was Gaumont. This venerable firm, founded in 1898 to distribute the films of its French parent company, was run by A. C. and R. C. Bromhead, the former of them president of the British National Film League. The French interest in the company had recently been bought out by Isidore, Mark, and Maurice Ostrer, merchant bankers born to immigrant parents in the East End, and from 1924 the company served as British distributor for Warner Brothers. Its own studio, however, was not thriving.

In addition to Gaumont, finance for Gainsborough's first film, *The Passionate Adventure*, which Cutts and Hitchcock started shooting at Poole Street in March 1924, came from the Selznicks. Though they were on the brink of bankruptcy, they had mounted a grand New York premiere for *Woman to Woman* in the ballroom of the Ritz-Carlton Hotel on 10 January 1924, followed by a wide release across the United States that included, from 30 March, a run at the Rivoli. Somehow there was also money for *The Passionate Adventure*, and Myron Selznick came to London with its star Marjorie Daw, his future wife, to supervise production. Though the Selznick companies did not survive long enough to release the film, Myron Selznick's visit created the bond that ultimately took Hitchcock to Hollywood.

Hitchcock and Brunel were not alone among British filmmakers in admiring the German films; Cutts too had spoken favorably of them. "A

'Caligari' is too violent a swing into the realms of mental experiences to be universally acceptable," he had written in February 1924, "but along that line future developments lie."[82] Four years after its German debut, *The Cabinet of Dr. Caligari* opened to the public at the Marble Arch Pavilion on 17 March 1924. Iris Barry, who called the story "as terrifying as any Poe ever wrote," wrote that it "should attract many new visitors to the cinema, including psycho-analysts, alienists, modern artists and all 'highbrows' who enjoy moving pictures but are usually disgusted with the banality of their themes."[83]

Gainsborough's alliance with Selznick and Gaumont was fleeting. In the summer of 1924 Balcon and Cutts resumed their arrangement with W. & F., and found a new partner in Erich Pommer of Ufa. In March *Woman to Woman* had become the first British film to be shown in Germany since the war.[84] Gainsborough's next film, *The Blackguard*, would be made not at Poole Street but at Neubabelsberg. The cast included the American star Jane Novak and Bernhard Goetzke, who had played Death in *Destiny* and the obsessive prosecutor in *Dr. Mabuse*. In this way, Hitchcock and Reville gained direct experience of the German studios. In one of his most treasured anecdotes of his time there, recounted by John Russell Taylor, Hitchcock saw F. W. Murnau, at work on *The Last Laugh*, shooting in forced perspective. "What you can see on the set does not matter, explained Murnau—the only truth that counts is what you see on the screen."[85]

A minor oddity of the Truffaut interview is Hitchcock's seemingly precise recollection that "Murnau's films came around 1923–24": none of them were released in Britain by then, but it is possible that he had seen them, since they were in private circulation in the screening rooms of Soho.[86] Mycroft had seen Murnau's *Phantom* by May 1924, and it was his knowledge that other such films were languishing in their cans that led him to call, on that occasion and others, for the establishment of a Film Society.[87]

Mycroft's review of *The Passionate Adventure*, which had its premiere at the Davises' new Shepherd's Bush Pavilion in August 1924, referred to "Graham Cutts and his coadjutors," and it is probable that Hitchcock's frustration under Cutts was already apparent among his friends.[88] Both Hitchcock and Reville, many years later, attested to Cutts's lack of professionalism at the time of *The Blackguard*, in the autumn of 1924, and its follow-up, *The Prude's Fall*, shot on location on the Continent and at Poole Street in early 1925, and there is evidence that Cutts's work on the latter fell short. In both instances Adrian Brunel was summoned to act as film surgeon, leading to Hitchcock's entry into "the world of Adrian Brunel" in late 1924, a year before the Film Society had come into being.

It was then that Brunel's burlesques, which had won praise from Barry and Mycroft when they were shown at the Tivoli in the summer, were taken up for distribution by W. & F., and Brunel's Soho film surgery became closely integrated into the company's operations. One of his first tasks was to produce a one-off burlesque to precede the trade show of Harold Lloyd's *Hot Water* at the Shepherd's Bush Pavilion on New Year's Eve. Brunel's first collaboration with Hitchcock seems to have concerned the preparation of backgrounds for *The Blackguard*. In November 1924 Balcon wrote to Brunel

> to remind you that in addition to the Albert Hall arrangements we discussed, Hitchcock wants good still photographs of one of the boxes, the whole organ and the orchestra.
>
> As I have explained, we are most anxious to get the crowd scenes but even if we are not successful, the above photographs are still required.[89]

The finished film includes a concert scene, using matte shots combining a still image of the inside of a box in the foreground, framing a moving image of the audience and orchestra in the background. In February 1925, as *The Blackguard's* premiere—held at the Albert Hall—approached, Balcon wrote to Pommer to say that Brunel "has been working for some weeks on the titles for the above mentioned production, first of all from the script while the picture was being finished, then with Mr. Hitchcock on his return to England, and finally after the print arrived here."[90] In response to an enquiry from Harry Wilson in 1947, Brunel wrote of Hitchcock that:

> If he had not been under contract to Gainsborough, I am sure he would have joined my brilliant gang of collaborators—for a time, at least—because he

always got a kick out of satire. He was always a good talker and his keen sense of humour was one of his most endearing characteristics.[91]

Nor was Hitchcock alone involved. In February 1925 "Miss Reville" reported to Balcon that the print of *The Blackguard* was of poor quality and needed to be replaced.[92] In March, Balcon wrote to "Hitch," asking him to "tell 'Rene' to go through the film and look out for the joins where she has put in titles and where flashes show on the screen, as per specimens attached, and then make fresh joins nearer to the heart's desire."[93] *The Prude's Fall*, a more modest production, required more drastic measures. It had gone on to the floor at Poole Street toward the end of February, with a cast including Brunel's close associate Miles Mander, the wayward son of Midlands industrialists and a fellow Old Harrovian. It was in the same month, at the premiere of Lubitsch's *Forbidden Paradise* on 10 February 1925, that a decisive step was made toward the foundation of the Film Society, when Hugh Miller, another actor cast in *The Prude's Fall*, introduced Brunel to his friend Ivor Montagu. At about the same time, Miller and Montagu made contact with Iris Barry, and, through her, Sidney Bernstein. It is only from this date that Montagu can be named as a member of the "Pack," or that "the world of Ivor Montagu and Adrian Brunel" can be evoked.

Balcon passed the first cut of *The Prude's Fall* to Brunel at the start of April 1925, for further editing, and with a number of retakes to be completed before Cutts returned to the floor to commence production on the film Brunel had once been lined up to make, *The Rat*; whatever his shortcomings, Cutts was, after all, a company director. "By full titles the length must be pulled out to at least 6000 feet," Balcon instructed Brunel, and there were serious continuity problems to be remedied.[94] Among other faults, Marie Ault's character "disappears from the picture without proper explanation." Balcon made clear that the film was not to be shown to W. & F. until it had been salvaged.

The Prude's Fall proved to be Hitchcock's last film as Cutts's assistant, and afterward Balcon offered him the chance to direct his first feature for Gainsborough, in association with another German studio, Emelka. One of the earliest announcements of *The Pleasure Garden* came from Mycroft, who wrote in the *Evening Standard* on 2 June 1925 of the coming "directorial début of Mr. A. J. Hitchcock, whose artistic settings helped so much in Graham Cutts' 'The Passionate Adventure' and 'The Blackguard.'"[95] Two weeks later, Mycroft announced that work had begun in Munich. The film's American stars were Virginia Valli, who had appeared in *Sentimental Tommy*, and Carmelita Geraghty, daughter of one of Hitchcock's supervisors at Famous Players-Lasky, Tom Geraghty. Mander played the villain. One of the few surviving pieces of Hitchcock's correspondence from these years is an undated letter he wrote to Brunel during production:

> I am very pleased to hear that the Prudes Fall has come out of your "film hospital" a new being. . . . I have seen very little of Munich since I have been out here—only the studio and my hotel room are the "sights" of this beautiful city I have been permitted to see.[96]

·   ·   ·   ·   ·

The Film Society had its first performance on Sunday 25 October 1925. In addition to Leni's *Waxworks*, the program included abstract films by Walter Ruttmann, Chaplin's Essanay two-reeler *The Champion*, from the distant days of 1915, a Broncho Billy one-reeler western of a similar vintage, and Brunel's burlesque of newsreels, *Typical Budget*. There one might have expected to find Hitchcock mingling with his social superiors. Thomas Elsaesser wrote with confidence that "we know that Hitchcock had seen Paul Leni's *Waxworks*, 1921, before he made *The Lodger*"; but in fact it seems unlikely that Hitchcock attended the first—or indeed the second—Film Society program, because by late October he was back on the Continent, making his second feature.[97]

Production on *The Pleasure Garden* ended in August 1925, but *Kinematograph Weekly* reported Hitchcock's return to Munich, "busy on preparation for his second production in the Emelka studios," on 1 October.[98] On 22 October, three days before the Film Society's first performance, the same paper announced that production on what was then titled "Fear-o'-God" would begin "in a few days' time," and that negotiations with "a well-known American screen actress" were continuing.[99] The previous day's *Variety* had a report datelined Paris, 10 October, saying that Nita Naldi had arrived to appear in a film of Vicente Blasco Ibáñez's *Queen Calafia*, to be directed by John S. Robertson.[100] Robertson had directed Naldi in

Jekyll and Hyde, opposite John Barrymore, in 1920, and since then she had starred in three films with Valentino. *Queen Calafia* was to be made at the Victorine studio near Nice, occupied and equipped by Rex Ingram, with MGM's money, the previous year. But no such film ever appeared, and in late November it was announced that Naldi had joined Hitchcock's cast, alongside Bernhard Goetzke.[101] Production on what became *The Mountain Eagle* had begun some weeks earlier, however. In the 1 November issue of the *Sunday Herald*, Walter Mycroft wrote that "Mr. Hitchcock is now at work in Munich."[102] He very probably missed *Waxworks*.

It was in the same column that Mycroft broke the news of Hitchcock's third film, before the first had been seen. Under the subheading "Filming the Fog," he wrote:

> Afterwards he talks of filming a certain stage play which was produced in London some years ago.
>   This will have two definite but difficult characteristics—it will be photographed as to certain scenes in precisely that London fog which is supposed to be such a handicap to our film production, and it will be without sub-titles.

A week later, almost exactly a decade after this "certain stage play" had made its debut, Mycroft named the author on whose novel it was based, but in keeping with the mystery that had surrounded it ten years earlier, he did not name the play, *Who Is He?*, or the novel, *The Lodger*.

4 The Autocrat of the Studio

With more than a hundred credits to his name, by the mid-1920s Eliot Stannard was the most prominent screenwriter in Britain and a prolific commentator on the screenwriting trade. Nevertheless, despite the scholarly interest in Stannard initiated by Charles Barr, the nature of his collaboration with Hitchcock is frustratingly hard to visualize. It began in the spring of 1925 when Michael Balcon assigned the novice director the veteran screenwriter's adaptation of *The Pleasure Garden*, a popular novel of 1923 by Oliver Sandys, pen name of Marguerite Jarvis, a writer whom Stannard had adapted once before. Recently, in March, Stannard's stage farce *The Man-Eater* had opened at the West Pier Theatre in Brighton, produced by and starring his regular collaborator Edwin Greenwood, a fellow member of Balcon's "Pack" whose later collaboration with Hitchcock, on *Jamaica Inn*, may have led to his untimely death.

Stannard had rehearsed his views on screenwriting with more frequency earlier in his career. "What constitutes a good scenario?" he had asked in a June 1920 issue of *Film Renter*.[1] "Surely, it is one that tells its story clearly, dramatically, temperamentally, and, above all, *pictorially*." By this he meant that the screenplay should enable the director to "visualise grouping, artistic composition, light and shade effects—in short, an immediate appeal to the *eyes* of his audience." In the same paper a month later, he discussed the craft of adaptation with Eve Unsell, head of the scenario department at Poole Street—and so possibly the woman who gave Hitchcock his start in the business. Both writers were in favor of adaptations over original compositions.

In a *Motion Picture Studio* article of 1923, Stannard described the position of the scenarist—his own—as that of a diplomat negotiating between author and director, with the latter acknowledged as a "sea captain."[2] Stannard claimed to have had good relations with the living authors he had adapted, despite taking "the most glaring liberties with their work. I have discarded great slices of their novels, omitted important characters, altered locations, and generally assumed the right to create or uncreate according to the exigencies of the medium in which I was working." The article was written in response to a symposium on adaptation published in a recent number of *John o' London's Weekly*, whose contributors included H. G. Wells, Marie Corelli, and Marie Belloc Lowndes. "I feel sure," the latter had written,

> that the cinema's great day will only dawn when novel writers direct for the films. To my view, the novelist should *always* collaborate with the cinema producer. I think the comparative failure of many a famous novel on the screen is entirely owing to the way in which the story has been altered and, if I may say so, mangled by the adapter. I have heard people say, "Don't go and see So-and-so on the film. It is not one bit like that splendid story." Soon the author will have his chance, for film producers have almost exhausted the vast reservoir of old and modern plays. They are now turning again to novels.[3]

It was not her first contribution to the literature on this perennial question. Lowndes had written on the "Art of Adaptation" in the same *Times* supplement in which Hitchcock's name had appeared in February 1922. "In the vast majority of cases, innumerable new scenes, sometimes grotesquely 'out of the picture,' are interpolated," she had said then, "and a new ending to the tale provided."[4] She identified Louis Mercanton's *The Call of the Blood*, her friend Ivor Novello's first film, as a rare exception. Nor was the 1923 article her last word on the topic. In January 1926, weeks before production began on Stannard's adaptation of her best-known novel, she again wrote that "I often feel that an enormous amount of money and a great deal of misplaced ingenuity have been spent in the screening of stories to which have been added a great deal of extraneous and unnecessary matter."[5]

These interventions were the fruit of bitter experience. In 1920 Lowndes had learned that her 1912 novel *The Chink in the Armour* was to be filmed; or, more precisely, that *The House of Peril*, Horace Annesley Vachell's stage adaptation of the same, first performed at the Haymarket in 1919, was to be filmed, and that Frederick Harrison, the play's producer, believed that he was entitled to sell the film rights for the property, play and book together, under the terms of the original contract that she had signed for the stage version, without consultation or significant additional payment. Legal opinion was sought, and Lowndes was disappointed to learn that, as a result of a poorly drafted contract, she was not at liberty to dispose of the film rights to the novel separately and would have to come to terms with Harrison. Harrison, in turn, grudgingly paid her £400, and never spoke to her again.

It seems most likely that *Who Is He?* was produced on the basis of a similar contract, and that—following the affair of *The House of Peril*—Harrison, Vachell, and Lowndes were reluctantly bound together in the sale of the rights to what was counted as one property, despite the vast differences between Lowndes's novel and Vachell's stage adaptation. In May 1922 she wrote to G. Herbert Thring, solicitor to the Society of Authors:

> Only yesterday I looked at the contract concerning the dramatization of "The Lodger"; it practically gives Mr. Vachell every conceivable right over the dramatization and film copyrights of this book, though he assured me that the play he had made on the book was so exactly like the book that it was only from a sense of honour he approached me at all. I am writing to him to try and persuade him to let me at any rate have the dramatic rights in the story itself—for, though his play closely followed the book in certain parts, my book is a tragedy, and the play he wrote is a farce.[6]

The evidence is partial, but in 1931 Lowndes told Thring's replacement that "full film rights revert to me next year," suggesting, perhaps, that a ten-year contract, removing ambiguities, was drawn up in 1922.[7] It was in late 1932 that the first remake appeared. That Walter Mycroft's announcement of *The Lodger*'s impending adaptation by Hitchcock, in November

1925, characterized the film as a version of the farcical play, rather than the tragic novel, may indicate Hitchcock's personal attachment to the former, but it also points to the complexity of the contractual arrangement. A document of obscure provenance in the BFI archive, a handwritten budget titled "Detailed Cost of Production" in two drafts, suggests that out of a low total budget of around £13,000, Lowndes was paid £225 and Stannard £405,10,6, figures to be compared with Novello's fee of £950, June's of £510, or with the average coal miner's annual wage of about £120.[8]

The play had never been published, and it may be wondered whether Stannard had seen it, or with what degree of detail even Hitchcock remembered it ten years after it was performed. The same had been true of the film of *The Chink in the Armour*: Lowndes claimed that its scenarist and director Kenelm Foss, a close associate of Stannard's at the time, had confessed to her that he had worked exclusively from the novel.[9] The time and place of Hitchcock and Stannard's collaboration is another matter for speculation, since neither they nor anyone else left any record of it. Unlike *The Pleasure Garden* and *The Mountain Eagle*, *The Lodger* seems to have been Hitchcock's choice of material, and it may be assumed that he was not presented with the script as a fait accompli. He was in Germany until the end of 1925, and if he and Stannard worked together in the same room, it was presumably during the first weeks of 1926.

In *Writing Screen Plays*, a pamphlet published in 1920, Stannard had written that "the Beneficent Autocrat Producer, by giving fair credit where it is due and by not sparing himself can rely upon being followed almost like a god and need not fear Labour-troubles nor Trade-Union disputes."[10] His collaboration with Hitchcock continued through eight films across two production companies; evidently it was good while it lasted, but on the question of credit he was to be disappointed. One of the few anecdotes about Stannard comes from the last months of his life, in 1944, when Gavin Lambert encountered him in a lowly position within the film trade, repeatedly accusing Hitchcock of credit theft.[11]

Mycroft's promise that *The Lodger* would be "without subtitles" was not to be borne out, but it would not have been unprecedented. The debate over subtitles was almost as old as that over adaptation, and there had been films without them before. Stannard had written on the question more

Kinematograph and Lantern Weekly,
11 September 1919.

ELIOT   STANNARD

than once. "The sub-title which could have been expressed by the dumb show of movement is a blemish," he had said in 1918, and he was far from being alone in this view.[12] Asked for his conception of the "Ideal Cinema" in 1924, C. R. W. Nevinson said that he wanted to see a story told "by the obvious means of dynamic visual composition rather than by the false introduction of 'captions.'"[13] The German films were praised—not least by Mycroft—partly because they kept titling to a minimum.

Two German films in particular set the standard to which Hitchcock aspired. Arthur Robison's *Warning Shadows*, which opened at the Tivoli in November 1924, was described by Mycroft as "devoid of written text—which is the ideal films should aim at."[14] In the same review, and in the same spirit, he wondered "How Poe would have revelled in this medium, which would have permitted the wildest flights of his dark imagination, whereas it had instead to be shackled to the comparatively limp and halting vehicle of the written word." The second instance was *The Last Laugh.* When Murnau's film debuted at the newly opened Capitol in March 1925, Mycroft hailed it as "(practically) sub-title-less."[15] Iris Barry spelled out the implication:

> As there are no sub-titles in this film, not only Jannings as the old man but the places which he frequents have to be very expressive pictorially. The eye of the camera treats the swinging doors of the hotel, the porcelain basins and mirrors of the cloakroom lovingly, sees them—I would say—freshly and intelligently. We know that hotel, take part in its subtler moods.[16]

Similarly, C. A. Lejeune found herself "conscious of the camera just ahead of us, like a vast superhuman eye. It fixes its beam upon some inanimate object, a door, a window, a staircase, and presently that door, window, or staircase becomes animate, a living actor in the drama."[17] Hitchcock himself recalled that the Germans "placed great emphasis on telling the story visually; if possible with no titles or at least with very few," and in *The Last Laugh*, Murnau "was able to do that, to dispense with titles altogether, except in an epilogue. I don't believe that was accomplished by anyone else."[18]

The first night of shooting on *The Lodger* was not the last occasion on which the press was invited to see Hitchcock at work. "We drove up to an old power house in a slum with great rounded Georgian windows," wrote the society columnist of *Vogue* in early April 1926;

> inside, however, the "Famous Players Lasky" have made it all new, and, really, film studios themselves have a beauty of their own. The blazing hectic violet rays throw long shadows that make ladders and stacked cardboard walls into things of beauty. The hugeness of it, like a cathedral, and the sweet pear-drop smell of the films themselves gave one quite a thrill; one felt like watching in the passages of that wonderful film, *Doctor Caligari*.[19]

That wonderful film *Caligari*, released to the general public two years earlier, had been revived by the Film Society on 14 March. Continued *Vogue*:

Laymen do not know that these very famous producers will spend over half an hour over a "close up," which takes a few seconds to be reeled off; first the number and section is photographed thus:

240
Hitchcock
Take I.

Then the producer speaks the script from an armchair to Novello, who registers it with his face; then another label is photographed with Take 2, then the same pose as before. This is done three times over—how elaborate and wearisome for the actor and producer, and all the time the clock is ticking minutes and hours away—no wonder fortunes are lost and won at the game! The whole marvellous organisation is run, so I have heard, by two girls of about twenty, who never forget anything and who take a constant commentary or diary of the script.

One of these "girls" was probably Alma Reville. The other, Renie Marrison—presumably the "Rene" whom Balcon had mentioned in connection with *The Blackguard*—gave an account of her role as "the hired memory of the film director" in the October 1926 issue of *Picturegoer*. The "continuity writer," she wrote, using the same title Reville had used in 1923—not "script girl"—had to notice changes in costume between shots which might be taken on different days, and not only that. "There are subtler points for her to remember, such as the angle of the camera, the position of the players' heads, feet and hands and so on, which are of vital importance in 'matching up' scenes which run on."[20] She had also to match facial expressions:

In *The Lodger*, for example, Mrs. Bunting had not to reveal suspicion of her lodger before a certain scene, bearing a certain number. All numbers below called for an innocent expression, and all numbers above for unmistakeable suspicion. (Film scenes, of course are shot not in numerical but in the most convenient order.) I think I may be forgiven for saying I had a struggle to hold the director to that arrangement.

Marie Ault, who played Mrs. Bunting, had dropped out of Theodore Komisarjevky's production of *Three Sisters* at the Barnes Theatre, pivotal in establishing Chekhov's reputation in Britain, to take the role.

An extensive account of the *Lodger* shoot by E. E. Barrett, paying special attention to the elaborate staircase that Hitchcock had constructed, "unusual inasmuch as it was three stories high," had appeared in the May 1926 issue of the same magazine:

> The difficulties of lighting this set were apparent to the merest amateur, for, unlike most sets, which are usually built with two sides left open, this had only one comparatively small opening on the left-hand side of the entrance hall, and the staircase itself boasted not only walls but ceiling.[21]

Also on set that day was Marie Belloc Lowndes, who was photographed standing alongside Hitchcock, next to the camera. "Unlike Mr. Hitchcock," wrote Barrett, "she thinks that an entirely new and different technique is not necessary in writing for the screen."

Iris Barry visited the set on almost certainly the same day as Barrett— and probably *Vogue*—Saturday 20 March, three weeks into principal photography, to observe part of the staircase scene being filmed. On the following Monday, she wrote in the *Daily Mail* that:

> all kinds of intriguing work was in process. Mr. Alfred Hitchcock, the young English director of whom so much is expected, was taking Mr. Ivor Novello through several short scenes. Mr. Novello, muffled up to the eyes and look- ing pale and furtive, tip-toed down the stairs, across the hall, and softly out of the front door of his boarding-house.
>
> But, no, he must bend forward more and stand and listen a moment before opening a door just sufficiently wide for him to pass through. After half a dozen rehearsals this scene was photographed and rephotographed, and finally close-ups of Mr. Novello's stealthy feet were arranged.
>
> Meanwhile Miss June appeared from her dressing-room to discuss the merits of an intensely golden wig she must wear in "The Lodger."[22]

The day after Barry's article appeared, Mycroft reported on the same scene:

> The novel and interesting experience of a British film in which the consist- ent endeavour has been made to avoid conventional photographic "angles" is promised in "The Lodger." Sometimes a sudden change of angle is shot into a film with the disturbing effect and lack of reason of the average close-up.
>
> Mr. Hitchcock in "The Lodger" will seek to present the scene from unex- pected viewpoints because such treatment will be in accordance with the character and atmosphere of the story. Murnau was successful in similar unconventionality in "The Last Laugh."

To suggest the furtive exit of a character from a fourth-floor room in "The Lodger," the English director has constructed in his studio a set of four flights of stairs. Just stairs and banister. Then he has had his camera fixed at the top, looking down, and all that the photographic eye (and the spectator's eye eventually) sees is the furtive sliding descent of *a man's hand*.

Mr. Hitchcock has also had the idea of having ceilings put up in his interior sets. Ceilings are as rare on the screen as on the stage. In this case, again, the device is employed essentially for the more facile expression of the story, as it was in "The Street," the only other ceilinged film I can recall for the moment.[23]

The Street, directed by Karl Grune, was another of the German films, shown in London to much acclaim in the spring of 1924. Continued Mycroft:

> Baron Ventimiglia, the camera man of "The Lodger," tells me that he has been set some interesting problems in the photography of this film, including no doubt those of the Embankment fog scenes, the fog having to be created in this metropolis of fog by the use of no less prosaic an agent than drain "bombs."
>
> "Venti" (studio brevity) is as romantic as an Italian ought to be. It emerges that he took part in the Black Shirt march on Rome.

Gaetano di Ventimiglia, after his apprenticeship in the Italian industry, had shot a feature for the American-born director Walter Niebuhr at Poole Street in late 1923, when it was a rental facility, and had gone on to work in Germany, shooting two films that happened to feature Hugh Miller, including Niebuhr's *The City of Temptation,* which was shot in Berlin at the same time as *The Blackguard* in late 1924. (Not only Miller but his American costar Julanne Johnston appeared in *The Prude's Fall* immediately afterward.) "Venti" had then filmed Miller in the Anglo-German coproduction *Venetian Lovers* at the Emelka studios in the spring of 1925—a film, according to Ivor Montagu, in which Cedric Belfrage "had persuaded his Harley Street father to invest money to give him a start."[24] It was after this that Baron Ventimiglia was hired to serve as Hitchcock's director of photography on *The Pleasure Garden,* and then *The Mountain Eagle,* at the same site.

In his interview with Richard Schickel, Hitchcock reflected on what had driven him to shoot the staircase scene as he did. Echoing what Mycroft had said of him nearly fifty years earlier, which perhaps echoed, in turn, things he had said to Mycroft, Hitchcock told Schickel that his style was "influenced [by] the German—angles of photography, the visual ideas," and then directly related the power of these visual ideas to the technological limitations of the medium at the time.[25] "There was no sound in those days," Hitchcock recalled—immediately before giving, as an example of his visual ideas, the Lodger's exit from the house being "shot from above a big staircase with a continuing handrail," in which "all you saw was a white hand going down." In the same vein, with reference to the transparent ceiling through which the Lodger is seen pacing about his room, Hitchcock told Truffaut that "many of these visual devices would be absolutely superfluous today because we would use sound effects instead."[26]

The Lodger was made during the first phase of the cinema's transition from silence, the other side of which few if any were able to foresee, in part because of sound's very familiarity. In November 1924 C. A. Lejeune had called sound films "hardy perennials."[27] There had been many variants over the years. Edison's Kinetophone, using a synchronized phonograph, had come to the West End Cinema in early 1914, and been exhibited all over the country. "We should miss a year that did not see them and their companion the colour film anew," Lejeune went on. "They are so brave and optimistic and look to a kinema with such a long, long future in which they can grow." The spring of 1926 saw developments in both sound and color that brought this future much closer. Far from there being "no sound in those days," sound was hard to ignore; and if there was appreciably more sound in the cinema when *The Lodger* was released than when it was shot, there was certainly not none even then.

The most conspicuous sound system in the mid-1920s, the subject of Lejeune's article, was Phonofilm, the evolving creation of the American inventor Lee de Forest and his colleagues. Phonofilms had first been demonstrated in London in June 1923, soon after their New York debut at the Rivoli in April. A separate British De Forest company led by the Australian radio pioneer Cyril Elwell, who had previously been associated with De Forest at a research laboratory in Palo Alto, was established that July. The program seen by Lejeune in November 1924, however, staged at the Royal Society of Arts, consisted of short films made at De Forest's studio in Manhattan, including a dance, a banjo player, a comic monologue, the violinist Max Rosen, the soprano Bernice de Pasquali, and President

Coolidge speaking in the White House garden. "As an instrument of reproduction the De Forest phonofilm has splendidly succeeded," she wrote.[28]
Iris Barry, who had been shown a similar program privately six months
earlier, used the same word: while it was "a most uncanny and delightful
experience, sitting at the back of a great empty theatre, to see and hear a
little film of Fokina performing the Swan Dance," and while Barry found
that her "prejudices and misconceptions about talking films have been
transformed into enthusiasm and interest," still the Phonofilm was "mere
reproduction."[29]

As such, it was perceived as a threat to the visual ideas that critics of
Barry and Lejeune's stamp cherished, and that their friend Hitchcock
sought to use in his films. "Personally," Barry continued,

> I do not see how Phonofilm plays can ever be anything but another kind of
> stage play, for the very use of dialogue in drama tends to hold the actors in
> one place, and therefore destroys the freedom of movement, so like that of
> the ballet, which distinguishes the "silent" films and gives them their pecu-
> liar aesthetic.[30]

Hitchcock would insist on the superiority of this "peculiar aesthetic" over
"mere reproduction" until his dying day. His advocacy of film's "entire severance from both the stage and the novel, and the command of a medium
of its own," stated thus in early 1928, just as the ascendancy of the talkie
went from highly probable to inevitable, was rephrased many times in
articles and interviews, most memorably in the formula he used in the
Truffaut interview, "photographs of people talking."[31] In fact, Cyril Elwell
agreed with such analyses, and told his audience at the Royal Society of
Arts in 1924 that the "ordinary silent drama, to which we have all become
so accustomed, will not in general be improved by the addition of the
voice."[32] By then his company was in the process of establishing itself in
a comically inadequate studio, described by the West End showman Vivian Van Damm as "a disused lavatory space, underneath some arches in
Clapham," South London.[33] Most of the films made by Elwell's unit over
the next few years kept within what he himself saw as the new technology's proper limits—but not all of them.

The Phonofilms made their public debut in Britain at the Wembley
Empire Exhibition in May 1925, and were first shown in an ordinary

cinema at the end of June, when the Tivoli, "unheralded," put on four—two British, two American—initially in support of the Lon Chaney film *The Unholy Three*.[34] Mycroft had mixed feelings but saw in them the possibility of superseding "sub-titles in 'Americanese.'"[35] Hitchcock was abroad at the time, shooting *The Pleasure Garden*, but sound films would return to London screens shortly before he began work on *The Lodger*. The fourth performance of the Film Society, on 17 January 1926, the first that Hitchcock is likely to have been able to attend, included a French abstract film synchronized with Liszt's *Mephisto Waltz* by the inventor Charles Delacommune, whose idea was "to make a moving pattern each motion of which shall correspond exactly to a note in the Liszt waltz."[36] (The same performance included René Clair's *Entr'acte*, possibly the inspiration for *The Lodger*'s transparent ceiling.)

Less than two weeks later, at the end of January 1926, the Phonofilms returned to the screen, technical improvements having been made—again with a handful shot in Britain. Iris Barry, who had played host to Delacommune during his visit, wrote in the *Daily Mail*:

> What was claimed to be the first complete performance in Great Britain of moving pictures in which the characters can be heard talking and sounds of movement are reproduced was given at the Holborn Empire, Holborn, W.C., yesterday morning, when the De Forest Phonofilms, Ltd., a British company, showed privately a number of films.[37]

The films on show included "the sounds of a native grass dance, a day in a German farmyard, a Swiss playing on a zither, an operatic duet, a jazz band, and a Scottish play"—not *the* Scottish play, but Graham Moffat's *Till the Bells Ring*. American Phonofilms tended to show vaudeville acts or popular songs, and lasted only a few minutes; *Till the Bells Ring* was far longer. It was not a great success. Though at first "the voices came naturally enough," reported the society columnist of the *Daily Express*, later "the sound was blurred. 'The box that held the projector and the whole apparatus became so overheated,' Mr. Moffatt explained, 'that it expanded the metal and caused the voices to go out of focus.'"[38] The program was nonetheless popular once it opened to the public, in the first week of the *Lodger* shoot in February, and it was held over for ten weeks running. At the start of April, *Bioscope* observed that "the Phonofilms make their appearance as part of a music hall programme," just as the early silent films had done. "How long will it be before they provide the whole of the entertainment?"[39]

In a more considered response to the Royal Society of Arts program, Lejeune had written that the "custom" was "to huddle together colour films and stereoscopic films and talking films as future developments of the kinema which will come, and should come, in the cause of artistic progress. But the three are not rightly allied."[40] The former pair, "things of the eye," could more easily be tolerated, even welcomed, at least in theory. In 1923 Lejeune had listed the "many substitutes for colour" she had witnessed "—many strawberry pink nightmares people with deformities, crude unearthly things in human semblance, ringed by iridescent auras, hovering in a limbo of horrid darkness"—but she nevertheless believed that color had a future; indeed, on that occasion she was writing in measured praise of *The Toll of the Sea*, a feature-length demonstration film of Technicolor's two-strip process.[41]

Hollywood's adoption of "natural" color, as distinct from the tinting and toning processes that were commonplace in the silent era, was far slower than its adoption of synchronized sound—it did not become the norm until the twilight years of Hitchcock's career in the 1960s—and was less consequential both for the structure of the industry and for the filmmaking process. Correspondingly, Hitchcock's attitude toward it was less antagonistic. In the same 1928 article in which he called for film's "entire severance," Hitchcock blandly declared that "The ideal film will be the coloured stereoscopic film."[42] Just as Lejeune suggested, short color films, and color sections within longer films, were not uncommon in the 1920s, and it is even possible that Hitchcock had worked on one of the latter himself. Cutts's *Flames of Passion*, from 1922, contained sequences in the Prizma process, Technicolor's main rival at the time.

Among the bursts of natural color found on British screens in the mid-1920s was a Technicolor Phonofilm of the "Parade of Wooden Soldiers" dance from the Chauve-Souris revue, shown at the Tivoli in July 1925. But the most notable achievement in color arrived during the *Lodger* shoot, when *The Black Pirate*, a Douglas Fairbanks production for United Artists, shot entirely in Technicolor, had its world premiere at the same venue—a few hours before its opening in New York—on 8 March 1926. Only a star of Fairbanks's magnitude could have insisted on using the still cumbersome process for a full feature, but the result was greeted with enthusiasm by the critics, happily oblivious of the consequences for the bottom line, including Barry, Montagu, and Mycroft. "Into the slack, depressing sameness of the colour," wrote the more ambivalent Lejeune, "Fairbanks has introduced here and there a flash of steel, a bright warmth of copper, a flaming dawn behind a dark ship, a stained glass window of ruby and emerald light."[43]

Her comments are of interest partly because they anticipate one of Hitchcock's first significant comments on color, which in fact appeared as a quote in one of Lejeune's reviews almost ten years later, in July 1935. The occasion was the release of Rouben Mamoulian's *Becky Sharp*, for MGM, the first feature to be shot in the three-strip Technicolor process. "The colour of 'Becky Sharp,'" wrote Lejeune,

> has all the exuberance of a travelling salesman. There is far too much of it, and it has not yet learnt the economic value of restraint. Alfred Hitchcock's idea of a colour picture, which starts off with a board meeting in black and white and grey, interrupted by the wife of one of the directors in a red hat, is much nearer the root of the matter.[44]

Hitchcock spoke on the topic at greater length in 1937, while making *Young and Innocent*. "I don't believe in colour for colour's sake," he told the British fan magazine *Film Pictorial*. "Colour should be used dramatically, symbolically—to add emphasis or point contrast."[45] To illustrate his point he used the same example Lejeune had quoted two years earlier—"a dark, panelled room, with men in dark suits and just one woman with a light coloured dress or hat." He also imagined shooting a London fog. "That's a thing nobody has tried to put on the screen yet—and how beautiful it would be in colour. Thick yellow fog, and a street lamp showing through it. It would create an atmosphere of drama at once." Hitchcock's use of sound and color was governed by the desire he expressed in his contribution to *Footnotes to the Film* in the same year—the desire "to put my film together on the screen, not simply to photograph something that has been put together already."[46]

The Pleasure Garden was trade-shown on the day Mycroft's set report from *The Lodger* appeared, 23 March 1926, at 11:15 a.m., at the Tivoli. Newspaper critics at the time tended to review films as soon as they saw them, regardless of release date, and *The Pleasure Garden* was noticed in both the trades and the dailies. The headline above the *Daily Express*'s review referred to Hitchcock as a "Young Man with a Master Hand" (as Hitchcock would accurately recount to Peter Bogdanovich).[47] Mycroft sought to distinguish the master from his material. Out of a "quite undistinguished" story, he wrote in the *Evening Standard*, Hitchcock "has made a film which it became a stimulating experience to see. He has developed the plot filmatically, not by sub-titles."[48] In the *Sunday Herald* he wrote that Hitchcock "demonstrates such a free and instinctive appreciation of genuine film technique, marked by such sudden strikes of innate virtuosity that a tawdry plot is transmuted by his treatment, despite a certain amount of over-emphasis."[49] Iris Barry's notice was brief, but hailed "a picture calculated to amaze even hardened kinema habitués by its originality, subtlety, and power."[50]

The reviews in the trade papers disclosed that W. & F. had scheduled the film's general release for Friday 14 January 1927. The gap was long, but not wholly out of the ordinary; block and blind booking filled exhibitors' calendars for months in advance. Ivor Montagu's claim that *The Pleasure Garden* had been shelved by its distributor, so that the later disagreement over *The Lodger* put his career in jeopardy, was simply a fiction.

The sixth performance of the Film Society took place on Sunday 11 April, with a supporting program that included Brunel's burlesque of Hollywood-on-Hollywood films, *So This Is Jollygood*, written with Edwin Greenwood. The feature was Marcel L'Herbier's *Feu Mathias Pascal*, making its British debut a year after its Paris debut. A year later, Mycroft, discussing the quest for novelty, recalled the most vertiginous staircase shot from *The Lodger* and how it was achieved. "Then we saw Marcel l'Herbier's "Late Matthew Pascal" with exactly the same device. Both directors had hit on the same means of conveying the effect they wanted."[51] It is unlikely that Hitchcock had seen L'Herbier's film before it was shown at the Film Society. "The odds against such a duplication occurring must have seemed about a million to one," wrote Mycroft.

The next day, late in the *Lodger* shoot, on Monday 12 April, *The Pleasure Garden* opened to the general public at the Capitol—a West End opening in advance of its general release, as was customary. As well as *The Last Laugh*, the Capitol had been used by Fox for the first run of John Ford's epic *The Iron Horse* in the autumn of 1925, but the cinema's short history was not untroubled. It had run into difficulty soon after its opening in February 1925, when the venue's leaseholders terminated their contract prematurely, and had then come under the direct control of Sir Walter Gibbons, the eccentric impresario who had built it. G. A. Atkinson, writing in June 1926, credited Gibbons with turning it "from a greyish-white elephant into what City prospectors call 'a paying proposition,'" though some credit was due to the manager he had installed, Leonard Castleton Knight, formerly of the Shepherd's Bush Pavilion.[52]

The Capitol was a white elephant principally because Sir Walter's plan to sell it to First National for use as a shop window had fallen through, though there were other problems.[53] Vivian Van Damm, who had turned down the job of manager, found that the stairs that all customers had to climb in order to enter the cinema were an "insuperable obstacle."[54] MGM's films went to the Tivoli; Universal's to the Rialto, as the West End Cinema had become; and now Paramount's new titles would go to the Plaza. At the end of 1925, Castleton Knight had cut prices and resorted to revivals—not what a two-thousand-seat venue in such a location, across the Haymarket from the theater of that name, was intended for. More recently, he had courted controversy by including in the program an exploitation film offered by W. & F., *Bonjour Paris*, filmed at the Folies Bergère. The film was hand-colored, so that "the actresses were given a certain amount more clothing."[55]

Nonetheless, it was some achievement for any British film to open there. *The Pleasure Garden* was replaced by DeMille's *The Volga Boatman*, made after his break with Paramount but still a major film. If, as Atkinson alleged, some distributors paid to have their films shown in the West End for promotional purposes, that only supports the argument that W. & F., far from shelving *The Pleasure Garden*, saw it as a possible hit, worth spending money on. An advertisement was placed in the *Sunday Express* on the day before it opened, specifying that it was "Produced by ALFRED HITCHCOCK, *England's Youngest Producer*," an unusual selling point for any film in 1926, let alone a debut.[56] Iris Barry praised it all over again, this time in the *Spectator*, where she wrote that "a new director

The Capitol, Haymarket. SOURCE: Media History Digital Library.

in the person of Mr. Alfred Hitchcock has astonished everyone with his freshness and power."[57]

The only German, indeed, the only non-American film that Hitchcock included in his "Ten Favorite Pictures" opened in London on the same day. E. A. Dupont's *Vaudeville*, which was shown at the New Gallery, about five hundred meters from the Capitol, contains a scene uncannily reminiscent of the opening sequence of Hitchcock's film, in which a scantily clad acrobat is seen reflected in the opera-glasses of her rapt audience. Hitchcock would use the film's art director, Oscar Werndorff, on a number of his films in the 1930s, including *The 39 Steps*.

Also on 12 April, A. Jympson Harman devoted half his *Evening News* column to a set report from *The Lodger*, giving the clearest picture yet of Hitchcock at work. "'Miss June, come back and wipe your shoes on this mat' . . . ," the account begins.[58]

> The floor glistened in the light of the arc lamps because the linoleum had recently been painted to simulate marble, and every footstep on it left a telltale mark.
>
> After the rehearsal of June's scene the floor had been wiped over with oily mops and now the scene was actually to be photographed she had to rub the soles of her dainty shoes on an oily mat, placed just outside the range of the camera to remove the dust.

Harman, who saw the final sequence being filmed, describes Hitchcock—whom he called the "autocrat of the studio"—giving direction even as the camera rolled.

> June was waiting on the set to welcome her lover. Round her feet, which were not to show in this scene, chalk marks had been made so that she should not move out of focus. Her back was turned to the camera. "I'm a great believer in backs," Mr. Hitchcock said to me. "You can get a lot of expression out of them if the owner can act."
>
> The camera began to work and Mr. Novello came down the staircase of the Park-lane mansion towards June. "Hold that, Ivor!" said the autocrat, and the hero stopped and "registered" pleased surprise. "Now come on," Mr. Hitchcock said, and the lovers met and kissed—not quite on the lips, I noticed.
>
> "Tell him, June," the director ordered, and Miss June, without using her voice, told Mr. Novello of the arrival of some visitors. "Turn round," said Mr. Hitchcock, and Mr. Novello turned his head and gave a welcome glance to the battery of lamps that was shedding fierce, hot rays on him. The visitors were not there; but they will be when the connecting parts of this scene are filmed.

At least one scene, however, had already been edited at this early date—the one that newspaper readers already knew about.

> Down in the cellars of the studio, whence tunnels lead direct to the Metropolitan Railway (for the studio was a power-station at one time) Mr. Hitchcock

JUNE AS FILM ACTRESS.

Alfred J, Hitchcock, the young British producer, directing Malcolm Keen in a scene with June in "The Lodger," by Mrs. Belloc Lowndes, a Gainsborough British film.

Evening News, 12 April 1926.

allowed me to see on the screen the result of the staircase scene. The effect was of looking over the banisters to the floor below, and all the action we saw was a man's hand sliding along the banisters of each flight of stairs. It was eerie indeed.

On another page was printed a photograph of Hitchcock playfully threatening June with a poker. His reputation as an autocrat was well earned. By her own account, June was put through twenty takes of her carrying "an iron tray of breakfast dishes up a long flight of stairs," when "I felt a strange sickening pain somewhere in the region of my appendix scar, but forbore to complain or ask for a rest, because delicate actresses are a bore and a nuisance, and in any case, this scene ended my work on the film."[59] The shot does not appear in the finished film.

·   ·   ·   ·   ·

Novello had problems of his own. The day after Harman's article appeared, on 13 April, the case of the Fifty-Fifty came before the magistrate at Bow Street police court. Novello and his partners were charged with supplying intoxicants—champagne in some instances—in breach of their license, and after hours. The second charge was dropped, but all were fined, and the premises disqualified from being used as a club for six months.

Apart from the synchronized Phonofilms, still running at the Holborn Empire, April 1926 saw two notable instances of live accompaniment, more evidence of the inescapability of sound during the *Lodger* shoot. On the evening of the day of *The Pleasure Garden*'s debut, 12 April, Richard Strauss came to the Tivoli to conduct the orchestra for the British debut of the film Robert Wiene had made of his opera *Rosenkavalier*. The performance, which was broadcast live on 2LO, inevitably prompted reflections on the possibilities of film music. Iris Barry wrote that Strauss "showed his appreciation of the new art-form by rearranging his score and by composing fresh passages to fit the picture," calling this "a significant occasion in the history of the kinema."[60] Ivor Montagu, who had become film critic of the *Observer* in November 1925, soon after launching the Film Society, wrote that judging "the picture as an expression of the music here performed, we can only find it exhilarating. Costumes, palaces, and gesture have all an operatic spirit, each sequence is carefully paced to fit the beat of the conductor's baton."[61]

Later the same night, 2LO broadcast from the Hotel Metropole, a short walk from the Tivoli, a performance of *Rhapsody in Blue*, also in the presence of its composer. Gershwin was in London for the opening of his musical *Lady Be Good*, starring Fred and Adele Astaire, at the Empire, Leicester Square. It had already been announced that the Paul Whiteman Band, which had originally commissioned Gershwin to write the *Rhapsody*, and had performed it at the Albert Hall the day before, would take up a residency at the Tivoli after touring the provinces. From Monday 26 April, the band played before the early afternoon and evening programs—then took a late-evening slot at the Kit-Cat Club. The plan to have the band accompany the main film was thwarted only by an intervention by the Musicians' Union on behalf of the Tivoli's orchestra. Angus MacPhail, Montagu's understudy at the *Observer*, wrote that "after seventy minutes of their fascinating harmonies and still more fascinating cacophonies any film short of genius would be disappointing."[62]

It is one of the curiosities of classical Hollywood cinema that the music most associated with it was more in the line of Strauss than of Gershwin. Of the four principal composers Hitchcock worked with, three were products of European conservatoires—though all but one had eclectic tastes. In the spring of 1926, Miklós Rózsa, the most conservative of them, was still a student at Leipzig; Franz Waxman, who had studied in Dresden, was in Berlin, where he would soon join a jazz orchestra, Weintraub's Syncopators; and Dimitri Tiomkin, who had been at the St. Petersburg Conservatory before the war, had recently arrived in New York, where he had already played piano in the pre-film program at the Mark-Strand cinema. Bernard Herrmann, meanwhile, was a teenager growing up in Manhattan, already inspired to become a composer by his reading of Berlioz's *Treatise on Orchestration.*

In between Strauss's appearance at the Tivoli on 12 April and the start of Whiteman's residency at the same venue two weeks later, a decisive step was made toward the adoption of synchronized sound by the American film combines. The partnership of Warner Brothers and Western Electric, manifested in their jointly created new company Vitaphone, was announced in a press release on 25 April, making the front pages of the principal Los Angeles newspapers, as well as that of *Film Daily* in New York, the next day, though without capturing the attention of even the trade press in Britain. "No attempt will be made to reproduce 'talking pictures,' it was announced," reported the *Los Angeles Examiner*, "but the invention will be confined to producing musical accompaniments by leading orchestras for motion picture productions, and to the presentations of musical programs."[63] The "first demonstration of the new apparatus" would be the John Barrymore production *Don Juan.*

In New York, Phonofilms were still being shown in the program of the Rivoli from time to time, as they had been for the past three years, but Western Electric's operation, behind which stood the mighty AT&T, dwarfed the unstable De Forest companies. Nevertheless, Vitaphone, despite its significance for the adoption of synchronized sound across the industry, was a sound-on-disc system—a technical dead end, redundant within a few years. The sound films of the future more closely resembled the Phonofilm, an optical sound-on-film format. Indeed, Theodore Case and Earl Sponable, whose sound-on-film technology was purchased by William Fox in July 1926, and branded as Movietone, had collaborated unhappily with De Forest and had borrowed some of his ideas, just as De Forest had borrowed some of theirs. Cyril Elwell, who had a separate relationship with Case, had set about improving the Phonofilm technology independently of De Forest, and partly as a result, the cutting edge of the sound film was, for a time, to be found in Clapham, in a cramped facility that was nicknamed "the ladies."

The 22 April issue of *Kinematograph Weekly* reported that Hitchcock "has just completed his studio footage."[64] The 1 May issue of *Film Renter* said that *The Lodger* had "entered its last week of production in the studio. A few days' exterior shooting round the London streets will complete the picture."[65] This probably involved the location work made possible by Walter Mycroft, who had

> persuaded the *Evening Standard* to allow scenes to be photographed in the printing and publishing departments. When the studio crew arrived with their arc lamps and paraphernalia and clearly expected to get to work during press time, a Shoe Lane sensation was created. The publisher came up and protested, all sorts of people protested; they hadn't bargained for anything like this.[66]

The resulting sequence provides the film's only direct trace of the historical moment of its making—the front pages, seen in the first reel, proclaiming Churchill's new budget, which was delivered in the House of Commons on the afternoon of Monday 26 April, and reported in that evening's newspapers.

Even as Churchill affirmed the wisdom of the return to the gold standard, which he had announced in his budget a year earlier, Stanley Baldwin, the prime minister, was making a forlorn attempt to escape its effects. John Maynard Keynes, in his instant critique of the return to gold, had written that the policy, which raised the value of the pound by 10 percent, was ruinous for Britain's export industries—especially the coal industry. In order to compete in the world market, exporters would have to reduce their prices by a corresponding 10 percent, and that could only be achieved by a reduction in wages, also by 10 percent. The mine owners had indeed demanded a reduction in wages, and even as Keynes's pamphlet appeared, in the summer of 1925, Baldwin was having to deny having said, in negotiations with the miners' union, that "the workers of this country have got to face a reduction of wages to help put industry on its feet."

The miners had held firm, and to prevent a lockout Baldwin had had to introduce a subsidy to the industry, capital and labor both, which was to expire on 30 April 1926. Meanwhile a royal commission, led by Sir Herbert Samuel, a former Liberal cabinet minister—and cousin of Ivor Montagu—was established to see what could be done with what Keynes called "a decadent, third-generation industry."[67] The commission's report, published in March 1926, proposed reform of the coal industry as well as wage reductions, and was duly rejected by miners and owners alike. By then the Trades Union Congress had committed itself to backing the miners with a general strike, which was destined to begin when the subsidy ran out. Neither Baldwin, nor the TUC, and still less the Labour leadership in Parliament, wanted it, and when it arrived Keynes sent an article to the *Chicago Daily News*—the British presses being closed—saying that the atmosphere was "one of depression and helplessness and dismay at the failure of reason and common sense."[68] Neither side had any solution to offer, only outdated ideologies, held without much conviction.

In that respect the coal crisis presented a parallel with the quota controversy. In both cases, Baldwin's government could not face up to the consequences of the prewar, laissez-faire approach it was itself attempting to revive. In the realm of film this was because free trade had, in practice, enabled an American near-monopoly over what was shown in British cinemas. Policy makers could not, however, imagine an alternative other than protectionism. The trade was still hopelessly unable to provide a voluntary solution of its own, and so on the day after the budget, 27 April, Sir Philip Cunliffe-Lister—who had had to recuse himself from the coal crisis because his wife Molly, having inherited a large Yorkshire estate, was a mine owner—told the House of Commons that the quota would go on to the agenda of the Imperial Conference in the autumn, making direct government intervention some degrees more likely.

The miners' lockout began on 1 May, the general strike at midnight on the 3rd. Not everyone experienced it as Keynes did. For Mycroft, who claimed to have made his car available to the strike breakers only because the TUC could not find a use for it, the strike was merely "an eight day long Bank-holiday."[69] For his Film Society colleague Ivor Montagu, meanwhile, the strike was "a semi-revolutionary situation."[70] Montagu had scandalized his father, the second Lord Swaythling, by joining the British Socialist Party while in his teens, and though he had not joined the BSP's successor, the Communist Party of Great Britain, he was active in the radical Holborn branch of the largely moderate Labour Party. Montagu spent May 1926 acting as a bicycle courier for the strike sheet *British Worker*, and lamented that his high-minded cousin had been used by both sides to bring about the strike's end, less than a fortnight after it began. But Montagu and Mycroft alike recognized that the cost was borne by the miners, whose struggle continued long after the excitement of May, largely unheeded, until they were broken.

5 To Catch a Thief

Michael Balcon arrived at Southampton aboard the White Star liner *Majestic* on the morning of 30 April 1926, just before the general strike began. He had spent six weeks in New York, staying at the Algonquin again, and so was absent for most of the *Lodger* shoot. He had taken copies of *The Pleasure Garden*, *The Mountain Eagle*, *The Rat*, *The Prude's Fall*, and a more recent Graham Cutts production, *The Sea Urchin*, with the aim of finding a distributor. In this he was only half successful. After the collapse of the Selznick organization in 1924, Gainsborough had relied on a small Times Square sales agency, Lee-Bradford, to sell into the United States. *The Blackguard* and *The Passionate Adventure*, the film Myron Selznick had personally supervised, had been taken up by the company after its president, Arthur A. Lee, visited Europe in the spring of 1925.

Lee-Bradford, however, sold to "state rights" distributors that served only the lesser independent cinemas. The prize that Balcon sought when he set out for New York was a contract with one of the combines; and yet when offered one he turned it down. Afterward, E. Bruce Johnson, foreign manager of First National, told *Film Renter* that "only recently I offered on behalf of my company a contract to Mr. Michael Balcon, of Gainsborough Pictures, whilst he was in New York, to finance a number of pictures to be produced by Mr. Graham Cutts for distribution by us all over the world."[1] First National, as Johnson mentioned, had recently part-financed two films by Cutts's former partner Herbert Wilcox. On earlier occasions Balcon had followed Wilcox's example—by bringing American stars to Poole Street, and by mounting major productions in Germany—but Wilcox's entanglement with the combines was another question.

In the autumn of 1925, Wilcox had begun shooting the second of these two First National–backed productions, *Nell Gwyn*, with Dorothy Gish in the title role, at Poole Street, but he ran out of money, only to be rescued by a newly formed company fronted by J. D. Williams, British National Pictures. After resigning from First National in 1922, Williams had managed Valentino's production company, but he had come to London in 1925 ostensibly without plans. British National's capital came from George T. Eaton, an Australian cattle dealer who had backed some of Williams's earlier ventures and since retired to Sussex. The British branch of First National had the British rights to *Nell Gwyn*, but Williams managed to sell the US rights to Paramount. Thus was *Nell Gwyn* chosen, in deference to patriotic sensibilities, as the first film to be shown at the Plaza, in March 1926. Williams went on to win distribution advances from Paramount for three further films with Gish, to be directed by Wilcox, eventually at the studio British National was building at Elstree, a village on London's northwestern outskirts. The first of the three, shot at Twickenham in the spring of 1926, and featuring scenes of the Paul Whiteman Band performing at the Kit-Cat Club, was titled *London*.

When the Paramount deal was made public, in the summer of 1926, Balcon raised an objection that explained his decision to turn down First National:

> I have in my office an exactly similar offer from an American house of eminence quite as great as that of Famous-Players. I have always understood, however, that the desire and hope of the people who count in this country is that England should make films unfettered and uncontrolled by foreigners, and should be in a position of equality with other countries in the marketing and distribution of these products.[2]

The First National deal, being global, would have meant cutting out W. & F.—and for a fixed fee rather than a percentage. In later years Balcon claimed that he had also declined a similar offer from MGM.[3] No doubt there was more to both stories than he let on, but Balcon returned from New York with only a fresh contract with Lee-Bradford, and this had been all but assured even before he left. In addition to the batch of five films that included the first two Hitchcocks, which Arthur Lee could have seen, the deal included *The Lodger*, as yet unfinished.[4]

A few weeks after his return, in mid-May 1926, *Cinema News* published an interview with a despondent Balcon about his visit. "When it comes to placing British films, unless one of the four big corporations takes the picture," the paper's correspondent paraphrased, meaning Paramount, MGM, First National, and Fox, "there is little chance of making a deal."[5] *The Rat* had been deemed risqué, and Mae Marsh, age thirty-one, was considered past her peak. "'No star that is not "run" by one of the four organisations is regarded as having a star value at all,' explained Mr. Balcon. 'But if you try to get a better star before commencing your picture the ruling companies will not part with one.'" Despite his having acquired a clearer view of the obstacles in the path of British producers, Balcon nonetheless continued to shrink from recommending concerted action against the American oligopoly, such as a quota. He "hesitated some time before venturing an opinion," but could endorse only "public opinion, led by the Press."

A prime example of what the "big four" could achieve, and of what effect press opinion might have, arrived in London the day after the interview appeared. MGM's war film *The Big Parade* opened at the Tivoli on the evening of Friday 21 May, preceded by "a wildly exciting half-hour of Paul Whiteman's irresistible jazz orchestra," as Iris Barry put it.[6] In that day's *Daily Express*, G. A. Atkinson had written that "there is strong doubt, even among the sponsors of the film itself, of the wisdom of showing it to the British public."[7] Sure enough, on the morning after, Atkinson's review was headed "How America 'Won the War'"—and so was Barry's in the *Daily Mail*. As she said, "no other Allied troops of any kind are even so much as casually mentioned."[8] That and the story's implausibility, she said in her longer *Spectator* review, were likely to repel British viewers. "The War was not a great game ending in twenty-four hours of fighting: no film dare show what it resembled."[9] Such views were reported in the New York papers, and these reports were in turn reported in London.

The doubts to which Atkinson referred were real. Alfred Davis said he would not show *The Big Parade* in his cinemas. Sir William Jury, whose distribution firm had mutated into the British branch of MGM, had put off showing the film, which had opened in the United States in November 1925, and eventually declined to involve himself in the launch, which was handled from New York.[10] In this instance, however, public opinion was not led by the press. *The Big Parade*, despite having a story that chafed at the tenderest point of the Anglo-American relationship, was a colossal hit. Its success embraced the whole equation of American pictures in Britain: control of distribution and exhibition; expertise in presentation and promotion; exploitation of star quality; mastery of screen craft; and, underlying all these, finance on a scale of which British filmmakers could only dream.

Most critics acknowledged the craft, and some wrote in the film's favor. "Judging it as a picture," wrote Ivor Montagu in the *Observer*, "we see at once that it is the lineal and worthy successor of those masterpieces of historic spectacle with which Mr. Griffith first worked the cinemagoer to a knowledge of how excited he could be."[11] Less visibly to British cinemagoers, it also represented a benchmark in studio organization, five thousand five hundred miles away in Los Angeles. In early June, the Tivoli's weekly newsletter said that because it had been decided to give *The Big Parade* an indefinite run—it lasted into late autumn—there were no coming features to promote, and that the space would instead be used to introduce some of the personalities involved in the film. Director King Vidor, author Laurence Stallings, and stars John Gilbert and Renée Adorée were all given brief lives, but no mention was made of the twenty-six-year-old responsible for the production, Irving Thalberg.

Still an obscure figure in Britain in 1926, by the time of his death ten years later Thalberg had become a legend. "Here was no ordinary impresario, showman or business man," wrote Balcon in tribute, "but a sincere craftsman who made films and made them well."[12] Thalberg's death came during the golden years of the studio system; in 1969, amid its ruins, Hitchcock wondered "how Thalberg would fare today."[13] Thalberg had been "quoted as saying in a recent biography that films are not made, they are remade," said Hitchcock, who reflected that *Rebecca* had had two weeks of retakes following its first preview. But now "this whole way of making pictures is impossible. The components of a picture leave as soon as production is finished." Himself a recipient, at the 1968 Academy Awards ceremony, of the Irving G. Thalberg Memorial Award, the older Hitchcock could afford to wax nostalgic. Closer in time to *The Lodger*, however, in an article published in the *Evening News* in November 1927, he wrote of "American film directors under their commercially minded employers," and lamented "that the author's story is made into screen form on paper by one man, who may have been overseen by some important executive, filmed by another, cut by another, and edited by another"—precisely the modus operandi perfected by Thalberg, as Hitchcock would have known by then.[14]

His article appeared shortly after the publication of a firsthand account of Hollywood's workings, *Films: Facts and Forecasts*, by L'Estrange Fawcett, film critic of the *Morning Post*. Fawcett had visited Hollywood in August–September 1926, and the reports he published in his column, expanded in the book, described the eclipse of independent-minded directors by committees presided over by production supervisors, "the re-making process" whereby "whole sections of the film are re-built and re-shot" according to the committee's wishes, and the use of multiple sneak previews to refine the film yet further.[15] Film direction, wrote Fawcett, "is no longer an individualistic enterprise," and *The Big Parade*, "an outstanding example of the success of these drastic methods," had come about after Thalberg, "an extremely clever young man," persuaded the company to expand Vidor's modestly proportioned film into an epic.

There were less happy examples of the Thalberg regime at MGM, of which Hitchcock would also have been aware. The fate of Erich von Stroheim's *Greed* was well known. The first announcement of the formation of the Film Society, in May 1925, carried on the front page of the *Daily Express*, included a claim from Ivor Montagu that he would show all "eight hours" of Stroheim's film, the truncated version of which had recently opened at the Tivoli.[16] Hitchcock would also have read Rex Ingram's repeated threats, at the time of MGM's creation in 1924, to quit filmmaking for sculpture, and noticed his refusal to work at its studio in Culver City in favor of Nice. At the start of 1926, the New Gallery's manager, Jean Norton, visited Ingram while he was at work on his adaptation of Somerset Maugham's *The Magician* and wrote, also in the *Express*, that "America has failed to grip him. He is 'agin the Government' behind the screen."[17] Had Hitchcock access to the American trade press, he would have registered the sacking of Mauritz Stiller from his protégée Garbo's second film for MGM, *The Temptress*, in May 1926, and Maurice Tourneur's sacking from *The Mysterious Island* in July. Neither Tourneur nor Ingram worked in Hollywood again.

The model provided by Thalberg was soon followed by the other studios. In July 1926, B. P. Schulberg, an old industry hand at thirty-four, was appointed to a similar role at Paramount. His son Budd compared the "two top intellectuals in town" thus: "frail, self-contained Irving who burned with a Jesuitical faith in the world religion of motion pictures; and B.P., a more profound reader and a more original mind but with all the traits that Irving piously disavowed: drinking, gambling, and wenching."[18] Thalberg systematized, rather than invented, the new way of making pictures; conversely, the system never quite froze in the manner suggested by the term *classical* Hollywood cinema—used somewhat in jest by Bazin, if not by those who followed him. Nevertheless, there was a consolidation of power within the Hollywood studios in the mid-1920s that Hitchcock had to reckon with when he contemplated going to work there.

At the time, what was most palpable in Hollywood was not the fixing of a new pattern but the breaking of an old one. "Old Hollywood, with its world-famous motion picture players wearing grease paint and an incongruous assortment of costumes is about to make a graceful exit," wrote Louella O. Parsons in her newly launched *Los Angeles Examiner* column in May 1926.[19] "But while the small village is singing its swan song a new Hollywood is arising to take its place." Land values in Hollywood had multiplied tenfold in little over a decade. "When the Lasky, and, I might say, the Fox studios, were built, there were few buildings anywhere near, the highest one of three stories was dubbed the skyscraper," and many of the stars had lived in the district.[20] As Hollywood became a boom town, however, its elite had decamped to Beverly Hills, still a "secluded village," and now the studios themselves were on the move. Hollywood had never been located only in Hollywood, but after 1926 almost none of it was.

"First National is locating in Burbank, where they will have room to expand. Fox is adding to its Hollywood holdings at Westwood and Famous is collecting its units at the United Studios which are far removed from the business center."[21] Paramount had bought the United Studios on Melrose

Avenue, a mile south of its first home at Sunset and Vine, in January 1926. Simultaneously, First National, United Studios' main occupant, had decided to build a large facility five miles to the north, close to Universal City. Construction at Burbank began in March and the site was in use by June, while Paramount overhauled the Melrose Avenue site with equal rapidity, ending production at Vine Street in mid-May and recommencing at Melrose a month later. Fox had bought a vast tract in Westwood, between Santa Monica and Pico Boulevards, in 1923, almost as soon as the area was made available for development, but had moved slowly. By April 1926, however, Fox Hills, as the area was called, was being used for Raoul Walsh's war epic *What Price Glory*, and the site's formal opening came at the end of August.

Together with Universal City and Culver City, these would remain the principal studio locations of Los Angeles for the rest of Hitchcock's career. *Lifeboat*, his only film for Fox, was shot at Westwood; *Rope* began the series of films he made at Burbank, long since controlled by Warner Brothers; and Paramount was still on Melrose Avenue when he shot *Rear Window*.

Not Thalberg but one of his bosses, Marcus Loew, traveled to England in the early summer of 1926, and attended the annual meeting of the Cinematograph Exhibitors Association, held that year in Brighton—once a center of world film production. The same conference provided the backdrop for the beginning of a twist in the convoluted tale of *The Lodger*.

In August 1925, immediately after the production of *The Pleasure Garden*, Gainsborough had been reorganized, with Charles Lapworth joining the board alongside Balcon and Cutts. The son of a Yorkshire coal miner, Lapworth had been active in left-wing politics and journalism before 1914, and was briefly editor of the radical *Daily Herald*. He had moved to the United States during the war, and, having gone to interview Charlie Chaplin, became part of his entourage. Afterward he had worked in a variety of roles for the Goldwyn company, both in London and in Culver City, where he assisted Victor Sjöström on his adaptation of Hall Caine's *The Master of Man*, reportedly advising "on English customs and habits," though the story is Manx.[22] Lapworth had left Goldwyn shortly before it was merged into MGM, and returned to London a year later, in the spring of 1925.

He joined Gainsborough as editorial director, and contributed two scenarios that went straight into production, one for *The Sea Urchin*, adapted from a recent play, the other for Hitchcock's *The Mountain Eagle*, an original. But it is probable that Lapworth was more valued for his knowledge of the American film scene, which he had shared during the spring and summer of 1925 as a vocal participant in the row over the fate of British cinema, author of a string of articles proposing, as an alternative to the quota, "reciprocity"—a scheme whereby British exhibitors would use their collective bargaining power to insist that the American combines take and show a certain number of British films each year.

More than once in these articles, which appeared in *Kinematograph Weekly*, Lapworth quoted Keynes on the disadvantage caused to British exporters by the return to the gold standard. "The whole country is in for a period of revision of political and economic principles, many of which may be discovered to be mere shibboleths," he wrote in one installment, published in July 1925.[23] "The hundred-per-cent. free trader and the hundred-per-cent. protectionist are beginning to review their positions in respect to the state of world trade. Party lines may become somewhat blurry and indistinct." Balcon wrote in the same issue, and while he was less explicit on the point than Lapworth, he too advised his notional American readers that it would be better for them voluntarily to provide "a guarantee of an outlet in their own home market sufficient to make profitable the modest program of British pictures which we are capable of," than to be compelled into a worse arrangement by the government.[24]

Lapworth had accompanied Balcon to New York in March 1926, and it was reported by *Film Daily* that their visit had a "semi-official aspect as British officials have requested they report back concerning the consideration they receive from American distributing organizations."[25] The pair, it went on, carried "letters of introduction from the Federation of British Industries" and other such bodies. In April they had had a meeting with Will Hays, the powerful head of the Motion Picture Association of America. Hays, "Postmaster-General in the Cabinet of the martyred Harding and an eminent Presbyterian layman," as H. L. Mencken once painted him, had been installed in the post a few years earlier to represent the film industry at government level.[26] On his return, Lapworth was outwardly proud to recite to the *Evening News* and other papers versions of Hays's noncommittal but apparently "deliberately spoken words: 'The British film situation is our major consideration at the moment.'"[27]

Lapworth had left New York before Balcon, for reasons unknown, and on his return Balcon was dismissive of reciprocity's chances. They parted ways after the Brighton conference. The talk Lapworth gave there, on 15 June, did little more than repeat more forcefully what he had been saying for a year, but it was written up on the front page of that day's *Evening News,* and elsewhere the day after, with incendiary headlines. "Exhibitors could put British films upon American screens," the *Daily Mail* paraphrased, "and if they did not do it they deserved the obloquy which would surely come when the public was made fully aware of their neglect."[28] The next week's trade papers carried fuller versions of the talk, accompanied by a letter from Gainsborough's publicist Bill O'Bryen, an old friend of Balcon's from Birmingham days, disowning Lapworth's remarks. The most savage criticism came from C. M. Woolf's right-hand man, Jeffrey Bernerd, who called Lapworth's speech a "joke" on the front page of *Cinema News.*[29] "The American market is absolutely dead to British pictures," said Bernerd, and by attacking exhibitors for not getting behind reciprocity, all Lapworth had done was to insult people with whom Gainsborough and W. & F. needed to do business.[30] Within a week Lapworth had resigned from the Gainsborough board, and the trade papers the week following, dated 1 July, announced that the company would be reorganized once more.

A few days after the Brighton conference, Marcus Loew, at a farewell luncheon in London, told his hosts that Britain lacked a "nucleus for an organisation" such as could be found in the United States or Germany; it had instead a dispersed group of small producers, none with a guaranteed outlet, the exhibition field being similarly dispersed.[31] Gainsborough's reorganization was intended to concentrate its resources. Under the name Piccadilly Pictures, Gainsborough was merged with W. & F., with C. M. Woolf as chairman, and Balcon as joint managing director alongside a new name, Carlyle Blackwell. Both Cutts and Lapworth were off the board, though Cutts was still part of the company. The new arrangement plainly put the distributor in control, but this was merely to ratify Balcon's decision, in New York, not to be swallowed up by the Americans.

The more eye-catching change is the advent of Blackwell, put "in control of production," while Balcon had "commercial control."[32] Carlyle

Blackwell, an American, had been a star of the early 1910s for Vitagraph and Kalem, and had continued his career in Europe after the war, notably playing Bulldog Drummond in an Anglo-Dutch film of 1922. He had first been mentioned in association with Gainsborough, as star and producer, in the autumn of 1925, but Blackwell was not a name to conjure with in the mid-1920s. Indeed, an elegiac article published in the *Los Angeles Times* on the demise of the original Lasky studio, reflecting on the "ghosts of former film fame," carelessly remarked that he was "in vaudeville in England."[33] He was not obviously qualified for the role of production chief.

On the other hand, he was married to a millionaire. Blackwell's celebrity at this time derived as much from his complicated marital affairs as from his film career. He and Leah Haxton had married in January 1925, in Berlin—four months before her divorce from Alfred Haxton went through the English courts, with Blackwell named as corespondent. The couple were said to have married a second time, again in Berlin, but felt that a third wedding, in London, was called for; and this was announced a few days after the Gainsborough reorganization, for 29 July.

Leah was the daughter of Barney Barnato. The semiliterate son of a Whitechapel rag-merchant, Barnato had gone out to the diamond fields of South Africa in 1873, been a rival to Cecil Rhodes, then sold out to him, becoming a life governor at De Beers. In his autobiography Michael Balcon, who was married to an Englishwoman raised in Johannesburg, wrote that his father had been in South Africa "with all the early pioneers— Rhodes, Joel, Barnato. The one difference was that he returned home broke."[34] Ultimately Barnato had not returned at all. He died in 1897, still in his early forties and very far from broke, having gone overboard, somewhat mysteriously, during a voyage back from the Cape to attend Victoria's Diamond Jubilee.

The implication of Blackwell's arrival at Gainsborough in these circumstances is clear, and yet it has rarely been made so, either at the time or since. However, one former Gainsborough employee, Cedric Belfrage, having moved to the United States in the summer of 1926, felt secure enough to write, in the October issue of *Picturegoer*, that "Leah Barnato is a useful acquisition to the impoverished British film industry; it was she, as those on the inside of things know, who made possible the purchase by Piccadilly Pictures of the Famous Players studio at Islington."[35] This purchase, it was said in the announcement of 1 July, had only "just now" been completed. One of Leah's brothers, Jack, had died in the influenza pandemic that swept the world after the war; the other, Woolf, known as "Babe," had become a celebrated racing-car driver, and Babe had a yet more direct connection to *The Lodger*: June was his girlfriend.

Adrian Brunel recalled meeting him "one night at the New Oxford Theatre during the run of the American crook-thriller 'The Gorilla,'" in the summer or autumn of 1925.[36]

> We were with his ex-wife and her husband, and sitting behind us were Babe Barnato, with June (later Lady Inverclyde). He and his ex-wife were sincerely hearty in their greetings & the presence of the husband and June did not seem to embarrass them at all. During the interval we three men met in the bar and had a jolly manly chat about the jolly, thrilling play and then parted.
>
> I liked Babe's easy manner. He was keen physically & mentally and seemed unspoiled by his riches.

At the end of 1925, June and Carlyle Blackwell had appeared opposite one another in one of a series of short films starring the jockey Steve Donoghue, produced at Poole Street "by Gainsborough Pictures for C. & M. Productions," essentially W. &. F. acting as producer. It was June's first film appearance in five years.

Gainsborough's access to the Barnato fortune puts a different complexion on Balcon and Woolf's rugged declarations of independence. "Let's win our better equipment like any other business, through our own ability," rather than seek state subsidy, Balcon the 100 percent free trader had written in 1925.[37] "The making of British films must, in my opinion, be the subject of individual endeavour," Woolf had written in March 1926.[38] Without the Barnatos' money, W. & F's future was bleak. Its most recent Harold Lloyd picture, *College Days*, as *The Freshman* was titled in Britain, premiered at the New Gallery in November 1925 and released in January 1926, was to be its last. Lloyd had signed a new worldwide distribution contract with Paramount, starting with *For Heaven's Sake*—which when it opened in September became the first film to run at the Plaza for more than a week.

Within a few months, virtually all major American productions would be in the hands of American-controlled distributors. Warner Brothers, the last significant studio to rent through an independent British firm, had announced in February 1926 that it would distribute its films on its own account—more precisely, through the venerable Vitagraph network, which it had recently acquired—once the Gaumont contract ended that autumn. British distributors were left with the output of Poverty Row, continental imports, and British films—and the first category left C. M. Woolf unimpressed, as he told G. A. Atkinson in August:

> "The most rapid process of brain-softening," he said, "is to look at a batch of average American films. When you have waded through that morass of vapid sentiment, sickly sex stuff, trite philosophy, and banal drama, without discovering one logical moment or sane impulse, you are a ripe candidate for the lunatic asylum. Film-renting is one of the dangerous trades."
>
> I should explain that Mr. Woolf is not concerned, except in rare instances, in studying the output of those American companies which have their own distributing organisation.
>
> They account for rather less than half of America's 800 films.
>
> He studies the output of independent companies and the smaller regular producing concerns.[39]

For Atkinson, this situation explained Woolf's investment in British production. The interview was timed to promote his company's coming schedule of trade shows, a schedule that included *The Lodger*. These would be W. & F.'s first trade shows since the company's reorganization, and it had put on just one since April, for *Her Betrayal*, a German film starring Lya de Putti. A year earlier W. & F. had claimed to be a fifty-two-films-a-year operation; no longer.[40] Woolf and Balcon may have disapproved of the protectionist legislation that now seemed likely to be enacted, but their company's new orientation toward British films depended on it, as Balcon had hinted on his return from New York.

Asked to improve on his remark that "public opinion, led by the Press" was a solution to the industry's problems, Balcon "gave it as his considered view that the solution was in this: that everybody who is now engaged in the business of making British pictures should carry on."[41] Asked whether this was viable, Balcon replied: "Yes, with care, and taking advantage of the present wave of public opinion, we are likely to get the same results as were proposed under the Quota scheme," meaning the voluntary scheme that the exhibitors had rejected in 1925. Producers needed only to bide their time. "And then, in the event of legislation being introduced, the

Industry would be equipped with the necessary material, and would be able to avoid the criticism—levelled before—that the British producer was not capable of carrying out what was required of him."

Increasingly squeezed out of the market in films—both American films in Britain, and British films in the United States—by the American combines, now financed by Wall Street at its most bullish, Woolf and Balcon were able to rest their small private company, no longer competitive, upon a cushion of capital accumulated at the height of the British Empire a generation earlier, until the hour of state protection arrived. It was during this interval, and using this residue of inherited capital, that *The Lodger* was completed.

Hitchcock's name was not mentioned in the announcement of Gainsborough's reorganization at the start of July. According to the myth, *The Lodger* was at that time languishing unloved on W. & F.'s shelves, awaiting Ivor Montagu's handiwork, with Hitchcock's career in jeopardy; perhaps Piccadilly Pictures had made a clean break with him. In fact, Hitchcock's career was in anything but jeopardy. On 20 May, less than a month after the end of production on *The Lodger*, Walter Mycroft had broken the news that "Mr. Alfred Hitchcock, the clever English director of 'The Pleasure Garden,' is joining British National, which company will soon have, at Elstree, the largest studios in the whole world."[42] Bill O'Bryen instantly wrote to the papers to point out that Hitchcock was contracted to Gainsborough until 28 February 1927, and that his next project would be an adaptation of John Buchan's *Huntingtower*, to star Carlyle Blackwell. Having printed this clarification, Mycroft then added color: "Mr. Hitchcock is to be paid the salary of £10,000 a year," he wrote on 1 June.[43] "Probably no British director has ever signed such a contract; certainly none in this country ever has." Hitchcock was then in Scotland, "engaged in the congenial task of hunting up castles for his new film."

Whatever Elstree's square footage may have been, it was certainly the only British studio complex comparable with those of Los Angeles or Berlin. Construction had begun in January 1926; in April, with two stages nearing completion, the trade papers had been invited to report on its progress. "Within a month or two *the whole of the present available studio space in this country will be doubled*," the correspondent of *Kinematograph*

Weekly had written.[44] Elstree was not intended for use by British National alone, but as a rental facility. At the time the enterprise was launched, in the autumn of 1925, some among those demanding government action advocated the building of a "national" studio, with government support. Elstree met the same need without direct subsidy.

In July 1926, Charles Lapworth, who had known J. D. Williams from his time with Chaplin, described Elstree as exactly the "nucleus" that Marcus Loew had recently claimed Britain lacked. "Here is a group of British capitalists who responded to the appeal made by the Trade to the Government twelve months ago for first-class central studios," he wrote in *Kinematograph Weekly*, without much regard for the capitalists' nationalities, "and themselves are providing that equipment; and such faith have they in the future of British production, they are actually spending their money in the making of big pictures without first bothering to secure markets."[45]

As with Woolf and Balcon, it is more likely that Williams and his backers built Elstree in the belief that a secure market was on the horizon. The quota would lead to a rush of investment, and demand for studio space. Williams favored a quota, he declared in July 1926, as a "temporary measure," and "a method of creating financial confidence in British film making."[46] By then his company had a major new investor, I. W. Schlesinger, an American whose companies had a monopoly over distribution and exhibition in South Africa. Schlesinger's association with British National was announced at the end of May 1926, about the time of the Hitchcock announcement. As L'Estrange Fawcett commented in the *Morning Post*, the news was "all the more interesting because hitherto South Africa has been practically a closed shop for American productions"—no others could get in.[47] In *Films: Facts and Forecasts* he expanded on the point. The South African market, wrote Fawcett, had been inaccessible to all except the American combines, but when "the possibility of the imposition of a quota became probable, Mr. Schlesinger joined the board of British International Pictures," as British National was later known, so that if the South African government were to follow London and "enforce a British quota," Schlesinger would profit from the arrangement.[48]

There is no date for the fateful screening of *The Lodger* for the staff of W. & F., during which Hitchcock and Alma Reville made their way around

East London, hoping for the best. The versions of the story given to Truffaut and Bogdanovich, the most detailed, provide clues, but also confusion. "When it was finished, Cutts was still in the company, and Balcon had gone to America," Hitchcock told Bogdanovich.[49] "When he returned, Cutts said to him, '*I've* been looking at the rushes and I can't make head nor tail of them—don't know what the hell he's shooting.'" Next—and here the Bogdanovich interview matches Truffaut's—"the film was shown to the distributors' publicity woman," Leila Lewis, "and chief accountant, and they went back and gave a very bad report." To Truffaut he said that their "big boss" in Wardour Street came to see it two days later; to Bogdanovich it was Balcon, who came "the following day."

Balcon, in his autobiography, claimed that the "jealous" Cutts had influenced not him but Woolf, who "didn't want to put *The Lodger* out and in fact it went on the shelf for a while" until he, Balcon, rescued it.[50] It is more likely that the big boss to whom Lewis and the chief accountant of W. & F. reported back was Woolf—whose office was on the corner of Wardour Street and Old Compton Street—and that Balcon would have seen the film before anyone from W. & F. The specificity of Hitchcock's recollection of Balcon having recently returned from New York is striking, but hard to reconcile with other parts of the picture. It is his remark to Truffaut that after this second screening with the "big boss," be he Balcon or Woolf, W. & F. "stopped booking it—because they were booking it on Novello's name, you see," that makes possible some anchorage in the record, because the film was indeed being booked soon after its completion—and for weeks after Balcon's return, making it all the more likely that the big boss was Woolf.

W. &. F. paid to advertise *The Lodger* on the cover of three of the four trade papers in late May 1926. The cover of *Cinema News* dated 20 May, its first full edition after the general strike, had the film as "Nearing Completion."[51] A news item in the same day's *Bioscope* had it as "just finished"; in both instances this may be taken to mean the process of editing rather than principal photography.[52] The issue of *Film Renter* published two days later had *The Lodger* on the cover, and the news of Hitchcock's poaching by British National inside. These advertisements presented the film simply as a Gainsborough production distributed by W. & F.; an advertisement in *Cinema News* on 3 June named Balcon and Blackwell—some

W. & F., corner of Wardour Street and Old Compton Street, June 1926. With thanks to the British Newspaper Archive.

four weeks before the official announcement of the latter's place on the board—as "presenting" it.[53] The placement of these advertisements does not give the impression that W. & F. wanted to shelve *The Lodger* at this date. Still less so does W. & F.'s decision to emblazon the entire frontage of its Soho headquarters with posters promoting the film, photographs of which appeared in the trade press in mid-June. *Bioscope* captioned theirs "What is described as the largest hoarding in London."[54]

According to the issue of *Film Renter* with the film on its cover— 22 May—the Manchester branch of W. & F. was "now booking 'The Lodger.' . . . Already quite a number of bookings have been made."[55] Two weeks later the section of *Kinematograph Weekly* covering distributors in the far north of England, a region including Newcastle, where W. & F.'s regional office was based, reported that "'The Lodger' and a sequel to 'The Rat' are booking up satisfactorily."[56] The latter film was still being shot. It was unusual for British distributors to make films available for booking before completion—after all, neither film had an official release date—but, as with the ads and the hoarding, the practice does not suggest a lack of faith in the film's in-demand director. Stills from *The Lodger* appeared in the issue of *Film Renter* dated 19 June, with the announcement that the film was "shortly to be Trade Shown."[57] Taking Hitchcock's story at face value, *The Lodger*'s travails must have begun around midsummer. The "Detailed Cost of Production" account in the BFI archive is made up to 16 June.[58]

To recapitulate, as of June 1926, Hitchcock had seen his first film not held up, as Montagu was to claim, but widely praised on its debut at one of the major West End cinemas. When he signed a lucrative contract with one of Gainsborough's rivals, Gainsborough's response was to point out in public that they had him for another nine months, and that he was at work on a new film based on a book by one of his favorite authors. Hitchcock recounted none of this context in telling of how W. & F. took against *The Lodger*—apparently after heavily promoting it. Nor, in saying that it was held up by a "couple of months," did Hitchcock reflect that *The Pleasure Garden* had been completed for six or seven months before being shown. W. & F. did not trade-show a single film during May, July, or August 1926, with just one in June, *Her Betrayal*; as had been the case in 1925, they made a sales push in September, with trade shows of a number of big films, and it was natural that *The Lodger* was included in this, rather than shown in the summer. It is one thing that Hitchcock was prone to spinning yarns to interviewers, more surprising that none of this context has been reconstructed since, because it is only within it that the film's reediting can be understood.

To have canceled bookings for any film would have sent a bad signal to exhibitors, and if such a step had been taken it would likely have been reported in the trade press. There was no chance that the investment in *The Lodger*, which starred the most popular British male star of the day, was going to be written off. There must be a grain of truth in Hitchcock's account of W. & F.'s reaction to the film, which necessitated the film's reediting, but reediting was standard practice at Gainsborough and W. & F.—it was a practice in which Hitchcock himself had participated—and the only especially curious aspect of the case of *The Lodger* is the identity of the re-editor.

"About 'The Lodger,'" Adrian Brunel wrote from the Hotel Splendide, Juan-les-Pins, to Ivor Montagu, at 6 Dansey Yard, on 30 July.[59] "I was very pleased you cabled me & I appreciate it. Funny, though, that when Gainsborough used to be in difficulties they came to that highbrow Brunel & now that they can't get me they fly to that highbrow Montagu!" Brunel had been on the Riviera about a week. Montagu had cabled on the 28th to ask, "CAN I ACCEPT INVITATION LODGER WITHOUT PREJUDICING YOUR QUARREL,"[60] while Brunel was "away in Nice seeing the studios." Rex Ingram had been absent on that day, "but I went all the same & am going to see him next week," Brunel wrote. He could not quite suppress his objection to "our helping other British films. There are other intelligent people in British film production besides our little gesellschaft—such as Hitch and Edwin—but obviously you and I can do so much more than Hitch, clever as he is, to the literary side of films."

After recounting his quarrel with Gainsborough, Brunel concluded, not entirely convincingly, that he was "glad for you to do the film. It's practice, it's money, it's reputation & it will show them that highbrows are not devoid of balance and perspective." Montagu recalled how the job had come his way in his autobiography: "One day that summer Adrian relayed to me from Mick an urgent invitation to lunch. I went at once. The lunch was in the Monico off Piccadilly Circus, and I even remember ordering (and enjoying) mashed potatoes and fried onions."[61] In a subsequent telling of the same story, Brunel was present, and devised the following syllogism: if *The Lodger* "was supposed to be highbrow, the most scarlet epithet in the film trade vocabulary," and if Montagu too was a highbrow,

The Shaftesbury Avenue entrance to Monico's, with Piccadilly Circus in the background. SOURCE: Historic England Archive.

then why not have Montagu re-edit *The Lodger*, "on the obvious analogy of setting a thief to catch a thief."[62] With the exception of the venue and possibly the meal, little of this rings true.

Gainsborough had indeed gone to "that highbrow Brunel" in the past, and not only with Cutts's films. In November 1925, when Hitchcock was abroad making *The Mountain Eagle*, Balcon was in communication with Brunel about what Brunel referred to as "the Hitchcock comedy," presumably *Number Thirteen*, shot three years earlier, which he had collected from J. G. and R. B. Wainwright, an import-export firm.[63]

> I have talked this over with Hitch himself and we agree that it will not be a cheap proposition, as so much new stuff will have to be shot. As it stands now it is about 3,400ft, much of which must come out.
>
> I have several ideas for expanding it, but I would ask you to see the picture first if you can possibly manage it.
>
> Please do not think that it is through lack of interest that I have not brought the matter up before. I have not pressed the question as I knew that it would entail more money than you anticipated to put the film right. But now with the Quota coming into force, the whole situation is different.

The last line may have been a joke: the quota had only just been proposed. By late 1925, Brunel's film surgery had begun to be used for the preparation—recutting and retitling—of imported prints for the Film Society, bringing Montagu into the operation alongside Brunel's assistants J. O. C. "Jock" Orton and Lionel "Tod" Rich. Its home Dansey Yard, as Montagu wrote in his autobiography, was "a cobbled alley running east-west between Shaftesbury Avenue and Gerrard Street," parallel with both, and No. 6 had "outside its front door a green *pissoir*."[64] On the first floor was a tiny office and a "claustrophobic projection theatre seating some four or five. The floor above had tiny cutting rooms."

There Montagu had learned to cut, and in little time he too became a film surgeon. The denizens of Dansey Yard did not receive screen credit, but in March 1926 Mycroft told his readers that Montagu was responsible for the "bright and pointed sub-titles" given to *The Waltz Dream*, a German production that had opened at the Capitol that month.[65] Even before then, Montagu had been in communication with Balcon. After the trade show of *The Sea Urchin*, in February, Balcon had written to thank

Dansey Yard. SOURCE: London Picture Archive.

Montagu, whom he addressed as "Observer," for his suggested revisions, received via Brunel, whom he called "Burlesque," saying that "we shall alter the titles before release."[66] On the film's opening a few weeks later, Montagu wrote in his *Observer* review (albeit unsigned) that Cutts "has little or no originality," but this did not prohibit a second and more significant brush with Gainsborough two months later.[67] In the last days of April 1926, Montagu received a letter saying the following:

> All proceeds as you wished. Hitchcock would not have anything to do with your letter, saying he was too busy. Instead he sent me off to Miss Reville, who has promised to carry out all your alterations faithfully. I saw her, you understand, at the studio yesterday afternoon, and explained the details very carefully to her. She had received your telegram.[68]

The writer was Angus MacPhail, a friend of Montagu's from Westminster School, where they had briefly been contemporary with Patrick Hamilton, the author of *Rope*—first performed in 1929, his play provides an insight into the latter-day aestheticism characteristic of their milieu. Montagu had gone down from Cambridge in 1924, MacPhail the year after; there they had been contemporary with Cedric Belfrage. There is no way of knowing what the letter referred to, but one possibility is *The Pleasure Garden*. Montagu had reviewed the film in the 18 April issue of the *Observer*, writing that Hitchcock "has made some of it so interesting as to make one eager and optimistic for his future."[69] In his reminiscences Montagu said that he had not met Hitchcock at the time of the Monico lunch, but the review reveals that he knew something of his biography before then: "Detail with which he is familiar is amazingly well done, the very dust of the London rooms seems significant and real." Montagu identified a handful of flaws, however, including the "sometimes sentimentally shocking" titles. "Throughout they are depicted on ugly and distracting pieces of scenery known technically—not even the lexicon can say why—as 'art' backgrounds."

The Pleasure Garden had ended its run at the Capitol by 27 April, the day of MacPhail's letter; possibly Montagu had been asked to make suggestions for revision before its general release. Whatever the case, Montagu was not the wildcard pick for *The Lodger* that he made himself out to be. Nevertheless, it was not wrong of Brunel to observe that ordinarily he would have been offered the job. His quarrel with Gainsborough, however, directly involved Hitchcock. In October 1925 Brunel had been named in the trade press as a future Gainsborough director. When nothing came of it, Brunel began to complain to Cutts, in March 1926, then to Balcon, in April, that while he was sitting on his hands "Hitch is talking about stars for his fourth picture."[70] Gainsborough's corporate response, in May, was that "this Company's plans were very materially altered in view of certain events which took place early in the year in connection with America" and which led to "very serious losses," probably a reference to the loss of the Harold Lloyd contract.[71] Gainsborough did not respond to Brunel's angry reply.

By July 1926 Montagu was "Observer" no more; he had resigned from the paper over its editing of his review of *The Big Parade*. There was still some doubt, in the correspondence between Montagu and Brunel at the end of that month, whether Montagu would go ahead with *The Lodger*. On 6 August, however, Balcon wrote to Montagu at Dansey Yard, in response to a letter of the day before, saying that "I am very relieved to hear there is a possibility of your covering up the particular eccentricity, which was rather troubling me. I am also very glad to have your comment on the general possibilities of the production when re-edited."[72] Three days later, Mycroft used his *Evening Standard* column to report, under the headline "Peer's Son For The Films," that Montagu "has now definitely identified himself with a sphere of activity which in this country is urgently in need of such fresh blood," and was "at present engaged upon a new British film, of which much is expected."[73]

The two main accounts that Montagu himself gave of his role in finishing *The Lodger* are consistent, and fairly modest: he "cut down the titles as far as possible,"[74] leaving "just an ordinary matter of re-shooting scenes where it seemed the intended effect had not quite come off."[75] Montagu was at once prone to a rhetorical underplaying of his intervention in what he called "a critical film in Hitch's career, maybe in British film history,"[76] and to exaggerating aspects of that intervention, such as his claim that "the titles were got down to eighty instead of the usual from three hundred and fifty to five or six hundred."[77] In neither account, however, did he claim to have recut the film itself in any important sense.

Moreover, Montagu could not have brought to bear upon it "the Eisensteinian influence," as would become part of the myth, since he had neither seen *Battleship Potemkin* nor met Eisenstein at the time. Montagu did not meet Eisenstein until 1929,[78] and while his accounts of his role on *The Lodger* mention other films that inspired him, he makes no mention of *Potemkin*; nor is there any other evidence of his having been in Berlin or having seen *Potemkin* in April or May 1926. There were press reports of *Potemkin*'s success in Berlin, but none described its cutting. There was nothing Soviet about *The Lodger*'s montage. It came out of all that Hitchcock had learned of cinema as a viewer and as a filmmaker—Brunel said that he "had grown up with films & had the cinematic sense to a rare degree"—though it was not unique to him.[79] Some conception of montage—"the art of switching," as Alma Reville had called it—was part of the ambience of the "Pack." Brunel once wrote of Jock Orton's apprenticeship at Dansey Yard that he "soon became the most dextrous manipulator of the smallest sections of film, so that when we encountered 'Russian cutting' it was already *vieux jeu*."[80]

The reshoots were announced in the issue of *Bioscope* dated 12 August, a few days after Montagu's involvement became public. The delay in completing the film was attributed with some plausibility to June's illness, "but the picture will be definitely completed in a few days' time."[81] June had fallen ill not long after her ordeal on set. On 17 June the *Evening News* reported that she was in a Wellbeck Street nursing home, recovering from a "second internal operation," following her appendectomy in January, and that "it may be four months before she is quite her normal self again."[82] On 7 July Hannen Swaffer wrote in the *Daily Express* that "June, who leaves her nursing home next week to go, first to Devonshire, and then to the South of France, will be back in October."[83] Two weeks later the *Daily Sketch* carried a photograph of her recuperating with Babe Barnato and others at Lulworth Cove, in Dorset.[84]

June's costar was also unavailable in June and July. Novello's new play *Down Hill*, written, like *The Rat*, with Constance Collier, opened at the Queen's Theatre on 16 June, and transferred to the Princes Theatre on 26 July, throughout which time Novello was also busy at Poole Street on *The Triumph of the Rat*, the sequel that had been rushed into production, under Cutts's direction, soon after the general strike. The final scenes were shot at Dieppe on the morning of Monday 9 August, whereupon Novello "crossed by aeroplane in time to appear at the matinée of 'Down Hill.'"[85] *Kinematograph Weekly*'s report of this exciting episode appeared on the same day as *Bioscope*'s report of the *Lodger* reshoots. Brunel told Harry Wilson that Hitchcock "was forced to alter the end,"[86] but Montagu wrote merely that the retakes were "principally fresh long-shots of the lynching chase."[87] They were not on the scale of *The Big Parade*.

Montagu did not cut the number of titles to 80, nor is it likely that he began with upwards of 350—a large number for any film, let alone one that was intended to have none. There are two sets of typed titles for *The Lodger* among Montagu's papers in the BFI's archives, one largely corresponding to the finished film and crediting Montagu, the other crediting Charles Lapworth as production editor.[88] Neither is dated; however, the earlier "Lapworth version," which names Carlyle Blackwell as producer, probably dates from May or early June 1926. The two title lists are quite different in tone, but the difference in number is small: Lapworth's version has 119 numbered titles after a set of unnumbered credits, whereas Montagu's has 107, including 6 given over to credits. The surviving print has 99, including credits. The Lapworth version is often facetious; one title, presumably referring to the murderer, reads "One Gentleman Who Preferred Blondes," a reference to Anita Loos's recently published novel. The line went, along with other bits of wordplay, some exposition—and Hitchcock's middle initial, J., which he had used for *The Pleasure Garden*, from his director credit.

The day after he announced Montagu's involvement in *The Lodger*, on 10 August, Mycroft hinted at a further development. "Mr. McKnight Kauffer, the distinguished British artist, is another recruit to the films. He is assisting in the editing of a new British film, his part being to devise the 'art titles,' that is to say, the design of the letterpress."[89] The Montana-born Kauffer had been an art student in Chicago at the time of the epochal "Armory Show" of modernist art at the Art Institute, and came to Europe in the same year, 1913. By his own account he "arrived in London as a painter" but eventually "saw the futility of trying to paint and do advertising at the same time. I wished also to keep my integrity as a painter free from depending on social hypocrisy and the necessity to paint pictures that would sell."[90] Having quit painting, however, he continued to be championed by the Bloomsbury art critic Roger Fry.

When Kauffer's posters were exhibited in a Bloomsbury gallery in May 1925, Fry wrote in the *Nation and Athenaeum* that with the decline of patronage, "art, in our modern life, has been forced, with that adaptability which is the special gift of parasitic life, to seek new hosts" in the mass market.[91] Though this was not always a happy arrangement, Kauffer had managed to bring modernist abstraction into advertising, and his posters had the advantage of being unencumbered by "the solemn traditional humbug that surrounds the painted picture." It was in the same month that Fry was named as a supporter in the very first announcement of the Film Society; Kauffer, who would join its organizing council, designed its logo. His work on *The Lodger*, including some animated titles in the appropriately Germanic Neuland typeface, and some illustrated titles that recall Paul Leni's designs for *Waxworks*, are as important a contribution to Hitchcock's film as Saul Bass's title sequences thirty years later.

Kauffer was not the only Bloomsbury figure to assist in the finishing of *The Lodger*. Another document among Montagu's papers strongly suggests that Francis Meynell was consulted to review Montagu's revisions. Meynell, scion of an illustrious intellectual family, had been associated with Lapworth in the *Daily Herald*, and had used one of Kauffer's woodcuts to advertise its relaunch after the war. Since 1922 he, his wife Vera, and David Garnett had run a small publisher, the Nonesuch Press, and its office, also the Meynells' home, at 16 Great James Street, not far from Iris Barry in Guilford Street and Montagu in Lincoln's Inn, housed Kauffer's studio. The handwritten document, included with Angus MacPhail's letters to Montagu, is headed "Ivor" and begins "Meynell was helpful," before relaying a handful of suggestions—a couple of reworded titles, one shot worthy of deletion, and the view that the synopsis was wrong to refer to Bloomsbury: "It must be altered to Westminster—or Pimlico."[92] This was accurate, but curiously not taken up; nor does it seem that the others were.

For his part, MacPhail wrote: "I was impressed by the picture. I take off my hat to Hitchcock. If I wore an ostrich feather in it, like Chase"— Chaz Chase, an American vaudevillian they admired—"I would take that off too." MacPhail also wrote that "I'm profoundly dissatisfied with the titles—and you can't have Daisy five times," with "can't" underlined four times and the pencil amendment "as the g.s.t.t.s." (girl said to the soldier). Montagu, in retrospect, was proud of this repetition, which he said was inspired by a similar title in Chaplin's *The Gold Rush* (one of Hitchcock's "Ten"), but in the finished version the "Daisy" title appears a mere three times. MacPhail ended by writing that he had "booked the stage box for the last house. Kauffer's coming with us. Rely on you too." Chaz Chase had been on the bill at the Alhambra, Leicester Square, since Monday 9 August; he was joined there on the 16th by the Houston Sisters,

Renée and Billie, a Scottish music-hall act MacPhail and Montagu followed obsessively. Whether MacPhail could rely on Montagu to be there is unclear. Montagu was in Berlin on and very probably before Tuesday 17 August, and remained there for some weeks.

The trade show of *The Lodger* was announced, along with the rest of the W. & F. slate for the coming season, in a lavish advertisement in the 19 August issue of *Kinematograph Weekly*, quite probably before the edit had been locked. On 1 September, Balcon wrote to Montagu at the Hotel Eden in Berlin, thanking him for a letter of three days earlier and his comments on *The Lodger*. "It is a great relief to hear that certain problems have been solved, and I am now looking forward to seeing the finished copy of the picture when I can let you know my definite opinion of the alterations."[93] It is unlikely that Montagu had seen the finished copy himself. The next day, 2 September, MacPhail wrote to him:

> I was speaking to Miss Reville this morning. She says that Hitchcock is beginning to think that he is not quite sure whether he approves of all the titles. She doesn't know whether he seriously contemplates any alterations, but she gathers that he intends to get in touch with you before he does anything. She's going to let me know at once, if Hitchcock arrives at any definite decision. If it seems prejudicial to your interests I will wire you, of course.[94]

Nothing more of the correspondence is known to have survived. As in the possible earlier case of *The Pleasure Garden*, MacPhail was at the very least an emissary for Montagu, and perhaps more than that, as *The Lodger* assumed its final form. In his autobiography Montagu introduced his friend as "a red-haired and rather gauche Scot," an intellectual "but totally blank as regards any form of politics or science."[95] Like Montagu, MacPhail would collaborate with Hitchcock again in the mid-1930s; unlike Montagu, he would continue to work with Hitchcock long after Hitchcock's move to Hollywood. Hitchcock mentioned him in the Truffaut interview; he did not mention Montagu, and in his interview with Bogdanovich, Hitchcock credited MacPhail with the invention of the MacGuffin.[96]

6 The First True Hitchcock

The Scala Theatre in Smallbrook Street, Birmingham, opened during the prewar cinema construction boom, on 3 March 1914. It was large for the time, seating 850, and luxurious, done out in marble and mahogany, its doorways "draped with costly rose-coloured curtains," as a local paper reported.[1] "A feature is made of the vari-coloured hidden lights over the main cornice, which illuminate the ceiling with all the colours of the rainbow." The opening ceremony was presided over by a local worthy, who spoke of the cinema's possibilities "as an instrument of education," but the first films to be shown there came from Selig, Essanay, and Edison. Jack Graham-Cutts was the Scala's manager from the start, appointed by Sol Levy, the local film distributor who had built it. Levy had traveled the world as a salesman, initially for his father's footwear business, and had been convinced of the cinema's potential while abroad. Later in the 1910s he was responsible for the provincial distribution of D. W. Griffith's epics, and by the early 1920s he had a nationwide chain of more than a dozen cinemas.

The Lodger's London trade show, at the Hippodrome, took place at 3 p.m. on Tuesday 14 September 1926, but its first screening had come four hours earlier in Birmingham. The Scala was an apt venue: apart from Graham Cutts, Michael Balcon had worked for Sol Levy, as had Victor Saville and Herbert Wilcox. The film's first reviews appeared in the next morning's papers, along with news of the belated ratification of the Locarno treaties at Geneva, Germany having joined the League of Nations a week earlier. Iris Barry, in the *Daily Mail*, seized upon the film's first reel: "Mr. Alfred Hitchcock, the talented young director," she wrote, "opens it with a terrified screaming woman's head, and swiftly follows with brilliant impressions of newspaper offices, the B.B.C., and paper-boys all bruiting abroad the news of a murder."[2]

Barry had called him "the clever young director" when he was scouting locations for the same sequence, less than seven months earlier. It was a sequence that Hitchcock himself would describe many times, perhaps more often, and in more detail, though not always with more accuracy, than any other in his oeuvre. In the lecture he gave to Columbia's extension students in March 1939, at Barry's invitation, Hitchcock, immediately after expounding his idea of "subjective suspense," moved on to discuss "springboard situations, where suspense starts practically in the first reel," using *The Lodger* as his example.[3] After the screaming woman's head is seen, and the eye-witness on the Embankment has given her statement to a policeman, and to a reporter, he said,

> I took the trouble to spread a description of this man all over London. I did it by every known means of disseminating news. The fact that he only went for fair-haired girls was broadcast, or that he wore a black cloak or carried a bag. I spent a whole reel on stuff like that.

For Truffaut he proudly described it—and in one instance drew it—virtually shot by shot, in one of the most rhapsodic passages in the book. The principle, Hitchcock explained, was that with each rapid transition, as the news spreads across London, "we give additional information."[4] The crucial question is by whom the information is received. The springboard situation, he said in 1939, "really comes under the heading of what I would call letting the audience into the secret as early as possible." Part of Hitchcock's mastery of suspense lay in his ability to orchestrate different levels of knowledge between the audience and the characters on screen—and to do this primarily through the eye. The first reel of *The Lodger* puts the audience one step ahead of the principal characters in the story: we know the identity of the killer before they do, and for much of the rest of the film they are having to catch up.

And yet the first reel is not only a springboard for suspense. Hitchcock took pride in it also as a kind of city symphony *avant la lettre*, preceding the genre's founding films. *Rien que les heures*, directed by Alberto Cavalcanti, debuted in Paris a month after *The Lodger*'s trade show. Walter Ruttmann's *Berlin*, the best-known example, was still being shot at the time. There are possible antecedents in montage sequences—also *avant la lettre*—from French and German films which Hitchcock may, in theory, have seen, for instance Abel Gance's *La roue* and Murnau's *Phantom*, both completed in 1922, but none that amount to a template. It was after *Berlin* was shown in London, in the spring of 1928, that Hitchcock expressed his wish to make such a film. "Between completing his present picture 'Champagne,' and beginning the next," reported Barry,

> Mr. Hitchcock hopes to secure many of the scenes of everyday London life. In the manner of the film "Berlin," recently shown at the Capitol, Haymarket, S.W., he hopes to blend them into a symphony of pictures which will introduce Billingsgate, perhaps the perambulator parade in Kensington Gardens, the changing of the Guard, the stream of debutantes on their way to the Palace and other fascinating glimpses of London life.[5]

Years later Hitchcock told Peter Bogdanovich that the "story of a big city from dawn to the following dawn" was "something I've wanted to do since 1928."[6] His failure to achieve it, he said, stemmed from his need for it to "be done in terms of personalities and people, and with my technique, everything would have to be used dramatically." The first reel of *The Lodger* achieves precisely the fusion of city film and story that he said eluded him later.

That it begins with a screaming woman's head—Maudie Dunham's—may be an instance of Hitchcock's rejection of Ivor Montagu's alterations. The top of the first page of Montagu's title list is marked in pencil: "Golden curls open. face follow" and "Rearrange 1st 2 shots."[7] In the finished film, the illuminated "To-Night 'Golden Curls'" sign, advertising a stage show, follows the face. The third shot shows the victim's body laid out on the Embankment with Big Ben in the background; in the fourth, the witness provides the crucial piece of evidence to the policeman and the reporter by miming a face half-concealed by a scarf.

A few brief shots later, when the crowd is dispersed and the witness is at a coffee-stall, her miming is reinforced by the film's first dialogue title: "Tall he was—and his face all wrapped up." Curiously, this is the one piece of information about the killer not to be included in Hitchcock's detailed retellings, whereas the bag and cloak are not mentioned in the film. The wrapped-up face—as the promoters of *Who Is He?* had known—was the most visually striking clue, and the one that Hitchcock used. Instantly, a joker in the queue mimics the witness, wrapping his collar around his face. With the arguable exception of the very first shot of the screaming woman's head, the witness's sight of the joker's distorted reflection is the film's first definite point-of-view shot, and, significantly, the character from whose point of view it is taken misrecognizes the joker for the real killer. Simultaneously, the witness's statement is relayed over the phone by the reporter to a wire service, along with the information that this is the "seventh golden haired victim" of the self-styled "Avenger."

The wire, shown being typed out, is received by, among others, a newspaper editor—Hitchcock himself, in his first cameo—and there follow the shots taken in the *Evening Standard* building near Fleet Street, capped by the first of E. McKnight Kauffer's animated titles (other than in the opening credits): "Murder: Wet from the Press." At least one of the shots of the *Standard*'s vans—as drawn by Hitchcock for Truffaut—distributing the papers to newsboys across London was taken in Shaftesbury Avenue. It is one of the newsboys who introduces a new detail: the Avenger strikes on Tuesdays, and from here the news spreads among the public. Hitchcock cuts from a group of newspaper readers to a crowd of bystanders reading the news on an illuminated "scroller," and then—after another Kauffer animation, "Murder: Hot over the Aerial"—from a BBC newsreader to his listeners, one of them almost certainly Alma Reville.

The next shot reintroduces the "To-Night 'Golden Curls'" sign, now in context. The first victim is not identified as having anything to do with "Golden Curls," and though the sign is reflected in water, it is not definite that it is near the Embankment, which was and is without places of entertainment, as its Victorian planners ordained. In this way the sign's first appearance, in the film's second shot, has a slightly abstract relationship with the rest of the sequence, functioning more as an ironic comment than it does to establish place. When repeated, however, it is to introduce a scene in the theater's dressing room, where a group of chorus girls learn of the murder from the *Evening News*, two in particular, one blonde and one brunette. Unnamed and uncredited, they are the first characters who will reappear later in the film. The blonde, like the witness, is momentarily tricked by a joker covering her face in mimicry of the killer—a second point-of-view shot, a second misrecognition—meaning that this crucial detail has gone into the paper.

Hitchcock shows another all-female dressing room in another part of town a few shots later, but the central figure in this next scene is—by contrast with the chorus girls—properly introduced. Daisy's first appearance is preceded by an animated Kauffer title announcing her name, the first of the five that Montagu wanted to use. It may be, however, that Hitchcock did not intend to give her any more prominence than the girls in the earlier scene. The "Daisy" title does not appear in the earlier version of the title list, and though her introduction is more elaborate than that of the chorus girls, the two scenes take similar amounts of time. Daisy is first seen in furs and jewelry, and it is only subsequently, when she is shown from another angle, that we learn that she works as a mannequin and is not a society lady, as she first appears to be—another misrecognition, this time on the part of the audience. Unlike the chorus girls, Daisy does not read news of the murder, but hears it being bruited abroad by a newsboy outside the salon where she works; she then passes it on to her friends backstage.

After the salon scene, there is a cut to another newsboy, who sells an avid reader a copy, practically on his own doorstep. It is only now, ten minutes into the film, that the major characters begin to be assembled. As in *Psycho*, which begins with a series of pans across the Phoenix, Arizona, skyline, before homing in on one window out of thousands, there is a sensation of randomness in the selection of this particular house, so many alternatives having been introduced in the preceding sequence. Mr. Bunting enters the house through the kitchen, below street level, and finds his wife baking and his prospective son-in-law, Joe, smoking. Having scanned the paper before entering, Mr. Bunting shows them—and the audience, in close-up—the "stop press" item on the murder, which says that it took place on the Embankment, that it was committed by the Avenger, that it was the seventh of his crimes to be committed on a Tuesday, and that the victim was once again a fair-haired woman—but not that the killer was wearing a scarf around his face. Unlike the chorus girls, Mr. Bunting has a copy of the *Evening Standard*, not the *Evening News*. It is hardly likely that any audience would register this detail on first viewing, but it is of some importance to the plot.

The essentials of the Buntings' relationships with one another and with Joe are established in the course of the next two minutes. Mr. Bunting's first line of dialogue discloses that Joe is a police detective. Next, Daisy arrives home, introduced again by Kauffer's animated title, followed by a title announcing her as the "daughter of the house." Joe is seen to get on with Daisy's parents, but his relationship with her is evidently lacking in something. While she reads the paper, he makes heart shapes from the pastry Mrs. Bunting has rolled, a gesture Daisy visibly finds mawkish. Whereas Mr. and Mrs. Bunting are oblivious to the problem, and see a successful, respectable couple in the making, the audience perceives that Joe is well-meaning but clumsy. Daisy could be said to have willed the arrival of danger on the doorstep—soon to arrive—in compensation. In the same vein, however, the scene also establishes a kinship between Joe, the detective, and his prey-to-be, the Avenger. They both prefer blondes, as Joe says, and the implication cuts deeper, establishing a parallel between erotic desire and the desire to kill, the power of which will motivate much of the action to come.

"By the end of the reel you were shown a house where the gas went out," Hitchcock told his class at Columbia, "and just as the man was putting a shilling into the meter, there was a knock at the door." In fact, we see the door being knocked—there is a cut from the darkened kitchen to the point of view of a visitor unknown, as he or she ascends the steps to the Buntings' front door and knocks on it—one of a small number of moving shots in the film. "The housewife opened the door," Hitchcock continued, "and just then the gas came up with a full flood of light on this figure. Now that is what I call the springboard situation. You then knew that Jack the Ripper was in a London boarding house." You, the audience, may have known—but not Mrs. Bunting. The audience knows because the figure in the doorway has his face wrapped in a scarf, but nothing in the film suggests that the Buntings or Joe are aware of this detail of the killer's appearance, included in the film's fourth shot and repeated numerous times thereafter, but left out of the only newspaper report that they have seen. If Mrs. Bunting is perturbed, it is because of the Lodger's appearance, not because she thinks he might be the Avenger.

The foregoing, taking about thirteen minutes from screaming head to the Lodger's entrance, did not occupy a discrete reel of film, but conforms to the looser meaning of "reel," more or less interchangeable with "act," that was employed by Hitchcock. *The Lodger* as shown at the Birmingham Scala and London Hippodrome was composed of six reels, but can most conveniently be broken down into five "reels."

The second such reel, taking about seventeen minutes of screen time, takes place entirely within the Buntings' home, as the Lodger settles in. The pace changes on his arrival—he himself moves slowly and deliberately, in sharp contrast with the other characters, taking a minute to cross the threshold and remove his hat and scarf, while Mr. Bunting's pratfalls consume Daisy's attention. The Lodger's rooms on the first floor are first seen in gloom, lit by flashes of car headlights coming through the windows. This lighting effect, possibly borrowed from Karl Grune's *The Street*, has the effect of suggesting a porousness between the house and the city it stands in: it is not the sanctuary that the Lodger seems to be seeking, as his behavior later in this scene demonstrates.

First, however, once the lights are on, he looks around the walls and sees looking back at him the portraits of various ladies. This is done as a moving shot from the Lodger's point of view, intercut with four reverse-angle close-ups, three showing the Lodger's at first fairly neutral reaction— Hitchcock's "purest expression of cinematic idea"—and one Mrs. Bunting's house-proud response to what she interprets as his admiration. This emphatic reverse-angle sequence is capped by an intricate composition that takes in both what the Lodger can see (the point-of-view shot) and his reaction to it (the reverse angle). On the left-hand side of the frame it shows the Lodger, looking slightly off camera, and, on the right-hand side, in a mirror behind him, a reflection of the painting he is looking at—it was the second he saw, of five, but now it disturbs him. As the Lodger walks toward the painting, and so toward the camera, spellbound, his back is reflected in the mirror, doubling or splitting his image, and by the end of

The mirror shot in *The Lodger.*

the shot he is enclosed in three frames—that of the shot, that of the mirror, and that of the painting. The sequence suggests obsession—an inability to see beyond a frame created in his own mind, a crisis in the faculty of sight.

Before his reaction can be explained, the Lodger goes in horror to close the window, prompted by a newsboy's cries outside, providing an image of the cross formed on his face by the shadow of the window frame—used to promote the film at the time and since. Mrs. Bunting seems oblivious to his distress in this scene. The audience may not exactly identify with him, but by sharing his secret, and by seeing the portraits with him, and seeing his grimaces as she does not, we are closer to sharing his perspective than hers. After Mrs. Bunting's exit, the Lodger having paid her a month's rent in advance, the audience's complicity is heightened as we see him lock away his bag in a chiffonier, though the bag's contents are kept out of sight and are to be guessed at.

There is a cut to the rest of the family downstairs, where Joe and Mr. Bunting celebrate the Lodger's contribution to the family finances while Daisy and Mrs. Bunting prepare him a snack. When Mrs. Bunting brings it to his room—scarcely a minute of screen time after departing—he is busy turning the paintings to face the wall. The camera scans the room from her point of view, in a brief echo of the earlier shot from his, and does so again, yet more briefly, when Daisy enters to help take the paintings down, at Mrs. Bunting's request. The Lodger's response to the portraits—eight etchings of "early Victorian belles"—is in the novel as one quirk among many, but in the film it carries more weight. The picture imbued with mysterious power belongs to a tradition in gothic, romantic, and decadent fiction that includes Poe's *The Oval Portrait* and Wilde's *The Picture of Dorian Gray*, and that would live on in *Rebecca* and *Vertigo*.

This scene of the paintings being removed occasions the Lodger's first encounter with Daisy, more specifically his first look at her. When she enters, his gaze follows her around the room just as it did the paintings—something she registers but does not fully reciprocate. So sustained and blatant is this look that it continues after another brief cut to downstairs, where Joe and Mr. Bunting are discussing the Avenger case—Mr. Bunting, as in the novel, being one among "the vast world of men and women who take an intelligent interest in such sinister mysteries," making him the archetype of a number of Hitchcock's characters. The second half of the Lodger's look is returned, equally blatantly, as Daisy leaves the room, with not a word being exchanged. He rejects the gaze of the portraits, but not hers. Daisy is not seen from his optical point of view in this scene, however, nor in close-up: their encounter is shown in a master shot taking in the whole room, intercut with reaction shots of the Lodger in close-up as he looks at her.

Having removed the paintings, the family reconvenes in the living room to discuss their new tenant's foibles. Neither Mrs. Bunting, who has shown forbearance, nor Joe, who has not met him, regard the Lodger as a threat, but when Joe declares himself "glad he's not keen on the girls," Hitchcock gives Daisy a close-up that tells another story. The audience has its interpretation of the Lodger's look, and Daisy has hers—once again, desire and homicidal intent may easily be mistaken for one another, and the Lodger could be Jekyll and Hyde.

138 T H E   F I R S T   T R U E   H I T C H C O C K

In the novel, Daisy is Mr. Bunting's child by his first wife, and Joe is the grandson of a former senior servant under whom Mr. Bunting worked long ago. Daisy lives with the Buntings for only part of the time, and the romance between Daisy and Joe blossoms over the course of the story, which ends with their engagement. She meets the Lodger—named Mr. Sleuth—only late in the tale, and there is no attraction on either side, only danger. Joe never suspects him. In the play, the young detective, named Tom, is Mr. Bunting's son from a previous marriage, and the Lodger (calling himself Mr. Parker, revealed to be Lord Twyford) takes a fancy not to any member of the Bunting family—there is no equivalent of Daisy—but to Irene, another of the Buntings' lodgers, who scrapes a living as a writer rather than as a mannequin.[8] Irene and Tom have almost nothing to do with one another, and because the play is a farce, her romance with Mr. Parker never takes on an aspect of danger—nor of real romance. The deadly love triangle that develops between the Lodger, Joe, and Daisy during this second act of Hitchcock's film was Stannard and Hitchcock's invention.

Among numerous triangle plots in Hitchcock's later films, the one that most invites comparison is the memorable scene in *The 39 Steps* in which Richard Hannay, on the run in the Highlands, is sheltered by a crofter and his young wife, played by Peggy Ashcroft. The crofter correctly comes to suspect Hannay of trying to seduce his wife, but is thereby blinded to what she perceives, and is able to overlook—that Hannay meets the published description of a murderer.

The first day's action ends with the transparent ceiling shot, as Daisy, Joe, and Mrs. Bunting listen to the Lodger pacing about upstairs, and see the chandelier shaking, concerned—but not suspecting that he might be a killer. The next day begins with Daisy taking the Lodger his breakfast. This is not a successful scene. The pair of them flirt, but then the Lodger makes stabbing motions with a butter knife that are hard to interpret; oafish rather than threatening, and certainly not seductive, this is horseplay of the kind Joe indulges in. Daisy's reaction is equally inscrutable. The scene ends, however, with an unmistakably flirtatious gesture: Daisy, as she exits, turns to look back at the Lodger, and briefly grips the doorframe. The breakfast scene functions largely to lay the ground for the next, more advanced stage of seduction, which takes place "one evening, a few days later," as one of Kauffer's illustrated titles announces.

In this next scene, Daisy, dressed up, and the Lodger, in a smoking jacket, play chess in front of an open fire—an opportunity for them to look into one another's eyes across a small table. When Daisy drops a piece and bends to pick it up, the Lodger takes hold of a poker, in a bit of fast cutting that might just about be seen as the germ of the murder sequences in *Sabotage* and *Psycho*, quickly curtailed with a cut to the kitchen, where Joe has just arrived. Pokers serve as murder weapons in *Murder* and *Stage Fright*, but the next shot in the Lodger's room shows him using it for its proper purpose—the first of a handful of feints. At one point, the Lodger catches Daisy looking lovingly at his hair, then looks lovingly at hers, before their eyes meet. "Beautiful golden hair," he says (in a dialogue title), almost stroking it.

A twentieth-century descendent of "the Fatal Men of the Romantics" anatomized by Mario Praz in his 1930 book *The Romantic Agony*, the Lodger has many of their attributes: "mysterious (but conjectured to be exalted) origin, traces of burnt-out passions, suspicion of a ghastly guilt, melancholy habits, pale face, unforgettable eyes."[9] Much as Julian Maclaren-Ross said, it was the irruption of a Fatal Man into "the world of kippers and aspidistras," the fussy decor, meticulously recreated at Poole Street, of the Buntings' lower-middle-class home, that was Hitchcock's contribution to the tradition. Novello's performance oscillates, rather jarringly, between two poles within the Fatal Man's constellation of traits— the lordly, Byronic seducer, as in this scene, and the neurotic, aesthetic type in others. In this he is the forerunner of many Hitchcock protagonists to come—Maxim de Winter, from *Rebecca*, and Norman Bates, from *Psycho*, combined. The two types face one another in *Rope*, in which the discourse on aestheticism is explicit, and *Strangers on a Train*, with Farley Granger playing the more sensitive, less dominant role in both. In those two films the element of same-sex attraction comes close to being made explicit; in *The Lodger* it can only be hinted at, as in Joe's remark about the Lodger not being "keen on the girls."

Joe, as he now tells Mr. Bunting, has been put on the Avenger case, and the next part of the sequence includes what Charles Barr has identified as the film's most resonant line of dialogue. Daisy arrives in the kitchen just as Joe is showing Mr. Bunting the handcuffs he will use on the Avenger. "When I've put a rope round the Avenger's neck," he says, miming the action, "I'll put a ring round Daisy's finger," the equation of marriage with confinement and punishment repelling her. (A wedding ring with equally symbolic power will be central to the plot of *Rear Window*.) Characteristically, Joe is oblivious, and chases Daisy upstairs, actually cuffing her in the front hall, a perfect image of her darkest fears about matrimony. It is now that the Lodger sees Joe for the first time. Brought out of his room by Daisy's cries, he witnesses the scene from the landing, shown as a shot of the couple from the Lodger's point of view intercut with three reverse-angle close-ups of him staring down, suggesting his intense jealousy, and ill intent toward Joe rather than Daisy.

Daisy forgives Joe, but dashes upstairs immediately afterward, leaving Joe behind with Mrs. Bunting in the living room. There is a brief repetition of the ceiling shot, now opaque, from her point of view, before Joe asks whether the Lodger means Daisy "harm." Mrs. Bunting laughingly assures him that the Lodger is "not that sort." "Even if he is a bit queer, he's a gentleman." The word *harm* does not appear in the earlier version of the title list, in which Joe asks, "Is that lodger of yours sweet on my Daisy?" and its inclusion, which is surely not intended to mean physical violence, obscures the fact that at the end of the film's second act none of the principal characters suspect the Lodger of being the Avenger. Joe, however, does suspect him of having designs on Daisy, despite Mrs. Bunting's innuendo, mistaking one sort of interest for another, as the audience might think. The handcuffs scene, meanwhile, has led the audience to share Daisy's contempt, and even the Lodger's hatred, for Joe. Whether or not we continue to believe the Lodger to be Avenger, our sympathies lie with the potential couple he forms with Daisy, and against the law and stultification, as represented by her family and fiancé.

The third act is the shortest in the film, occupying less than a reel—though its start did coincide with the start of the third reel. Occupying the film's central section, it contains its most celebrated shot. After a Kauffer illustration at its beginning—"Late that night"—it includes not a single title, and so realizes what had been Hitchcock's intention for the whole film. This was not Montagu's doing; there were none in the earlier version of the title list. In contrast to the rest of the film, this sequence is in plain, untinted black and white. It is the most intricately constructed part of the film, and earns the epithet that Hitchcock prized, "pure cinema." The first act plays out across the breadth of London; the second takes place exclusively in the Buntings' home. The third cuts between the two, while introducing an oneiric quality to the film, putting into question the nature of what the characters within it, as well as the watching audience, can see.

The reappearance of the "Golden Curls" sign after the introductory title establishes that the next scene will take place in the theater last seen in the first reel. At the stage door the unnamed brunette chorus girl is driven away in a big, chauffeured car with an older man in a top hat, while her friend—the unnamed blonde—waits to be picked up on foot by her younger and evidently less well-off beau. Invented for the film, these brief scenes at the theater recall *The Pleasure Garden*, whose plot revolves around the love lives of two chorus girls. Brief shots of Big Ben getting toward 11:30 p.m. and a troop of policemen marching in line establish that it is Tuesday night and that the chorus girl is at risk. The next cut shows the audience what it might have anticipated from this setup—the Lodger stalking out of his room and onto the landing, his scarf back around his face, shot from a low angle on the staircase.

However, the shot that follows puts this one half in doubt: Mrs. Bunting, stirring in her bed. Logically, she must have heard the Lodger, but it can be seen that he moves stealthily. Her apparently uncurtained window frame casts a giant shadow on the bedroom wall opposite—the most *Caligari*-like shot in the whole film, appropriately, since it raises the possibility that the Lodger's actions are being imagined. Even if audibly real to her, what is shown might be in her mind's eye. The next few shots alternate between Mrs. Bunting in bed and the Lodger on the landing, both listening for each other, both seeming to look. The pattern continues as the Lodger goes down the stairs, producing the famous shot taken from directly above. "There is much virtue in a staircase," C. A. Lejeune had written in 1923, giving numerous instances of their symbolic use in films, including Ingram's *Scaramouche* and Lang's *Destiny*. "And much danger too."[10] In *The Lodger*—and in *Vertigo* and *Psycho*—the shot evokes peril, relieved only when the Lodger reaches the front door. It is then that Mrs. Bunting lays eyes on him, from the window, as he crosses the street.

The sequence this most resembles is in *Rear Window*, when James Stewart's character, having been deserted by Grace Kelly's, drifts in and

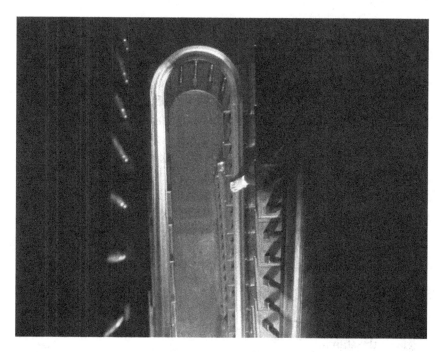

The staircase shot in *The Lodger*.

The staircase shot in *Vertigo*.

out of sleep in his wheelchair one rainy night, while beginning to notice some strange behavior on the part of one of his neighbors, who leaves and returns to his flat on multiple occasions—his third exit unseen except by the audience. Like other sequences in *Rear Window*, there hovers over this one the sense that the goings-on across the courtyard are at once real and projections of the character's inner conflict, and the same is true of its predecessor in *The Lodger*. Both sequences are pivotal also for Hitchcock's orchestration of point of view. In *Rear Window*, the third, missed exit is the first time that the audience departs from the protagonist's point of view. In *The Lodger*, conversely, the sequence marks the first time that Mrs. Bunting assumes the audience's point of view, as she catches up with what the audience already knows. This continues as she steals into the Lodger's room.

First, however, there is a cut back to the chorus girl and her companion walking through central London—actually alongside Westminster Hall, the most ancient part of the Palace of Westminster, though this is not made obvious. They quarrel in front of the statue of Oliver Cromwell, then go their separate ways. In a small courtyard, apparently within the palace precincts, she bends down to remove a stone from her shoe. We see the Avenger's shadow on her back before she notices him coming up behind her, but she turns and screams in horror before he attacks. Her cries bring an assortment of people to the scene, including a policeman and a carload of Bright Young People, but she is already dead. The policeman seems to see but does not pursue someone walking directly away from the camera— a shot Montagu wanted to remove.

Mrs. Bunting's search of the Lodger's room follows. She is shown descending the stairs from as steep an angle as the Lodger was—the sense of peril returns; now it is she who may be discovered. Again passing traffic illuminates the room. The sequence has already used intercutting to generate suspense; now, however, Hitchcock employs the principle of subjective suspense described in his Columbia lecture, showing only one side. Both Mrs. Bunting and the audience can imagine that the Lodger is on his way back without him being shown. All that she discovers, however, is that his chiffonier is locked. The intercutting resumes on his return; as before, Mrs. Bunting, back in the safety of her room, is shown listening as he climbs the stairs. The sequence ends at midnight, with the Lodger on the landing, shot from a high angle, giving a suspicious glance around before going into his room. Once again, what is seen may be half real, half what Mrs. Bunting imagines, but whatever doubts the second act has introduced about his intentions toward Daisy, for the audience, more than for Mrs. Bunting, who is as yet unaware of the new murder, the Lodger is once again prime suspect.

The fourth act begins in the kitchen, with Daisy exiting to take the Lodger's breakfast up. It is only when Mr. Bunting learns from his newspaper that there has been a murder "just round the corner" that Mrs. Bunting shows any concern—indeed she is almost overcome by it. Here the film loses its touch momentarily: if she was worried enough to search the Lodger's room, neither her lack of concern at Daisy seeing him alone, nor her shock at the news, makes sense. Joe arrives after a night on duty to tell of the foulness of the Avenger's new crime, whereupon Daisy's cries and a crash of crockery, shown in flash cuts, summon the three of them upstairs. The audience is prevailed upon to imagine that the Lodger has attacked her; instead, Joe sees what he had feared to see—Daisy in the Lodger's embrace. Their excuse—she was scared by a mouse—is thin from Joe's point of view within the film, and thinner still from the audience's. The scene serves to bring Daisy closer to the Lodger—she again grips the doorframe on her way out—but is otherwise another feint. It ends with a high-angle shot of a reconciled Daisy and Joe embracing downstairs, but with Daisy's look over his shoulder, toward the chandelier, revealing her true feelings.

The scene that follows is the original of many like it in Hitchcock's films: Mrs. Bunting has to persuade her husband to share her suspicions. After he has rebuffed her and returned to his pipe and paper—she is cleaning the fireplace—two shots, referring back to earlier scenes, stiffen her resolve. In the first, taken from her point of view, Mrs. Bunting scans the living room walls, seeing the paintings taken from the Lodger's room, a direct recapitulation of the earlier shots taken there; in the second, again from her point of view, Mrs. Bunting looks up at the chandelier. Mr. Bunting is duly persuaded that the Lodger is a threat to Daisy, and at the end of the scene they both look up at the ceiling in fear, literally sharing a point of view. Mrs. Bunting is the central character in the novel, which is largely told from her perspective; Hitchcock and Stannard's most notable omission in adapting it is her reluctance to suspect the Lodger, and even her willingness to cover for him, motivated by a well-founded fear of poverty and loss of status. Both ex-servants, the Buntings of the novel live "near that deep pit which divides the secure from the insecure."

The Lodger has been seen in a brief cutaway leaving the house in his top hat; the next scene begins with him looking directly into the camera, seated on what might almost be a throne. Subsequent shots reveal that he is at Daisy's salon, last introduced in a similarly misleading fashion in the first reel; then the scene began with Daisy being looked at, now it begins with the Lodger looking. Surrounded by society ladies, who regard him with unconcealed desire, his own gaze does not deviate from the parade in front of him, even when lighting a cigarette for his neighbor—a brief premonition of the tennis scene in *Strangers on a Train*. It is Daisy, announced with the third and last of her special titles, he has come for, and during her walk she obliges him with a direct look—again full face to the camera—which he returns, after a full 180-degree cut, and which she acknowledges, after another such cut. The whole of their relationship consists of an escalation of returned gazes, from their first meeting in his rooms up to this point—the first such exchange in which the two characters are shown in close-up, and from each other's points of view. The Lodger then buys her the dress she is modeling. Described in the fan magazine *Picture Show* as "a filmy affair of eau-de-nil georgette embroidered with silver," it came from the house of Péron, which had its salon in Regent Street.[11] Earlier, Daisy took the place of paintings; now the Lodger will try to make her conform with an image in his head.

As an instance of the place of the look in the culture in which Hitchcock was formed, the narrator of *Trilby*, George du Maurier's novel of 1894, which Hitchcock is sure to have encountered in one form or another, offers the following:

> But a beautiful eye that lets the broad white light of infinite space (so bewildering and garish and diffused) into one pure virgin heart, to be filtered there! and lets it out again, duly warmed, softened, concentrated, sublimated, focused to a point as in a precious stone, that it may shed itself (a love-laden effulgence) into some stray fellow-heart close by—through pupil and iris, entre quatre-z-yeux—the very elixir of life!

"Entre quatre-z-yeux"—*The Lodger*.

It is only after this consummation, manifested in reverse angle shots, that the forces of law and propriety come for the Lodger and Daisy.

The police have barely featured up to this point in the film; Joe has been seen strictly after hours. Now, however, immediately following the salon scene, Joe is shown telling Scotland Yard's "Big Four"—the officers in charge of the CID—of his discovery: "If one makes a plan of the Avenger murders," he says in a dialogue title, "one can see they have been moving steadily in a certain direction." Looking at his map, they deduce that the next murder will be "near these lodging houses," which the audience might infer to include the Buntings'. A line can be traced from the Embankment to Westminster to Pimlico, but the map itself, once seen, does not obviously show this pattern, nor reveal how the deduction has been made. *The Lodger*, though its plot begins with a murder and reaches its climax with the unmasking of the culprit by a detective, is not a whodunit. While Hitchcock situated himself within a tradition of crime literature dating back to Wilkie Collins, he all but excluded from that tradition the new school of detective fiction that was coming into vogue in the mid-1920s.

Agatha Christie had published her first Poirot novel in 1920, Dorothy Sayers's first Peter Wimsey novel appeared in 1923, Philip MacDonald created Anthony Gethryn in 1924, and Anthony Berkeley Cox had introduced Roger Sheringham in 1925. Christie's *The Murder of Roger Ackroyd*, having been serialized in the *Evening News* in the summer of 1925, appeared in book form at about the time *The Lodger* was being edited, in May 1926. Meanwhile, detective stories were beginning to receive serious historical treatment. August 1926 saw the publication by Oxford University Press of *Crime and Detection*, an anthology edited and introduced by E. M. Wrong, a history don at Magdalen College. Across the Atlantic, the literary critic Willard Huntington Wright's essay "The Detective Novel" was published in the November 1926 issue of *Scribner's Magazine*. Both authors traced the genre's evolution from Poe's Auguste Dupin stories to the present. But Wright, then launching himself as the detective novelist S. S. Van Dine, wrote that "it is significant that the cinematograph has never been able to project a detective story. The detective story, in fact, is the only type of fiction that cannot be filmed."[12]

The British whodunit writers were near-contemporaries of Hitchcock's, and he shared their fascination with one murder in particular, the case of

Edith Thompson and Frederick Bywaters, who were executed in January 1923 for the murder of Thompson's husband. The murder had taken place in Ilford; Hitchcock knew Thompson's father, who had taught him to dance, and his sister was a friend of Thompson's sister. In his chapter in *Footnotes to the Film*, Hitchcock said that he wanted to film the trial "verbatim."[13] By then it had inspired Sayers's novel *The Documents in the Case*. At the height of the whodunit craze, in 1930, Hitchcock would direct *Murder*, adapted from a novel by Clemence Dane and Helen Simpson, but perhaps because of his proximity to a real and not very ingenious murder, Hitchcock deprecated whodunits—once at a safe historical distance—as puzzle-like, emotionless. "You simply wait to find out who committed the murder," he told Truffaut.[14]

G. K. Chesterton, firmly in Hitchcock's preferred tradition of crime literature, had made similar criticisms at the time. In 1922 he wrote in his *Illustrated London News* column that the author of detective stories "cannot tell us until the last chapter any of the most interesting things about the most interesting people," so that they ought to be brief.[15] Earlier, in his well-known "Defence of Detective Stories," collected in his 1902 collection *The Defendant*, Chesterton had called the detective story of the time the "only form of popular literature in which is expressed some sense of the poetry of modern life," and credited it with the "realization of the poetry of London."[16] The new school of detective fiction was proverbially identified with the country house.

Marie Belloc Lowndes was not of this school and literary historians have found her difficult to place, partly because crime literature was not all she wrote. The longer version of Wright's essay, published as the introduction to a detective story anthology of 1927, mentioned her as the author of "two interesting and noteworthy contributions to criminal literature," *The Chink in the Armour* as well as *The Lodger*, but more might be said.[17] From one aspect, Lowndes's *The Lodger* is an anti-detective story, with its titular protagonist resembling a malevolent Sherlock Holmes. Apart from his unlikely and surely significant name and his cape, Mr. Sleuth exhibits more than one Holmesian trait—"he walked and he walked, up and down, and up and down, until I was weary of the sound of his footstep," Holmes's landlady Mrs. Hudson complains in *The Sign of Four*, as might Mr. Sleuth's landlady, Mrs. Bunting. In the same novel, Holmes, like

Mr. Sleuth, conducts scientific experiments in his rooms. The Buntings of the novel live somewhere very near Baker Street.

Lowndes's significance for Hitchcock may be gauged from the fact that her other works include a collection of nonfiction titled *Noted Murder Mysteries*, in 1914, and a version of the "lady vanishes" legend. In the original, an Englishwoman and her daughter visit Paris during the 1889 Exposition; while the daughter makes a brief excursion, her mother disappears from their hotel room without a trace, and on the daughter's return the hotel staff refuse to acknowledge that either of them was ever there. *The End of Her Honeymoon*, as Lowndes's novel on this theme was titled, was published in 1913, the same year as *The Lodger*. When she heard about Hitchcock's *The Lady Vanishes*, in the summer of 1938, Lowndes took legal advice.[18] It was not the first time she had felt herself to be the victim of plagiarism: though she tended to write crime literature rather than detective stories, Lowndes was also the creator of a French detective called Hercules Popeau.

Another criticism of Chesterton's provides another possible reason for Hitchcock's aversion to the whodunit, and his preference for Lowndes. In 1920, also in the *Illustrated London News*, he had written that detective stories tended not to make good plays,

> for the drama depends on what was called the Greek irony—that is, on the knowledge of the audience, and not the ignorance of the audience. In the detective story it is the hero (or villain) who knows, and the outsider who is deceived. In the drama it is the outsider (or spectator) who knows, and the hero who is deceived.[19]

From at least as early as 1935, Hitchcock wanted to adapt Anthony Berkeley Cox's novel *Malice Aforethought*, a deliberate break with the whodunit, published under the pen name Francis Iles in 1931. During Hitchcock's first visit to New York, in August 1937, an interviewer wrote that this was "because he likes the first line of it. The line reads, approximately, 'It was not until three months after Dr. X decided to murder his wife that he took any steps toward doing so.'"[20] This was Greek irony, suspense rather than surprise. In the event, Hitchcock used the second Francis Iles novel, *Before the Fact*, also a departure from the principles of what had by then been dubbed the "Golden Age of English Detection," as the basis for his fourth Hollywood film, *Suspicion*—a film with abundant similarities to *The Lodger*. Hitchcockian suspense depended on varying levels of ignorance and knowledge, and the master detectives of the Golden Age knew altogether too much.

From Joe's map, Hitchcock cuts to another, similarly annotated map, just as its unseen author, evidently the Avenger, adds another mark. Neither his identity nor his location is immediately revealed, but the next shot shows the Buntings where they were last seen, in their living room, and by now the audience is likely simply to assume that the Avenger is the Lodger, working on the map in his room. Daisy enters and shows off her new dress, to her parents' dismay—though they seem more concerned about the transfer of her affections away from Joe than about the threat to her life. A disgruntled Mr. Bunting returns the dress to the Lodger, and is received with disdain. After he leaves, however, the Lodger is shown looking dejected in a shot held long enough to raise suspicions about what he might do.

"The same evening," as an illustrated Kauffer title announces, there follows what irresistibly appears as a premonition of the shower scene in *Psycho*. While Daisy, her nakedness hidden by the steam, runs a bath, the Lodger works at his desk—on what a cut confirms to be the map. The rain against the window, however, leads him out of his room, and to the door of the bathroom. Starting with a shot of his hand testing the handle, Hitchcock cuts between Daisy in the bath and the Lodger on the landing, his intentions initially unclear until the scene resolves itself into a third feint—the Lodger has come to apologize about the dress, to which Daisy responds by asserting her independence from her parents. In the next scene they step out of the house together, under her parents' rather inattentive noses; and, as Mrs. Bunting is shown to say, "it's Tuesday night!"

Seemingly to suggest the proverbial criminal returning to the scene of his crime, the Lodger and Daisy are next shown at the site of the film's second murder. Sitting under a lamp in the courtyard, about to kiss, they are interrupted by Joe—an improbable coincidence that wisely goes unexplained. The two men face off, only for Daisy to tell Joe she has made her choice. After the new couple moves on, Joe sits down to mull things over. Staring at a footprint in the muck, he and the audience see, briefly

superimposed, a series of images from earlier: the turned-around paintings, the bag, the Lodger and Daisy embracing, and the chandelier.
Somehow the penny drops, and he too catches up with the audience. The
Lodger is not only a cad but a killer. The nearest equivalent in Hitchcock's
later films is the wordless sequence in *Notorious* in which Claude Rains's
character, alone, comes to realize that Cary Grant's character is not only
attempting to steal his wife, played by Ingrid Bergman, but using her to
spy on him. In both instances, the first suspicion is not wrong, just insuf-
ficient. Sexual jealousy has blinded both men to what is in front of them,
to what the audience has already seen.

Mrs. Bunting is so distressed at having missed Daisy's exit with the
Lodger that she also manages to miss their return. In his room, once he
has removed her hat, to see her golden hair, they finally kiss. The scene
is awkwardly blocked, and discontinuous, both between shots and in its
emotional flow, but it is the prototype of the elaborate kissing scenes that
Hitchcock included in *Spellbound*, *Notorious*, *Rear Window*, and *Vertigo*.
It begins with the shot that Hitchcock would go on to use to introduce
Grace Kelly's character in *Rear Window*—the Lodger's face seen from
Daisy's point of view, coming toward the camera, in this instance until
only his lips and nose are visible. As she did with Joe, though perhaps
more dreamily, Daisy is shown looking at the ceiling. For his part, the
Lodger at one point rather roughly pushes her away—possibly, the audience may infer, wrestling with a split in his personality. The scene is intercut with shots of the Buntings worrying in the kitchen; eventually they
determine to go outside in search of Daisy, only for Joe to arrive in a police
car. The Lodger and Daisy's kiss has brought the law down upon them;
their love is a danger to the public safety.

So begins the climactic fifth act, with Joe again interrupting Daisy and
the Lodger in his room, this time with a search warrant, though it does
not prevent the couple from remonstrating with him, even as Joe's fellow
officers retrieve the Lodger's bag from the chiffonier. It contains a pistol
as well as the map, and newspaper cuttings about the Avenger's murders.
Joe also finds in it, to the Lodger's great distress, a photograph—of his
first victim, accuses Joe. Now the Lodger begins to tell his story: the map
indeed gives the location of the murders, and the photograph depicts "My

murdered sister." Francis Meynell had recommended that Joe answer this with "Tell that to the jury," but in the film it remains "judge." The truth is deferred. The Lodger is arrested, and—after a pointless attempt to strangle Joe—cuffed. Joe, on the way out, sees Daisy gather her things, and is given a moment's screen time to reflect, we may imagine, that putting cuffs around the Lodger's wrists, as a prelude to putting a noose around his neck, has had the opposite effect from the one he intended, and that he and Daisy are now permanently estranged.

In the hall, after the Lodger's long descent of the stairs, Mrs. Bunting faints, causing a distraction that gives him the opportunity to disappear through the front door into the fog, first telling Daisy—though somehow no one else—to meet him in the courtyard. The three detectives race out before she does; though she has protested his innocence, the pistol gave her pause. But in the courtyard she duly finds him, and there, at last, he tells his story. It *was* his sister's photograph, he confirms—with this the photograph is shown for the first time, before a cut to a flashback of sister and brother dancing together at the coming-out ball where—the audience may have gathered from the newspaper cuttings—she was murdered. The flashback was probably shot, or reshot, during the period of reshooting, though Montagu does not mention it. The scene is not included in the earlier version of the title list, and the two main actresses who appear in it, Eve Gray and Daisy Campbell, playing the Lodger's sister and mother, were mentioned in the trade press in connection with the "additional scenes" in August.[21] Walter Mycroft described a process shot from the sequence in the same month.[22] To add to the mystery, however, it is claimed in John Russell Taylor's biography that this shot, or one very like it, was one of those that turned the studio against Hitchcock, and that it did not make the final cut.[23]

But what is most remarkable about this flashback, indeed most remarkable about this film, is not made explicit in either extant version of the title list; nor has it been commented upon in any of the criticism of the film, contemporary or retrospective, or in any of the histories and biographies. It is this: the Lodger's sister is wearing Daisy's dress. To put it the other way around: the Lodger bought the dress to make Daisy resemble his slain sister.

When Poe, in his essay "The Philosophy of Composition," wrote that "the death, then, of a beautiful woman is, unquestionably, the most poetical topic in the world," he was displaying a candidness about his craft—that

The Lodger's sister's dress.

or cynicism—which Hitchcock was to imitate in his interviews and writings, consciously or otherwise. Poe claimed to begin writing "with the consideration of an *effect*," then work backwards. Beauty, rather than truth, or passion, was the province of poetry; melancholy, because beauty induces it, was the appropriate tone; and death the most melancholy of all themes. Hence his conclusion. The most suitable voice for such a poem was that of a bereaved lover, and such a character would narrate the stories *Berenice, Morella, Ligeia*, and *Eleonora*, all of which concern the death and apparent return to life of beautiful women, in some cases in the form of another woman. If *Rebecca* and *Vertigo* are plainly in their bloodline, *The Lodger*—with its authentically Poe-esque dash of incest—hides its debt, in the manner of *The Purloined Letter*, in plain sight.

Like the later films, *The Lodger* adds to this complex the Lodger's conscious desire to remake Daisy in his sister's image—a Pygmalion twist, to be found elsewhere in the popular fiction of the time, in *Trilby* as well as Shaw's *Pygmalion*. As in *Vertigo*, the remaking begins at a mannequin parade. Unlike the heroines of *Rebecca* and *Vertigo*, who are coerced into resembling the dead woman, Daisy does not become aware of her lover's designs. On the contrary, the Lodger's flashback establishes their relationship on a new basis of trust. It was, he tells her, his mother's dying wish that he bring the Avenger to justice. He made the map to that end; here Stannard and Hitchcock, as if following the logic of Lowndes's decision to call him Mr. Sleuth, make the Lodger Holmes to Joe's Lestrade. Only Daisy believes him—a pattern repeated in *The 39 Steps, The Lady Vanishes*, and *Rear Window*. As in *Spellbound*, where the male protagonist's guilt also relates to his sibling's death, she alone can help him confront his trauma, her first step being to propose that they go to the nearest pub for a restorative brandy, the Lodger concealing his cuffs beneath his cape while she lifts the glass to his lips.

This is swiftly noticed, and the couple leave in a hurry, somehow without running into Joe, who enters the pub immediately after their exit, to telephone headquarters. His mention of the handcuffs alerts the rest of the pub to the identity of the strange man who had the brandy, and they go out in search of him. It is only then that Joe discovers from his boss that the real Avenger has just been caught red-handed. The Lodger is now confirmed as a Wrong Man on the run, though not Hitchcock's first, since

"Entre quatre-z-yeux"—*Vertigo*.

Malcolm Keen, Joe in *The Lodger*, had that role in *The Mountain Eagle*. The crowd that chases the Lodger through the streets recalls the groups of people seen in the first reel, whipped into a state of fear by the newspapers and radio; as the film reaches its climax, the narrow focus on the Buntings and the Lodger widens again. The Lodger manages to get himself suspended by his cuffs from some railings, and is almost torn apart by the terrifying mob, even after the police arrive. The police have less authority than the press, and the Lodger, bleeding from his mouth, is only rescued when a newsboy arrives with the *Evening Standard*, telling of the real Avenger's arrest.

At the hospital, a doctor tells Daisy, with what might be irony, that the Lodger's "youth and vigour will pull him through." Above the Lodger's bed, and above the others in the ward, is an empty-looking frame, probably a medical chart but bound to bring to mind the turned-around paintings. On the day after the trade show, Angus MacPhail wrote to congratulate Montagu: "The omission of the hospital scene is a considerable improvement. The tinting is less disgusting than you had led me to believe."[24] The dialogue titles for this scene are crossed out of the later version of the title list. Without it, however, the transition to the final scene would be too abrupt, and at some point it was reinserted. Introduced with a self-conscious title—"All stories have an end"—the final scene takes place in the Lodger's mansion. The Buntings bow and scrape, Daisy having bagged herself an aristocrat and become the society lady she at first appeared to be, and the film ends with a clinch. Hitchcock, in later years, was rightly embarrassed by *The Lodger*'s happy ending, which he blamed on the star system. Novello the matinée idol could not have been guilty, any more than Henry Ainley. "He should have gone on into the night and we should never have known," Hitchcock told Truffaut; whereas to Bogdanovich, at about the same time, he said he "should have been the ripper and gone on his way."[25]

In fact, the film follows the play, in which the Buntings go into service for their former lodger, once he has revealed his true identity and married Irene; nevertheless, Hitchcock introduces at least a hint of uncertainty. The film's penultimate image, before the end title, shows the Lodger and Daisy embracing in front of a window that overlooks both Big Ben and the "Golden Curls" sign, pushing in until June's face occupies most of the frame. The two landmarks strongly evoke the film's first scene, which includes the two in separate shots, and simply by showing that the Lodger had the theater in sight—as Novello, who lived opposite the Gaiety Theatre, really did—the scene suggests a connection. The shot of June's smiling face that ends the film is taken from the same angle as the screaming face with which it begins.

7 Stories of the Days to Come

At the end of September 1926 a new batch of Phonofilms went on at the Capitol, in support of a double-bill of John Ford's western *3 Bad Men* and Garbo in *Torrent*. It was more than a year since the Phonofilms' last engagement at a major West End cinema, and while they had attracted interest, the new ones attracted more. In the interim, as had been widely reported in Britain, the first Vitaphone feature, *Don Juan*, had opened in New York, on 6 August. *Kinematograph Weekly's* reviewer, probably Cedric Belfrage, who was in New York and writing for the paper at the time, wrote that it was "universally admitted that no earlier experiments had achieved anything like the same degree of success in regard either to exact synchronisation, volume or tone."[1] Meanwhile the British branch of the De Forest company had begun to break free from its moribund parent company, now embroiled in a legal dispute with Fox, and brought in new blood, including Vivian Van Damm as manager.

"Long and arduous research on the part of a British electrical genius, Mr. C. F. Elwell, was necessary to perfect, not the basic invention, but the reproduction," wrote Iris Barry during the first week of the Capitol show.[2] "After combing every European country for a satisfactory amplifier, Mr. Elwell trained several boys in Clapham and eventually succeeded in making his own amplifier, which is by far the finest in existence." Moreover, as Van Damm told the *Observer*, the Phonofilm surpassed the cumbersome Vitaphone system as a practical proposition. By this time, some of Britain's leading music-hall performers had visited the Clapham studio. The films they made were simple shorts, usually consisting of a song or sketch performed as if on stage, and shot from one angle, as if from the stalls, with few or no cuts, but Van Damm described these as a means of introducing the public to the new technology; longer "dramas and comedies" would follow.[3]

In October, an emissary from Warner Brothers told *Cinema News* that Vitaphone, as yet unseen and unheard in London, "is not an example of 'talking pictures.' It is a method of fitting a picture accurately with an orchestral accompaniment."[4] British critics, however, discussed both systems as though the age of talking pictures had arrived. Most of them were impressed by the Phonofilms' technical advance on those shown at the Holborn Empire earlier in the year; nevertheless, some continued to defend the silent film's "peculiar aesthetic" as Hitchcock himself would do. "The film is one thing, the Phonofilm is quite another," wrote Walter Mycroft, accusing its champions of "a fundamental inability to understand the function of the film, which is universal not merely because everyone the world over can understand action, but also because it does something no other medium can do."[5]

From another direction, Louis Levy, musical director of the Shepherd's Bush Pavilion, wrote that "the idea of the talking film is reversionary," whereas "cinema music is rapidly coming into its own."[6] He found "consolation in remembering the position of painters when photography was introduced." Just as the painter had not, as had been feared, been replaced by the photographer, so the cinema orchestra—albeit recorded—would prevail over dialogue since "it idealises the emotional content of the scene into its music, I venture to think, with far greater effect than words could have." From Hitchcock's point of view, the pessimists were proved right; not only had talkies "temporarily killed action in pictures," he said in 1933, but they had "done just as much damage to music."[7] Levy began working with Hitchcock in the same year, and would be engaged again, a decade after Hitchcock's move to the United States, on *Under Capricorn* and *Stage Fright*.

C. A. Lejeune met "the kinema's bright future" with irony:

At last the shadows we have invested for years with the characters of our own fancy will reveal themselves in all the nakedness of words.

How beautiful it will be to hear them speaking to us, those mute mouths which have framed so many sub-titles in the past! . . . I can think of nothing more romantic than a summer night on the waters of Venice, with the gondolier whispering "Gee, you're some baby" under the moon.[8]

Unlike Mycroft, however, she did not see a future for the silent film in parallel with the Phonofilm, and conceded defeat. "There are no longer movies and speakies. The movies speak. The speakies move."

The Phonofilms remained in the Capitol's program into November, supporting films by Lubitsch, Frank Borzage, and Howard Hawks. Meanwhile, De Forest equipment began to be installed in cinemas across the country, including Sol Levy's. The first cinema outside the West End to show Phonofilms, just a week after they began appearing at the Capitol, was the Empire in Plumstead, South East London, part of the chain Sidney Bernstein had inherited from his father; the program included a Phonofilm of Bernstein himself explaining the new technology.

Hitchcock's second film had its trade show after that of his third, on 1 October, at the Hippodrome. *The Mountain Eagle* was not fated for success. It was assigned a release date of 23 May 1927, and was duly released, but never had a West End opening of the kind *The Pleasure Garden* had had, and *The Lodger* would have, and it does not survive. The trade press was polite toward Hitchcock, reserving most of its criticism for Charles Lapworth's story. *Film Renter* called it "reminiscent of some of the Swedish photoplays," well acted, well photographed, but "far too slow" a judgment shared by *Kinematograph Weekly*.[9] Hitchcock's friends were no more positive in their brief notices. Mycroft saw a "clever" treatment of "a poorly devised, unimportant story."[10] Barry found it "far less entertaining" than *The Lodger*.[11]

Officially, the same day, 1 October, saw the US release of *The Pleasure Garden*, by Lee-Bradford. The date, together with dates for the other Gainsborough films Arthur A. Lee had acquired from Michael Balcon earlier in the year, had been announced in *Film Daily* in late August. *The Rat* was to go first, on 1 September, followed by *The Prude's Fall* on the 15th, *The Pleasure Garden* on 1 October, *The Mountain Eagle* on the 15th, and *The Sea*

Urchin on 1 November.[12] However, *The Rat* had been shown in New York cinemas as early as July, and *The Pleasure Garden*, too, was presented to the American public before its allotted date. Lee had announced the sale of the five films to local distributors in Illinois and Indiana at the end of May, a few weeks after he bought them, and so it was that on 29 August *The Pleasure Garden* opened at the Grove, an eighteen-hundred-seat neighborhood theater on the south side of Chicago.[13]

Serving a district dominated by railway lines and stockyards, the Grove played films for two days at a time from Monday through Saturday, and 29 August 1926 was a Sunday. It was the weekend after the death of Valentino, and much of the cinema-going world was in mourning. It is possible that *The Pleasure Garden* was shown at a similar venue at an earlier date, but the Grove or somewhere like it was where Hitchcock made his American debut. On Sunday 12 September the film had a further one-day engagement at the Parthenon in Hammond, Indiana. The 1st and 15th of October came and went without publicity, trade show, or reviews for either *The Pleasure Garden* or *The Mountain Eagle*; nevertheless, both of them went on general release in the United States before their general release in Britain.

Lee had been in London in September to visit his suppliers, taking back with him prints of *The Lodger*, *The Triumph of the Rat*, and Maurice Elvey's *Mademoiselle from Armentières*.[14] The latter, a Gaumont film trade shown the night before *The Lodger*, was Victor Saville's first production since his partnership with Balcon three years earlier. "During the past summer," Lee told *Cinema News*, "I visited all the Exchange centres in the United States, and was successful in signing up contracts for the release of a series of six pictures commencing on September 1, 1927"—the three named, and three more unnamed and as yet unmade.[15] He gave a melancholy reason for the British films' relative success, lying "in the fact that the independent American producer finds it rather hard to continue in business; there are not so many of them now, and the independent exchanges have to seek elsewhere for their supply." Lee predicted that within five years the independent exchanges would be gone, and distribution would be run nationally from New York.

In late 1938, with his transfer to Hollywood fast approaching, Hitchcock claimed that "I have always wanted to make films with some sociological importance—but I have never been allowed to do so."[16] He gave a surprising example. "Soon after the general strike in 1926 I wanted to put the whole thing into a film." The censor would never have permitted it, he said, but "I wanted to show fist-fights between strikers and undergraduates, pickets and all the authentic drama of the situation." Few of Hitchcock's films, British or American, have political themes, and there is no contemporary evidence of plans for a film about the general strike. *Huntingtower*, the film Hitchcock was planning at the time, is an anticommunist adventure story. But another film that Hitchcock announced he wanted to make in the same year does have sociological importance, albeit of a different sort.

Rumors of this project found their way into the press soon after *The Lodger*'s trade show. The same issue of *Kinematograph Weekly* that carried reviews of *The Lodger*, dated 23 September, also reported that Hitchcock was "busy upon preparations for his first subject for British National Pictures—a striking departure on unusual lines. J. D. Williams is to be congratulated on securing this unassuming but genuinely creative artist."[17] Elsewhere there were rumors of a film to star Alan Cobham, who was then making another much-publicized return flight, from Australia; during the outward journey his engineer had been shot dead over Iraq. Gaumont had released a film of his earlier expedition, *With Cobham to the Cape*, during the summer. On 1 October he landed his seaplane in the Thames next to the Palace of Westminster, and was knighted shortly afterward.

"It is true that a great 'super-picture' of the air is to be produced," wrote Mycroft on 16 October, and "it is true that Sir Alan Cobham will be associated with it. But the air-knight is not to be a screen actor; his role will be that of technical adviser."[18] The film was "to be made by Mr. Alfred Hitchcock." This "air picture," Mycroft went on, "with its projection into the life of a generation ahead, a life of giant air liners, and such developments as television in terms of telephone call boxes, is the fruit of the director's own imagination." A few days later *Kinematograph Weekly*'s reporter connected this "screen forecast of days to come" with "H. G. Wells's imaginative genius," and Lang's still unseen *Metropolis*. "Television will be used dramatically, and Sir Alan Cobham will probably be consultant on big episodes of the air."[19]

In Wells's novels *When the Sleeper Wakes* and *The War in the Air*, published in 1899 and 1908 respectively, aviation serves to epitomize what Wells called the Scientific Age, begun in the late nineteenth century. *The War in the Air*, which is set in the early twentieth century, evokes "the wild rush of change in the pace, scope, materials, scale and possibilities of human life that then occurred," and traditions "not simply confronted by new conditions, but by constantly renewed and changing new conditions." The protagonist of *When the Sleeper Wakes* falls asleep in 1897 and awakes in 2100 to discover that the rush of late Victorian London was "the mere beginning." Among other features of the "new order," whole fields of the economy have been monopolized by great "trusts" under a dictatorship. In a preface of 1921, Wells described the corporatist dystopia he had conjured up as "a practical realisation of Mr. Belloc's nightmare of the Servile State"—a telling comparison in view of Wells's and Belloc's opposite political views.

Both television—"kineto-tele-photographs"—and home video—"kinematograph-phonographs"—with color and sound are prominent features of the world of *When the Sleeper Wakes*, the former used for surveillance and broadcasting, the latter in place of novels. Some of what Wells had imagined in the year of Hitchcock's birth was becoming reality in 1926, which was punctuated by press reports of fresh developments in what its inventor John Logie Baird called the "televisor." This had been given its first convincing demonstration before a small audience in his rooms at 22 Frith Street, Soho, on 26 January, a month before the *Lodger* shoot began. By August, the company set up to exploit Baird's invention, Television Ltd., was making experimental transmissions between the company's office in the West End and a receiving station in Harrow, a northwestern suburb, and by September the prototype was on display at the Science Museum in South Kensington. The technological roots of the post-cinematic world in which Hitchcock, in the 1950s and early '60s, would thrive, lay in the earliest years of his career; and Wells had anticipated it even before then.

As Wells was moved to write in his 1921 preface, not all of his extrapolations were being borne out. The world of *When the Sleeper Wakes*—and that of *A Story of the Days to Come*, his novella of the same year—consists of "hypertrophied cities" with vacant countryside between them; but as

Wells confessed in his 1902 book *Anticipations*, he had already begun to perceive a different future. In a chapter of that book titled "The Probable Diffusion of Great Cities," Wells wrote that whereas he had till then assumed that the trend toward "densely-congested 'million-cities'" like London, New York, and "the Hankow trinity of cities" in central China would continue, the city of the future "will present a new and entirely different phase of human distribution."[20] It would be enabled by modern means of transport and communication, and characterized by the "little private *imperium* such as a house or cottage 'in its own grounds' affords," equipped with "photographic and phonographic apparatus."[21] Dense cities would be superseded by diffuse "urban regions."[22] The population of Los Angeles County in 1902 was around two hundred thousand; by 1926 it was easily a "million-city" of this new kind.

"This Broadway," wrote L'Estrange Fawcett in *Films: Facts and Forecasts*, "is a loud, noisy thoroughfare. By day, a wild, scurrying jumble of humanity and motor vehicles; by night, 'The Great White Way,' ablaze with scintillating signs and winking luminous words." He had visited in the autumn of 1926. "It seems like a huge, flaming ravine, full of adventure, excitement, and soundless explosions of brilliant electricity."[23] Standing in Times Square, one could see "the Rialto, the Criterion, the New York, the Paramount, the Loew State, the Rivoli, the Embassy, the Gaiety, the Colonial, the Mark-Strand, the Capitol, Warner's, and, largest of all, the Roxy."[24] Two of the biggest, the Paramount and the Roxy, were still under construction at the time of Fawcett's visit, but were about to be unveiled— the Paramount in November, and the Roxy in March 1927. Nor was this panorama all that the district had to offer. "Partially out of sight in the Forties and Fifties, which cut Broadway and the Avenues, there are half a dozen other stage-theatres given over to films." It put the West End in the shade.

The last week of October was a little flat. "Only house that approached anything like normal was the Capitol, where Rex Ingram's 'The Magician' drew $54,344—not what it should have been," reported *Variety*.[25] By now there were two Vitaphone features on show—*Don Juan*, approaching its third month at the Warner Theatre, and *The Better 'Ole*, at the Colony. "You cannot be in New York without hearing Vitaphone on every street corner, in every restaurant and at every party," Louella Parsons had written during a visit earlier in the month.[26] But the two main Paramount houses, "the Rivoli, with 'London,' British National picture starring Dorothy Gish, and the Rialto with 'Kid Boots,'" starring Eddie Cantor and Clara Bow, both "felt a slump." The big disappointment was D. W. Griffith's adaptation of *The Sorrows of Satan*—the book that the young Hitchcock had adapted on spec—at the George M. Cohan. The same paper reported rumors that the film's poor performance cast Griffith's future at Paramount into doubt—as it proved.[27] *The Sorrows of Satan* had taken just over $10,000 in its third week, half what *The Big Parade*, at a comparably sized theater, the Astor, took in its fiftieth week, and not much more than *Ben-Hur* took at the smaller Embassy in its forty-fourth.

Fawcett perceived that the vast, cheap cinemas—the Roxy would seat six thousand—courted a different audience from the smaller, more expensive theaters. "The Capitol people rarely go to the $2.20 house, and *vice versa*, and neither audience goes to the no less popular Loew's New York, where on the roof second-rate pictures are shown continually day and night at very cheap prices."[28] Loew's New York, on Broadway between Forty-Fourth and Forty-Fifth Streets, changed its program daily, and its box-office returns, from 40-cent tickets, were not listed in *Variety*. It was at Loew's New York, on Tuesday 26 October 1926, that Hitchcock made his Broadway debut. There and on that day, *The Pleasure Garden* both opened and closed in New York, having been shorn by its local distributor, Aywon, of one thousand feet, and billed with a Poverty Row production, *Dangerous Friends*. Some of the trade papers, though not the news dailies, sent reviewers; none were impressed. *Film Daily* called it a "sex picture wholly unsuitable for the exhibitor who aims to show good clean entertainment," and deplored "the rare skill of a director gone far wrong in the art of suggestion."[29]

The disappointing opening of *London*, attended by J. D. Williams and Herbert Wilcox, was of more consequence for Hitchcock's career. In London, the film had first been shown to a small audience at the Savoy, two days after the trade show of *The Lodger*, and provoked a controversy in the *Evening Standard*. Mycroft reviewed it together with *The Lodger* and *Mademoiselle from Armentières*, and found it wanting: "because it is assured of an American market (whereas the other films I have mentioned are not), I regret that this film will go across the Atlantic to be regarded as the best of which British film producers, including Mr Wilcox himself, are capable."[30] In the next day's *Standard*, its nominal author, Thomas Burke, a friend of Mycroft's, disowned the film. On the day *Variety*'s withering assessment appeared, Mycroft quoted a cable from Williams in New York, rebutting rumors of personnel changes inside British National.[31]

Mycroft said in the same column that Williams was in the United States partly in relation to "the question of a subject for Mr. Alfred Hitchcock to precede that young director's ambitious air film." Although Gainsborough had claimed at the time of Hitchcock's deal with British National that he remained under contract till the end of February 1927, there is every indication that this arrangement had not held. British National had begun giving details of its plans for him even before *The Lodger*'s trade show. In August Iris Barry had announced that Charles Rosher, "an Englishman who once worked with a firm of Broad-street Court photographers and became Miss Mary Pickford's cameraman," was "coming to work in an English film studio shortly for Mr. Alfred Hitchcock."[32] But as the autumn wore on, British National's prospects started to fade. Elstree's opening continued to be postponed. Rosher, who had shot Lubitsch's first Hollywood film, *Rosita*, went to Fox to shoot F. W. Murnau's first, *Sunrise*. *London* was meant to establish the company in the eyes of the world, and it had flopped.

Opening at the Rivoli created expectations; opening at Loew's New York less so. *The Pleasure Garden* did not go on to box-office glory, but nor was it sunk by its reviews. Indeed, it was still being booked as late as January 1930, when it played in Atlanta. More immediately, it opened in Los Angeles on 28 November, playing for seven days downtown at the Hippodrome, which charged 20 cents for a mixed bill of films and vaudeville—less than a third of the lowest-priced ticket at the grander venues. In Hollywood itself, Grauman's Egyptian was showing *The Better 'Ole*; Vitaphone had made its Los Angeles debut there a month before, on 27 October.

The big draw that week in Los Angeles was the world-premiere run of *What Price Glory* at the Carthay Circle Theatre, a new venue off Wilshire Boulevard, which stretched from the ocean to a point just short of the downtown area. Carthay Circle was about halfway between the two, just east of Beverly Hills. The area was still only part-developed and considered remote in some quarters, but as a supportive article in the *Los Angeles Times* pointed out in the same week, it was blessed with "unusually fine parking facilities," since its builders had anticipated that "95 per cent of its patronage would come from persons arriving in their own cars."[33] The site was adjacent to a section of Wilshire Boulevard that property developer A. W. Ross was then battling zoning ordinances to turn into the "Fifth Avenue of the West." Within a few years this was known as Miracle Mile, in Reyner Banham's estimation "a unique transitional monument to the dawn of automobilism," which he dated to 1927, precisely because it was not like Fifth Avenue, or Oxford Street, but was, like Carthay Circle, designed for drivers, the "first linear downtown."[34] Such was the pattern of life in a diffuse urban region.

Alfred Hitchcock and Alma Reville married on 2 December, while *The Pleasure Garden* was still playing in Los Angeles, and took their honeymoon in Switzerland. While they were away, the situation at British National deteriorated. On the 6th, the company's board held a press conference to announce that J. D. Williams's contract as managing director had been terminated. On the same day, Williams's lawyers announced that he had sued for damages; soon afterward he departed for the United States. The second film that Wilcox had made with Gish, *Tiptoes*, had not been seen, and so Paramount had not paid for it, and production on the third, *Madame Pompadour*, had not yet begun, construction at Elstree having been further delayed by the continuing coal shortage. British National's capital was depleted, and I. W. Schlesinger had stepped in until payment from Paramount arrived, putting him "in practical control," *Film Renter* reported.[35] The same paper observed that the company had "no future plans beyond the making of 'Madame Pompadour,' and its program after that appears to be extremely nebulous and dependent on the finding of further finance."

At the press conference it was disclosed that the company "had been approached to loan the services of Mr. Hitchcock for the making of one picture, and would probably do so if a convenient arrangement were proposed."[36] *Film Renter* noted that his salary at British National was to have been £2,500 per film, and that he would be farmed out "if and when there is a Company that can afford to pay this salary."[37]

Film Renter underestimated British National's promise. Though a renewal of the Paramount deal was unlikely, the market for British films was all but guaranteed to improve. Just as was promised in April, the quota question had been put on to the agenda of the Imperial Conference, held between 19 October and 23 November. In the weeks before the conference, the *Daily Mail*, the paper that had done the most to agitate for a quota, called attention to the difficulties British producers faced in selling their films into the Dominions, the self-governing countries with large white populations—Canada, Australia, New Zealand, and South Africa—whose leaders were about to foregather at 10 Downing Street. Barry reported that Gainsborough had been offered just £180 for the South African rights to *The Lodger*, less than it might make in a week at a single location in Britain, and Balcon joined the controversy in the *Johannesburg Star* when it disputed her claims.[38] I. W. Schlesinger's African Theatres Trust was the culprit.

In an early session of the conference, Sir Philip Cunliffe-Lister raised the specter of what effect "tens of millions of people seeing American films, staged in American settings, American clothes, American furniture, American motor-cars" might have on the cohesion of the Empire, and on British exports.[39] At this juncture the justification for protecting British film production was that to reverse the rising American tide within the Empire would require an adequate supply of adequate films from the "Mother Country," or produced elsewhere within the Empire. Corresponding action by the Dominion governments to ensure that such films would in fact be shown in their territories, in preference to the American output, would have to come later—if it came at all.

There were weightier matters on the agenda. Since the Great War, it was tacitly recognized that the Dominions could no longer be expected to join Britain in making military commitments in Europe, and the Dominion governments had been neither represented nor consulted at Locarno. This was not uncontroversial, and at the Imperial Conference the Dominion leaders were invited to associate themselves with the Locarno treaties if they so wished. The Canadian premier Mackenzie King made clear that he did not, and with the probable exception of New Zealand nor did the others.[40] The conference confirmed that there was no going back; the Empire was becoming a Commonwealth of Nations, equal under the Crown, but autonomous in foreign and domestic affairs. Within this larger frame, close coordination of film policy was unlikely, and the conference, in its last days, approved only the general aim of increasing intra-imperial trade. In the event, only New Zealand and the Australian state of Victoria would introduce imperial quotas. In India, notably, there was a significant body of opinion in favor of a quota to protect not British but Indian films.

From the point of view of its political sponsors, one of the quota's primary objectives had been effectively half abandoned; nevertheless, the domestic quota had become inevitable, and it would change the British film industry forever. In the week after the conference, on 27 November, the *Daily Mail*'s political correspondent reported that the Board of Trade had almost finished drafting quota legislation, which would be put before Parliament early in the next session.[41] Balcon called the news "highly satisfactory," albeit because it was "the only thing which will ever settle the problem."[42]

With the quota on its way, British National's films, and moreover its plant at Elstree, were therefore more valuable than *Film Renter* reckoned. In the first days of January 1927 the *Daily Film Renter*, a new publication founded to cover what was bound to be a fast-moving period in the business, announced that the company had a new board member, John Maxwell.[43] Truly a gray eminence, the opposite of J. D. Williams, Maxwell was a Glaswegian solicitor who had come into the business during the prewar construction boom. By the early 1920s he had significant interests not only in Scottish Cinema and Variety Theatres, one of the biggest chains in Britain, but also in distribution. Wardour Films mostly traded in the output of the lesser American studios, but in 1925 it began to act as distributor for Ufa; since then Wardour had handled *The Last Laugh*, *The Waltz Dream*, and *Vaudeville*, and it was about to release *Metropolis*.

By integrating production, distribution, and exhibition under the umbrella of state protection, Maxwell's British National was well placed to mimic the American combines. For the moment, however, while the company reorganized itself, Hitchcock was loaned back to Gainsborough. In the week before Christmas it was announced that he would again direct Ivor Novello, in an adaptation of *Down Hill*.[44] In a rather pointed article in *Film Renter* a week later, Balcon wrote that Gainsborough "can respect a director in other ways than negotiating an overdraft at the bank in order to pay him an extravagant salary."[45]

Also around Christmas, the Phonofilms returned to the Capitol. The new batch was more ambitious than those shown only a few months earlier; as Van Damm had promised, his studio was now turning out dramas. During the autumn the company had hired three experienced directors—Charles Calvert, George Cooper, and Thomas Bentley—and one novice, Miles Mander. Nor was Mander the only one of Hitchcock's associates to be involved; one of the new films was a scene from *Julius Caesar* performed by Malcolm Keen with Basil Gill. Of this Mycroft wrote that "George Cooper, the director, contrived to get changes of angles and close ups into a purely stage situation," and that the films in general "reveal an endeavour to apply kinematograph principles to the talking films, instead of being content to film the sight and sound of a stage show, as hitherto."[46] A few days before the New Year, Mycroft, on the front page of the *Evening Standard*, revealed that George Bernard Shaw was considering making a visit to Clapham with Sybil Thorndike (later to appear in *Stage Fright*). "One act of 'Saint Joan' would be given, and Mr. Shaw himself would appear on the screen to give a preliminary lecture, which would be the cinematographic equivalent of one of his famous play prefaces—but probably rather briefer."[47]

The Lodger opened to the public at the Marble Arch Pavilion on Monday 17 January 1927, playing three times a day, at 3:30, 6:30, and 9:30 p.m. Though it was by now outsized by the Tivoli, Plaza, and Capitol, the Pavilion remained one of the West End's prime cinemas. In December 1926 it had had the British premiere of Buster Keaton's *Battling Butler*, an MGM release, and it had secured the first run of *Metropolis*—originally booked for November 1926 but running late. Partly because the American firms had their own cinemas to use, the Davis family favored British films, but they were opposed to the quota.[48] It had become known that *The Lodger* would open there when Mycroft reported a row between E. McKnight Kauffer and W. & F., which had refused to use his proposed posters for the film. Jeffrey Bernerd was quoted calling them "sort of Futurist and quite attractive, but for one thing we did not want the public to think the film was one

The frontage of the Marble Arch Pavilion. *Kinematograph Weekly*, 15 October 1925. Reproduced by kind permission of the Syndics of Cambridge University Library.

Marble Arch Pavilion, seen from the northwest. © Historic England.

of these expressionist pictures like 'Dr. Caligari.'"[49] However, Mycroft went on, Alfred Davis had vowed to put them on display at the Pavilion.

The venue's musical director, in place since its opening, was William Hodgson, commanding an orchestra of some twenty players; along with Louis Levy, who had provided music for other films shown at the Pavilion at about this time, he is the most likely candidate for *The Lodger*'s musical arranger. At the Hippodrome trade show it had been presented in silence.[50] William Hodgson's Marble Arch Pavilion Orchestra, as it was billed, had a weekly program on 2LO, broadcast from the cinema on Tuesday afternoons. On 18 and 25 January the program went out between 4 and 5 p.m., during the first screening of the day. The BBC's records do not include the content of the program on the 18th, but on the 25th the Pavilion Orchestra played:

Unfinished Symphony, 1st Movement	Schubert
Norwegian Rhapsody, No. 1	Swensden [*sic*]
Gipsy Suite No. 1	German
The Merchant of Venice	Rosse
Scenes Alsaciennes	Massenet
Incidental Music to Faust	C-Taylor
Impressions d'Italie	Charpentier
Introduction to the Sun (Iris)	Mascagni
Petite Suite	Debussy[51]

According to the listings published in the London papers, *The Lodger* began at 3:30 p.m., and the second feature at 5 p.m., so that—assuming all this is accurate—Schubert would have accompanied the "Late that night" section that includes the staircase sequence, half an hour into the film. The compositions named in the BBC document are far longer than can have been played within the hour: Samuel Coleridge-Taylor's *Incidental Music to Faust* alone takes about fifteen minutes to play in full. Nevertheless, this is the kind of music that was used to accompany *The Lodger* during its first run. It did not arouse public comment, but it must have interested Hitchcock, who had, as Mycroft would recount, "developed an almost fantastic passion for music."[52] His tastes "ranged from and included Gershwin, Eric Coates, Elgar and Beethoven, to his equal content." Mycroft meant these words to have an edge, and there is an echo of it in Bernard Herrmann's claim that "left by himself, he would play 'In a Monastery Garden' behind all his pictures," this being a piece of British light music, such as Coates specialized in, from 1915; but Herrmann liked British light music, and revered Elgar.[53]

On the day *The Lodger* opened, the Capitol had Lon Chaney in *The Road to Mandalay*, from Herman Mankiewicz's first screenplay, replacing Garbo in *The Temptress*—both MGM releases kept out of the Tivoli by *Ben-Hur*, which had replaced *The Big Parade* in November and would continue there for months to come. The New Gallery had Keaton's latest, *The General*, billed with Tourneur's *The Desert Healer*, his last completed American film, while the Plaza had *Hotel Imperial*, whose pan-European provenance—produced by Erich Pommer, starring Pola Negri, directed by Mauritz Stiller from a story by Lajos Biró—attracted the attention of more than one reviewer. "Hero and heroine take their final close-up kiss as they have done in a thousand worse pictures," commented Iris Barry.[54] "Hollywood wins. They really do do these things better in Europe."

The Pavilion's second feature in *The Lodger*'s second week—none was named in the first—was *Irene*, a Colleen Moore comedy from First National. Moore plays a mannequin who, like Daisy, marries up the social scale, but unlike *The Lodger*, its fashion parade sequence is in Technicolor. Except for the Capitol, which had Ingram's *The Magician*, the other principal cinemas also retained their main features on 24 January, but there was a noteworthy general release in circulation that week—*The Pleasure Garden*. Hitchcock's debut opened at a number of London venues including the large Stoll Picture Theatre on Kingsway, often as part of a double-bill, on the 24th, ten days after its listed release date.

The same day's papers carried photographs of the last night of the old Empire, Leicester Square. *Lady Be Good*, running since Gershwin's visit in April 1926, was the last live musical to be staged there. Henceforth, following reconstruction, to be overseen by Thomas Lamb, Scottish-born architect of many of the Broadway cinemas, it would become MGM's new shop window in London, replacing the Tivoli. Much of the capital came from Solly Joel, Barney Barnato's nephew.

The Lodger's general release date was officially Monday 14 February; however, it opened in Dublin and Birmingham on 31 January, and in

Manchester on 7 February. It did not play at Sol Levy's venues in Birmingham, which had become the focus of a bitter row within the trade. In December it had been revealed that Paramount, which already had control of the Theatre Royal in Manchester, had bought a controlling interest in both of Levy's sites in Birmingham, the Scala and the Futurist, effectively closing them to British productions—the kind of ill that the quota was intended to remedy. Instead *The Lodger* opened at the West End Cinema, part of the Provincial Cinematograph Theatres chain, in Birmingham, at the Gaiety Theatre in Manchester, and the Metropole in Dublin—all leading cinemas in their respective cities.

On the morning of Tuesday 8 February, the King and Queen left Buckingham Palace in a golden carriage, observed by their baby granddaughter, the Princess Elizabeth, whose nurse held her up to a window. Twenty-five minutes later they arrived at Westminster for the state opening of Parliament. The King's speech, setting out the government's legislative agenda for the new session, "took less than ten minutes to deliver," *The Times* reported.[55] A few seconds were devoted to a bill "to encourage the production and exhibition of British films." Sir Philip Cunliffe-Lister had continued to meet members of the trade and the draft bill had continued to be revised since November. In late January, for instance, he had seen a delegation that included John Maxwell and Michael Balcon, in part to discuss the problem of defining the Britishness of the British films whose production was to be encouraged.[56] King George was listened to, *The Times* continued, "with unmoved attention. Germany and China, leasehold reform—even a reference to the films evoked no sign of approbation or dissent from what is probably the least demonstrative Assembly in the world."

During the week of 14 February, most of *The Lodger*'s bookings were in London, including the Shepherd's Bush Pavilion, one of Europe's largest cinemas. There and in numerous other instances it was billed with a Paramount programmer, *The Crown of Lies*, starring Pola Negri.

Also on the 14th, *The Lodger* opened in Sheffield, and at the Oxford Super Cinema, where it is likely to have been seen by Hitchcock's future writer Joan Harrison, then an undergraduate at St. Hugh's College. On 21 February it opened in Cambridge, Brighton, and in Alma Reville's native Nottingham. On the 28th it came to Bristol and Coventry, and a week after that to Belfast. On the same day, 7 March, it opened in Leyton-stone, at the Gaiety. In Glasgow, where it opened on 14 March, advertise-ments requested patrons "not to divulge the name of THE AVENGER," though it is not divulged in the film.[57] It opened in Edinburgh on 11 April. A week later, on the 18th, it arrived in Cardiff, Novello's hometown, where it played the giant Capitol. By the time *The Lodger* opened in Newcastle, in July, it had begun to make return visits to other cities—and all the while it was being shown in towns and suburbs across Britain. It was still being shown in smaller cinemas more than a year after its release, by which time Hitchcock had completed and shown three more films.

The release was accompanied by a novelization in the *Picturegoer*, writ-ten by John Fleming, and publication of a tie-in edition of the novel, the cover of which featured Novello's name more prominently than that of its author. At the end of February the anonymous author of a syndicated column wrote that he or she had met Mrs. Belloc Lowndes and

> found her naturally enough very elated at the extraordinary success of her film, "The Lodger," in which Ivor Novello and June are delighting cinema audiences all over the country. I think I detected, though, a certain regret that the conventions of the cinema made it necessary to alter the original novel so much.[58]

C. A. Lejeune made her first comment on the film in early March, in another column on what she considered to be the central but still unnamed art of montage, four years after she and Alma Reville had first published articles on the topic. "It was D. W. Griffith's perception of the way in which cutting and assembling could be turned to dramatic pur-pose that first brought the suspense scene into the kinema," she wrote.[59] "The modern film describes nothing—it hints, suggests, sketches, flashes from expression to expression," she went on. "When the producer of 'The Lodger' wants to create a sense of dark mystery for his theme he opens with a series of cuts and flashes of mouths screaming, faces horrified and distorted, newspaper telegrams, rushing news-vans, words on a sky sign, words across the ether, all sorts of startled images." This "school of jostled vision," she concluded, "in spite of its kinship with modern painting, lit-erature, and stagecraft, is peculiarly the kinema's own."

A week later *The Lodger* was reviewed in the *New York Sun* by the paper's former critic John Grierson, who had recently returned to the mother country and was about to take charge of the Empire Marketing Board film unit, another outcome of the Imperial Conference. Grierson, the future godfather of documentary, set out to argue that British cinema lacked the virtues he intended to instill in it, and declared *The Lodger* to be "bogey-bogey murder and mystery stuff, laid on with a shovel as in the days of ancient hokum, but its tedium is relieved by some excellent camera work."[60] A week after that, however, Grierson called Hitchcock "the most outstanding" of British directors, "a young man of twenty-six, with a fine sense of camera, but somewhat untutored emotionally. He is very good with types and experiences of which he has personal knowledge. His worst fault is a tendency to stage trickery."[61] This would become Grierson's standard line on Hitchcock in years to come.

At one of Levy's houses, the Futurist in Lime Street, Liverpool, *The Lodger* was shown with Phonofilms.[62] It opened there on 7 March, by which time Miles Mander had made what history records as the most significant of them all. *As We Lie*, in which Mander directed himself alongside Lillian Hall-Davies, was first shown in late February. Mycroft described the film as a "bedroom comedy" that used sounds from a radio as well as dialogue.[63] About the time it was made, Mander had been cast in *Downhill*, which began production at Poole Street on the day *The Lodger* opened, 17 January, but he had fallen ill and did not appear in the film. He would later claim to be "the first man in the world to apply modern film technique to the talking picture."[64] His films of early 1927 "contained sound, music and dialogue. I used exteriors, talking 'off,' tacit periods and angular set-ups, but although I used no titles, I obstinately refused to put dialogue on every foot, as one of the financiers suggested. In one film I think I had as many as 51 shots in 1,300ft." This romantic account appeared in the spring of 1929, when Hitchcock was about to present *Blackmail*, which was similarly conceived on the principle that "too much talk has ruined many a promising talking film."[65] In the interim, Reville had written the script for Mander's first feature, *The First Born*, adapted from his play *Common People*, first performed at the Hampstead Everyman in April 1927, and costarring Madeleine Carroll; and Hitchcock had twice directed Lillian Hall-Davies.

In light of these and other connections, it is highly likely that Hitchcock was aware of Mander's obscure doings at Clapham in the first months of 1927, and not unlikely that their films were shown together: *The Lodger* was shown with Phonofilms in Leeds as well as Liverpool, and quite possibly elsewhere. It is also likely that Hitchcock would have known from the trade press of the progress of synchronized sound in the United States. In January and February there were widely publicized demonstrations of Fox's Movietone and General Electric's sound-on-film system, RCA Photophone, and on 23 February it was announced that the "big four" combines except Fox would form a committee to decide how synchronized sound should be adopted, settling the problem of standardization.[66] Fox went ahead with Movietone, which together with Warners' Vitaphone productions would make sound films part of the landscape rather than a novelty over the next year, while RCA would create RKO, the fifth Hollywood combine, to exploit Photophone. It was with this system that Hitchcock would make *Blackmail*; according to Lejeune, in her obituary of John Maxwell, he used a secondhand set that had been sent to the University of Cambridge for laboratory tests.[67]

In the same months, wittingly or otherwise, Hollywood was beginning to attract writers who were equipped to make the pictures talk. In January 1927, Robert Sherwood, days before the Broadway opening of his first play *The Road to Rome*, commented on the "strange fact that few of the men and women who have approached Hollywood with reputations have accomplished anything in the citadel of the cinema."[68] Celebrated playwrights, such as he was about to become, "have flopped in Hollywood, while previously unidentified graduates of newspaper sporting pages have achieved glory and prosperity." Within the trade, Laurence Stallings, of the *New York World*, was considered the first of the newspapermen; his war stories lay behind both *What Price Glory*, adapted from a play he had written with Maxwell Anderson, and *The Big Parade*.[69] Stallings, however, had not settled on the Coast, and it was Mankiewicz, considered the second of the breed, who in Pauline Kael's words "spearheaded the movement of that whole Broadway style of wisecracking, fast-talking, cynical-sentimental entertainment onto the national scene."[70] Ben Hecht, credited writer of *Spellbound* and *Notorious*, must have received Mankiewicz's famous, possibly apocryphal invitation to Hollywood in late 1926;

he had been hired by Paramount by December, and his first screenplay, *Underworld*, went into production in March 1927, directed by Josef von Sternberg. Few of Hitchcock's films of the 1940s were made without a contribution from the "Algonquin-to-Hollywood group" of the late 1920s.

"One of the most dramatic days," wrote Balcon in his autobiography, "in my association with C.M. was the day of the passing of the 1927 Cinematograph Act."[71] The bill had its first reading in Parliament—a formality—on 10 March, was debated on the 16th, and was voted on after the debate resumed on the 22nd. It was carried by 243 votes to 135, thus becoming an act—known ever after as the Quota Act. The day Balcon remembered was more likely 14 March, when the *Evening News* covered the bill's progress with a photograph of Balcon, "giving my connection with the matter a disproportionate prominence," which threw Woolf into a fury; after all, both of them had publicly opposed it. That evening, however, Woolf, without referring to the fact he had vowed never to speak to Balcon again, told him that later that night he had a meeting with Isidore Ostrer at the Carlton Hotel—to discuss the absorption of W. & F., and therefore Gainsborough, into the Ostrer brothers' Gaumont company. Balcon felt that he had talked him out of it, but the contract was signed within a few days. The creation of the Gaumont-British Picture Corporation, of which W. & F. and Gainsborough became parts, was made public on the day after the Quota Act's passing, 23 March.

That the Ostrers were expanding Gaumont into a combine on the American pattern cannot have been news to Balcon. Late the previous year, the brothers had acquired the Biocolor circuit of about fifteen cinemas, and they were rumored to be bidding for the Capitol. In early February, in her husband's absence, Lady Cunliffe-Lister had attended a ceremony to mark the expansion of Gaumont's studio at Shepherd's Bush. Making the launch of Gaumont-British coincide with the coming of the quota that would ensure that the new corporation had a protected market was a theatrical flourish. Days later it was announced that the Ostrers had won control of the Davis chain, reportedly paying £550,000 for the four cinemas it now comprised—almost all of it for the Marble Arch and Shepherd's Bush Pavilions. Isidore Ostrer and Israel and Alfred Davis had taken the Train Bleu to Monte Carlo to negotiate the sale with the chain's original boss, Minnie Davis.[72] In April, Gaumont-British was floated on the stock market, and it continued to grow. In 1928 it acquired a stake in the Bernstein chain, then Provincial Cinematograph Theatres, and soon it formed half of a virtual duopoly that would dominate the British film industry into the 1950s and beyond.

The other half was formed by British International Pictures, as British National became on the last day of March 1927, when the new company, representing John Maxwell and his allies—and no longer I. W. Schlesinger—acquired the old company's assets. Those assets included Hitchcock, though on the day the new company came into being he was in Nice, preparing to shoot his last film for Gainsborough, an adaptation of *Easy Virtue*, Noël Coward's "deliberate farewell to the well-made play," as John Russell Taylor would characterize it.[73] It was probably during this visit that Rex Ingram, born Reginald Hitchcock in Dublin, told Hitchcock to change his name if he wanted to get ahead. British International, like Gaumont-British, grew and grew, becoming, in 1933, while still under Maxwell's chairmanship, the Associated British Picture Corporation. Gaumont-British eventually formed part of the even larger Rank organization, but ABC, originally BIP's theater chain, survived into the next century.

There were parallel responses to the American film oligopoly elsewhere, of a comparably corporatist character. Throughout the first months of 1927, it was reported that Ufa sought refinancing and an exit from its arrangement with Paramount and MGM. At the end of March, within days of the formation of both Gaumont-British and BIP, the combine came under the control of a syndicate led by Alfred Hugenberg. Immediately before the deal was made, the Berlin correspondent of the *Manchester Guardian* reported "persistent rumours" of his "intentions of producing on 'anti-Jewish' lines."[74] Thoroughly opposed not only to Versailles, Locarno, and the League, but to the Weimar republic itself, Hugenberg would still be at the helm of Ufa at the time of the Nazi victory in 1933, in which his party's support was instrumental, and remained the dominant shareholder until 1937, when Ufa came under direct state control.

Hitchcock would work for both British combines in turn. His first film for BIP, *The Ring*, shot in the summer of 1927, was written with Mycroft, who joined the company at the end of the year as a script editor. "The friendship remained—until I left Fleet Street," Mycroft recalled.[75] "Then we became enemies." Within a few years Iris Barry felt that Hitchcock had "in all the magnificent equipment of the Elstree studios lost a trifle of that very personal touch which won such immediate recognition for his films."[76] He never made his "screen forecast of days to come." By the time Hitchcock left in early 1933, Mycroft was production chief. In Mycroft's account, Maxwell caused Hitchcock's departure by rejecting his plans for *The Return of Bulldog Drummond*. According to Hitchcock, it was Mycroft who "was intriguing against me and the picture."[77] Hitchcock had been negotiating a move to Alexander Korda's London Films for some months before the film was announced, in January 1933, and it is not surprising that it was canceled once the deal with Korda—fruitless as it turned out—was done. *The Man Who Knew Too Much*, as the project was retitled, became Hitchcock's first film for Gaumont-British, where he was reunited with Balcon, as well as Montagu and MacPhail, among other characters from the *Lodger* saga.

The Lodger was already a relic. It had been made at the end of one epoch and was released at the beginning of a new one. The change within the British film industry in 1927 was palpable—the studio in which the film was made, and the cinemas where it was trade-shown and opened were swept away. In the same moment, the almost total dominance of the American film was checked. Though both of the new combines would be closely entangled with their American counterparts, the shift in the balance of power was unmistakable. *The Lodger*, however, was made at the high point of American dominance. Except for the growing rumble of the rival sound systems, the change in Hollywood during the same timespan was less dramatic, but in crucial respects it became the Hollywood Hitchcock would come to know when he first went there. He was wedded to the ways of an earlier era, and so was perhaps better suited to a later one—the period of Hollywood's decadence, amid the rise of television, in the 1950s. Many of his important collaborators in that decade were children when *The Lodger* was released. The screenwriter Ernest Lehman, who conceived of *North by Northwest* as the "Hitchcock picture to end all Hitchcock pictures," was born in December 1915, the month—so to speak—when the seed of the true Hitchcock picture was planted.[78] The first true Hitchcock, the template for all the films to come, was fixed in a world that was about to disappear.

8 Wilshire Palms

On Thursday 12 September 1935, *The 39 Steps* opened at the Roxy, one of New York's and the world's most famous cinemas. Its first screening was a late-evening preview, following the outgoing film *Diamond Jim*; the full opening came the next day. Nearby the Capitol had Garbo in *Anna Karenina*, a David O. Selznick production for MGM, while Radio City Music Hall, RKO's showcase, had Fred Astaire and Ginger Rogers in *Top Hat*. Selznick had already announced his departure from MGM and was, at the time, staying at the Waldorf, putting together the finance for his next venture, Selznick International Pictures.[1] Hitchcock's name was not used in the ads, but the critics were aware of him. Many of them compared the new film with *The Man Who Knew Too Much*, which had opened six months earlier at a lesser Times Square theater, the Mayfair, and won admiring notices. On Friday 20 September, *The 39 Steps* was held over for a second week.

In November, when the film went on general release in Britain, C. A. Lejeune wrote that its maker "is the first national institution, along with the 'Cheshire Cheese' and the Savoy Grill, that itinerant American journalists demand to see."[2] Such was the American interest in Hitchcock that the interview was reprinted a month later in the *New York Times*. Lejeune recalled their first meeting, "when he was writing and ornamenting sub-titles for silent pictures. . . . All his instincts were towards visualisation, and all his training towards draughtsmanship. It was obvious to everyone except the commercial nabobs of the industry that some day he would direct pictures, and direct them supremely well." The American journalists, she went on, "expect to find a lean, tough, grim fellow, compound of Dashiell Hammett, Sherlock Holmes, and Perry Mason," a notion of which they were quickly disabused.

One such journalist, Eileen Creelman of the *New York Sun*, had published her account of meeting Hitchcock a few days earlier. They had met at the Palace Hotel in Kensington, halfway between Shepherd's Bush and the West End, and a short walk from 153 Cromwell Road, the Hitchcocks' home since their marriage. Hitchcock, she told her readers, "studies in what spare moments he can find the folders of steamship companies, railroads, travel agencies, airplane firms all over the world," and wanted to know "how the New York subway differed from the London underground," and "the best way to reach Jersey City from Manhattan."[3] After all, he "might make a picture about America some day. He might even make one here." Hitchcock had recently returned from Greece, where he had been researching his next film, *Secret Agent*. "'You can't do it,' he insisted; 'you simply can't do a picture unless you've seen the place.'"

Hitchcock was not a complete unknown before *The Man Who Knew Too Much*. Both British International and Gaumont-British had attempted to export him into the United States, and more than half of Hitchcock's sixteen preceding features had been shown there. To begin with, the two companies had put their hopes in the same familiar figure, J. D. Williams, who reemerged on the scene in the spring of 1928, having won a High Court action against his former colleagues in British National, at the helm of a new distribution company whose ambitions were expressed by its name, World Wide Pictures. In June that year Williams arrived in New York, amid a blizzard of press releases, with a consignment of British films that included no fewer than five Hitchcocks. In the event only one of these, *The Farmer's Wife*, was shown, more than eighteen months later, and at probably no more than one cinema.

The Lodger, having been sold to Arthur A. Lee, was not among the five, and it happened to open in New York in the same month, on 9 June 1928,

A program for the Fifth Avenue Playhouse, 1928.

under a new and unexplained title, *The Case of Jonathan Drew*, at the Fifth Avenue Playhouse. Located between Twelfth and Thirteenth Streets, the Playhouse was one of New York's first art cinemas—or, as *Variety* had recently dubbed them, "sure-seaters," so-called because "one is always sure of a seat."[4] Managed by Michael Mindlin, a Russian-born theater producer, it had opened as a cinema in October 1926, in the week *The Pleasure Garden* played on Broadway, announcing itself in the press as being "for the special presentation of motion pictures of distinction in an atmosphere of Old World charm. It will be known as the 'theater of unexpected things.' Anything may happen, a recitation or a recital, a solo or a harangue, a speaker or an uncensored film."[5]

Occupying part of the ground floor of an eight-story office building, the Playhouse seated 264, and the orchestra amounted to a piano and a violin. *Variety* saw it as "out of the way for all but the Greenwich Village contingent."[6] By June 1928 it was part of a small but growing chain, and *Jonathan Drew* had had its US debut at the Playhouse's sister venue in Chicago at the end of May. Run by Mindlin's brother Frederick, the Chicago Playhouse, seating 573, was in the Fine Arts Building, facing Grant Park. It had opened in September 1927 with *Battleship Potemkin*. As was the practice in the New York sure-seaters, the Chicago Playhouse offered free coffee and cigarettes, and its staff would project on-screen jokes at the expense of the features. "You're not only supposed to be an intellectual when you go to this theater," wrote Mae Tinée, pseudonymous critic of the *Chicago Daily Tribune*. "You're supposed to be an intellectual with a lusty sense of humor."[7] *Jonathan Drew* "went above house average to $3,200" for the week.[8]

When it arrived on Fifth Avenue, *Jonathan Drew* replaced Ruttmann's *Berlin* as the main feature. The program included an American experimental film, *Rhythms of a Great City*, directed by Harry Sweet, formerly a director at Mack Sennett Studios, and an old Chaplin short, *The Cure*, from 1917. It had a mixed reception. The *New York Times*'s Mordaunt Hall noticed its "very, very excellent beginning,"[9] though Mordaunt Hall, according to Hitchcock, was a former colleague, assistant to Tom Geraghty in the editorial department at Poole Street during the last days of Famous Players-Lasky's tenancy.[10] Recalling that it "was rather highly praised by John Grierson, the Scotch critic," Richard Watts of the *New York Herald Tribune* found that although "it is hard to be enthusiastic about the direction, save in a scene or two, it is undeniable that the production is much less amateurish than is usually the case in works that come to us from the English studios."[11] *Variety*'s reviewer reported that "Mike Mindlin has written a special leader for the feature, setting forth that Alfred Hitchcock is the best director the English industry has."[12]

After a week on Fifth Avenue, *The Case of Jonathan Drew* was moved to the 55th Street Playhouse, a sure-seater in the heart of the entertainment district that had recently joined the Mindlin chain. A converted stables seating 299, it had lost money under a succession of managers including Symon Gould, the director of the Film Arts Guild, New York's equivalent to the Film Society. Mindlin and his associates Joseph Fliesler and Louis Lusty had turned it around, though the three had latterly parted company when Mindlin put his wife, Betty, in charge of both houses. In August, *Jonathan Drew* appeared at the St. George Playhouse in Brooklyn, very recently but no longer part of the Mindlin chain; by the autumn both the St. George and the 55th Street Playhouses had been ceded to Fliesler, and the lease on the Chicago venue had expired, leaving the Mindlins with only the Fifth Avenue Playhouse and an unfinished site on Fifty-Seventh Street.

The Case of Jonathan Drew was on Arthur Lee's books, and may have played elsewhere, in houses like those where *The Pleasure Garden* had played; or it may not have done. The new market represented by the Mindlin cinemas—the film art movement—had barely existed when Lee took the rights to *The Lodger* in 1926, and was still at an early stage in 1928. In particular, there were few consistent outlets for film criticism outside the trade press and the dailies. The Greenwich Village contingent only fitfully found its voice, in publications like the *New Republic*, which—in common with the other weeklies—did not review *Jonathan Drew*. That *The Lodger* was shown across the Mindlin chain is in itself evidence of a critical reputation in the making, decades before critics began the arduous task of making Hitchcock safe for highbrow consumption. But without critics, without repertory programming, and without the kind of publicity that was generated by a hit like *The 39 Steps*, it was practically difficult to sustain such a reputation.

The next Hitchcock release in the United States was *Blackmail*, handled by Sono Art–World Wide, as it had become after Williams's inevitable departure from his own company. In the hope of attracting a more powerful distributor, John Maxwell's lieutenant Arthur Dent traveled to New York and booked the film into the Selwyn Theatre, where it opened on 4 October 1929 and was kept on for more than a fortnight, closing just before the onset of the Wall Street crash. As the first British talkie, *Blackmail* had won international attention on its London opening, and the

New York trade show was reviewed on the front page of *Film Daily*. But in November the *New York Times*'s film correspondent in London, Ernest Marshall, wrote that *Blackmail*'s reception in the United States "is a very sore point at Elstree, where it is generally believed that the verdict of the American critics should have secured for it a much warmer welcome from the trade."[13]

Sono Art–World Wide did find some bookings for *Blackmail*. In October 1930, a year after its opening in New York, *Blackmail* made its Los Angeles debut at the city's first sure-seater. The Filmarte, on Vine Street between Sunset and Santa Monica Boulevards, had been a weak link in the Fox chain, and in 1928 was given over to Regge Doran, a former Fox publicist, to run as she saw fit. Seymour Stern, writing in the little magazine *Experimental Cinema*, characterized its audience as "a stormy combination of Los Angeles radicals with 'White Russian' emigres."[14] Through 1930, having come under new management, it had specialized in silent "Red Russian" films. *Blackmail* was the second sound film to be shown there, and the first talkie.

In the interim, a handful of Hitchcocks, silent and sound, had had runs in New York sure-seaters, but the next opening of consequence was *Murder*, also in October 1930, at the George M. Cohan, which British International had leased for a season. *Murder* was well reviewed, and had a marketable star in Herbert Marshall, and in December 1930 it was picked up for distribution by Columbia, a former Poverty Row studio whose fortunes had recently risen with the release of Frank Capra's *Ladies of Leisure*.[15] This was a modest victory, however, and led nowhere. *The Skin Game*, which was booked into the Little Carnegie, the sure-seater Mindlin had built on Fifty-Seventh Street, in June 1931, was the last of Hitchcock's films to open in New York for four years.

At the end of May 1935, the sales team of the Gaumont-British Picture Corporation of America gathered at the Warwick Hotel in midtown Manhattan for their first annual convention. Among the ninety salesmen present were "Mop 'Em Up" Max Mazur from Chicago, complaining about the heat, and J. H. "Ole Mint Julep" Butner from Atlanta, complaining that nothing stronger than lemonade was being served to fight it, *Motion Picture Daily* reported.[16] Leading figures from the industry had been booked as guest speakers, including Sidney Kent and Spyros Skouras, the most powerful men within the Fox empire, though the latter could not attend—Fox's merger with Twentieth Century was being formalized in the same week.

The first day's speakers were Howard Cullman, trustee of the Roxy—once Fox's flagship, now in receivership—and Morris Lightman, president of Malco Theatres, around Memphis. Both had contracted to take the whole of the Gaumont-British export offer for 1935–36, sixteen films, five of which were screened for the delegates, one of them being *The 39 Steps*. There was, said Cullman, "no longer a distinction to be made between Hollywood and British films." Gaumont's US branch was the work of George Weeks, sales manager, and Arthur A. Lee, vice president. The dalliance with J. D. Williams notwithstanding, Lee had remained Gaumont-British's man in New York since the 1920s. The connection with Fox went back almost as far. In 1929, during his most exuberant phase of expansion, William Fox had bought 49 percent of Metropolis and Bradford Trust, the holding company that controlled Gaumont-British, with the Ostrers owning an equal share. Fox had done this on the assumption that the Gaumont chain would favor Fox films, but Gaumont had failed to live up to its side of the bargain, or so it was alleged, and by 1932 Fox's successors were suing the Ostrers to recover their £4 million investment. Both sides pulled back from the brink. Sidney Kent, Fox's new president, joined the Gaumont board; Gaumont would carry Fox product in Britain; and in 1933–34 Fox would release half a dozen Gaumont films in the United States, with Lee handling the rest. In early 1934 Madeleine Carroll, the star of Victor Saville's Gaumont-British production *I Was a Spy*, which had opened at the Roxy that January, was sent to Fox to star in John Ford's *The World Moves On*.

This was a substantial advance for Gaumont and for British cinema, after years of near-invisibility in the United States, but the arrangement was not renewed. Both sides claimed responsibility. Some Fox salesmen said that the British films "have been difficult to sell"[17] while Gaumont was frustrated that they had taken only six of them.[18] Rather than retreat, Gaumont decided to build up its own distribution organization around Lee for the 1934–35 season, though Fox would handle physical distribution, and "Ole Mint Julep" and his colleagues would operate out of Fox's branch offices. The new policy was launched with much hoopla in the autumn of 1934. In October the Skouras brothers' circuit "signed a deal for the entire list."[19] In November, Weeks "closed deals with A. C. Hayman's first run houses in Buffalo and Niagara Falls and with Elmer Rhoden, Fox Midwest circuit, for first run in Kansas City and 60 other spots."[20] A national network came together bit by bit.

The Man Who Knew Too Much was not a lead title. When the second half of the 1934–35 slate was announced to the trade papers, it was fourth on the list.[21] The venue chosen for its opening, the Mayfair, seated twenty-two hundred, fewer than the Roxy or the Music Hall, both of which had been used for Gaumont titles in the same season. It opened on 21 March 1935, and managed to take more in its second week—$16,000—than in its first.[22] Eileen Creelman was among those who gave it a rave. "It's not big time," *Variety* advised, "largely because of paucity of names for the U.S., but it ought to please any audience that can be coaxed in."[23] At the time it opened, Michael Balcon was in Hollywood, seeking "names" for future productions. Its second holdover marked "the first time in three years that a picture has run this long" at the Mayfair.[24] During its third week, *Waltzes from Vienna*, the film Hitchcock had made before *The Man Who Knew Too Much*, opened at the tiny Westminster Cinema, nearby on Forty-Ninth Street, as *Strauss' Great Waltz*. At the start of its fourth and last week at the Mayfair, RKO booked *The Man Who Knew Too Much* "for first-run in its 45 theaters in New York and Brooklyn, beginning May 1."[25]

By then it had begun to open across the United States. "On May 3, 1935, a Gaumont-British picture called 'The Man Who Knew Too Much' opened at the Fox Theater with a minimum of fanfare," wrote Mildred Martin, veteran critic of the *Philadelphia Inquirer*, on the occasion of the remake twenty-one years later.[26] "English films, so American movie goers complained, were not only on the dull side, but just plain hard to understand because of poor sound technique," she went on. The Fox, on Market Street, seated some three thousand. "There was nothing especially exciting, either, about the cast." She considered Peter Lorre the best known, for *M.* "Well, those, including this reviewer, who did go to the Fox on what now seems a more or less historic occasion, sat up and took notice." It took $13,500, above average for the house.[27] Hitchcock's was "a new name but one which was to blaze to fame later that year when his 'The 39 Steps' began making the movie rounds." Also in May, *The Man Who Knew Too Much* played in Kansas City, Minneapolis, Pittsburgh, Buffalo, Newark, Boston—mostly in cinemas seating more than two thousand.

In Los Angeles, however, where it opened on 28 May, Paul "Prize Winner" de Outo—another of the salesmen present at the Warwick—had managed to book only the eight-hundred-seat Filmarte, now under the management of Hugo Riesenfeld, the Vienna-born composer who had held sway at the Rivoli and the Rialto in their 1920s pomp. But through June and into July *The Man Who Knew Too Much* continued to play in large venues elsewhere—the RKO Albee in Providence, the State-Lake in Chicago, the Missouri in St Louis. *The 39 Steps*'s first engagements in the United States preceded its opening at the Roxy. During August, while *The Man Who Knew Too Much* was still playing across the continent, Hitchcock's follow-up opened in San Francisco, Cincinnati, Baltimore. It opened in Los Angeles at the twenty-one-hundred-seat United Artists Theater, downtown, on 7 September, five days before it opened in New York. When it was held over at the Roxy, Lee wrote to Mark Ostrer, "We are pretty well bucked up by the success of 'Thirty Nine Steps' at the Roxy. I believe it is putting new life into our sales force and is going to help tremendously. This is the first time we have made any money for the exhibitors."[28]

In London a month later, before meeting Hitchcock, Creelman spoke to Balcon and Ivor Montagu, who explained Hitchcock's secret: "It doesn't matter really what you do so long as you do it so fast no one has time to know what it's all about."[29]

At the end of 1935, the *New York Times* reported the troubled birth of a "'kibitzer' prize committee," conceived in opposition to the Academy of Motion Picture Arts and Sciences on the grounds that "Hollywood was too insular a community to appraise the motion picture with complete non-partisan honesty."[30] Trade and fan publications were ineligible, but even with these exclusions, the composition of the New York Film Critics, later the New York Film Critics Circle, was unstable. Creelman left it before the first vote was cast because she found the anti-Hollywood publicity to be undignified, though of the Academy she declared that "I have never taken it seriously enough to grow upset."[31] Meanwhile, according to the *Times*'s film editor Frank Nugent, the "male clique" sought to remedy the original panel's near-gender parity by trying to include "the film critics (all men) of The New Yorker, Time, The New Masses, The New Republic and The Nation."[32] The latter three were voted out by "the feminine contingent" because of their radical politics, leading John Mosher of the *New Yorker* to quit, "since only one other weekly magazine is included," whereupon said magazine's critic, that of *Time*, followed him out.[33] At the same meeting, Nugent continued, "the question arose about the propriety of admitting foreign pictures to the eligible list." Nugent claimed that the opposition believed "that Europe was still remiss in its debt payments to the United States," incurred during the Great War; they were outvoted.

The NYFC's inaugural ceremony, presided over by Robert Sherwood and broadcast by NBC, was held at the Ritz-Carlton on 1 March 1936. It is doubtful that anyone expected Greta Garbo to attend, but nor did any of the other winners—not Ben Hecht and Charles MacArthur, for the script of *The Scoundrel*, not Charles Laughton, not John Ford, though he spoke over the radio from Hollywood. Although Ford's *The Informer* had been the unanimous choice for best film, his victory as best director was narrower. According to the *Times*, when the critics voted on 1 January, Ford had come in second on the first ballot, losing by one vote to the only foreigner on the list—Alfred Hitchcock. A majority vote was required, however, and on the second vote "the critics swung almost entirely to Mr. Ford, with Mr. Hitchcock getting minority recognition."[34] The presence of Creelman or of the radical magazine critics might have produced a different result, but even without them Hitchcock was identified, on the basis of just two films, as a director with a distinctive style. It fell to one of the radicals, Otis Ferguson, the *New Republic*'s film critic since 1934, to attempt to capture it in words. He had not, in fact, been convinced by *The Man Who Knew Too Much*, and did not review *The 39 Steps* at the time of its release; his encomium was occasioned by *Secret Agent*, when it came to the Roxy in June 1936.

"Later on I often wondered about the fact that I made no attempt to visit America until 1937; I'm still puzzled about that," Hitchcock told Truffaut.[35] Gaumont-British was in the midst of a power struggle in 1936–37, played out in boardrooms, courtrooms, on the stock exchange, and via transatlantic telephone calls made from Mayfair flats in the dead of night. In November 1936 Angus MacPhail told Adrian Brunel that the company was "only going to make a few pictures next year" and that his department had "had the weed killer liberally applied."[36] MGM had tried to acquire joint control of the company with Fox; when they were thwarted in this endeavor, partly through the intervention of John Maxwell, who called it his patriotic duty to keep Gaumont British, MGM poached Balcon to head up a new British production unit, and MacPhail went with him. Montagu had gone to make films for the Republican cause in the Spanish Civil War. Charles Bennett, Hitchcock's principal screenwriter, left for the United States. Interviewed by the *New York Times* as he passed through in March 1937, Bennett "wished aloud that Alfred Hitchcock might see all this as we plodded through the cobbled streets that wind under Brooklyn Bridge."[37] He made his way to Los Angeles by car, "in order not to miss anything—Chicago, Arizona, the cowboys, the oil towns."[38]

Hitchcock, Alma Reville, their daughter Patricia, and writing assistant Joan Harrison, arrived in New York on 23 August 1937. He told reporters that he was the only director still under contract to the ailing Gaumont, but also—falsely—that he "doesn't plan any huddles with film execs" during the twelve-day trip.[39] Two years earlier, Creelman had written that Hitchcock "wanted to know on what floor of Radio City was the Rainbow Room, and how it appeared."[40] On this visit he was shown around by its manager; five years later he would include it in *Saboteur*. Hitchcock also went downtown to the Eighth Street Playhouse, a sure-seater built by the Film Arts Guild in 1929, to see *The 39 Steps*—"for the first time," according to the *New York Sun*.[41]

On the evening of the day his Gaumont contract expired, 31 May 1938, Hitchcock took part in a press conference at the Regent Street offices of Mayflower Productions, Erich Pommer and Charles Laughton's new venture, backed by John Maxwell, to announce the title of his next film, *Jamaica Inn*, from Daphne du Maurier's bestseller. The next morning he and Alma Reville left Southampton aboard the RMS *Queen Mary*, bound eventually for Los Angeles. Creelman, who had been on the Coast during his first visit, interviewed him in New York, at Twenty-One. "He collects information greedily, asking what he may expect to see in Hollywood, how this is done, where this or that place may be," she wrote. "Usually he knows such details. For years he has collected time tables, taking much pleasure in planning imaginary trips. He knows thoroughly the geography of this city, knew it even before he arrived."[42]

Hitchcock did not know Los Angeles in the same way. On his return he wrote a series of three articles about his first visit for the *Evening News*. "Hollywood amazed me," he wrote. "Sixteen years in British studios have taught me something of the huge organisation that is necessary to make a picture. But the efficiency of Hollywood was a surprise."[43] Hitchcock had said in an interview a few months earlier that David O. Selznick was the only Hollywood producer he would work for, but his agent—Myron Selznick—had other ideas, and made sure his client was shopped around the other studios before signing with his brother. In the *Evening News* articles, Hitchcock claimed that "although they are brothers their deals are conducted on strictly business lines," but in reality the Selznicks' relationship was a combustible mix of rivalry and collusion.[44]

At Paramount the Hitchcocks were honored with a luncheon in the commissary, where they dined with the leading directors of the day— Mamoulian, Capra, Hawks—as well as Adolph Zukor, who had been at the top of the company when Hitchcock joined at the bottom and Reville near it. In one studio Hitchcock "saw a full-sized trawler in a huge tank for some sea scenes," and while he was familiar with back projection, "the background of this scene I saw was made up of *three* screens showing a wide panorama of seascape and each part blended into the other without noticeable join."[45] The Filmarte had gone over to Hollywood revivals, but in the last week of June, with or without Alma, Hitchcock could have visited the Grand Theater downtown to see the new subtitled import from Sweden, *Intermezzo*, and its rising star, Ingrid Bergman.

Selznick International was in the spotlight. It was the summer of *Gone with the Wind* casting rumors and within a few days of the Hitchcocks' arrival it was announced that Selznick would have to partner with MGM in order to cast Clark Gable and Norma Shearer. On the morning of 6 July, Carole Lombard—then in a celebrated romance with Gable— began a week in the role of press agent for the company, essentially as a screwball routine. Her first job was to announce a new Selznick production to a throng of journalists including two syndicated columnists with a long rivalry ahead of them, the veteran Louella O. Parsons and the neophyte Hedda Hopper, of the *Los Angeles Examiner* and *Los Angeles Times*, respectively. Lombard, said Hopper, "put on a swell show. Sirens shrieked, guns popped. Carole dressed in black tailored suit, wearing orchid, sat beside bowl of American beauties, and was in her usual form—tops."[46] Her news, said Parsons, was that "Hitchcock has signed with her boss, David O.," to make *Titanic*. "'Better story,' we told the new P.A., 'if you can name a few actors.' 'Well, I think any director who comes six thousand miles to put his name on a contract as Mr. Hitchcock did, is worth a head-line story,' was her reply."[47]

In 1969 Hitchcock would write that on arriving in Hollywood, "I found myself a minor figure in a vast film industry made up of entrepreneurs who headed the studios, and I became involved in the making of a picture under the producer system."[48] In this conventional portrait of the golden age, the producer, epitomized by Irving Thalberg, "was king," and what had emerged since the 1950s was to be lamented as the "package deal" sys-tem in which "anyone can be a producer, provided he is able to purchase a property, interest a star, and 'put it together.'" Yet in 1938 Hitchcock had written that the "development of the agent system in Hollywood was the thing that impressed me more than anything."[49] The agents, he had learned—"they are called 'flesh-peddlers'"—were the "uncrowned kings of filmland," and did more than negotiate on behalf of talent. The agent "buys stories and so, altogether, is in the position of universal provider for the producers." If Hitchcock exaggerated the power of agents at this date, it served the purpose of his own.

"Like a bombshell into the Hollywood summer lull," Parsons had writ-ten a few days before Hitchcock's article appeared, "comes Agent Myron Selznick's hat-in-the-ring announcement that he will become a producer himself."[50] This was, she went on, "an open challenge," since Selznick pro-posed to package together talent, bypassing the producers, and paying on a percentage basis. The first film to be made under the arrangement was to have been Lubitsch's *The Shop around the Corner*; Lombard and William Powell—both clients of Selznick, both named in Hitchcock's arti-cles—would star in the second.[51] The scheme swiftly fell apart because, in David Thomson's account, the moguls combined to deny Myron distribu-tion; intriguingly, "it is not certain what role David played."[52] Neverthe-less, Hitchcock, at the height of the producer system, had witnessed the birth of the system that would succeed it.

"Distances are great in Hollywood and you seldom see people walking," Hitchcock reflected after his three weeks there.[53]

> To walk is like being a tramp and you may invite the sort of attention from the police that tramps expect. An Englishman, just arrived, was once arrested "on suspicion" because he was found walking in Hollywood at 11.30 p.m.
>
> Everyone runs a car and usually drives it himself. The sidewalks—pavements we would call them—are deserted even in the busiest hours of the day. The only section of the sidewalks which I would describe as well used is that part between the hotel I stayed at and the office of my agent. I walked that bit for exercise, much to the dismay of my hired chauffeur, who kept pleading with me to take a lift.

A few months before the Hitchcocks' visit, Cedric Belfrage had published a novel, *Promised Land*, as the February 1938 selection of the Left Book Club. Taking place against the backdrop of Los Angeles's growth since the late nineteenth century, the novel's characters include a journalist who returns to the city in the early 1920s after a long absence during which Hollywood has become the center of the film world, and Beverly Hills the home of its elite. "The sidewalks were beautifully neat ribbons of smooth concrete slipping past and behind. Practically nobody walked on them and their virginal appearance suggested that practically nobody ever had or would."[54] The journalist writes that this is part of what makes Los Angeles "the ideal location for the movie factories," since movies, being a branch of the "international dope trade," should be made "far from what the ordinary man and woman know as the realities of life."[55] Myron Selznick's office was in Beverly Hills at 9460 Wilshire Boulevard, practically next door to the Beverly-Wilshire hotel. "Whether I shall be able to keep up the tramp stuff when I return early next year to make a film there," wrote Hitchcock, "I cannot say."

Talk of remaking *The Lodger*, in sound and color, got into the press in January 1941. Hitchcock was about to release *Mr. and Mrs. Smith*, his comedy with Carole Lombard, whose Bel Air house he was then renting, and was about to shoot *Suspicion*. Both films were for RKO, whither his flesh had been peddled by the Selznick brothers. Selznick International had been dormant since the opening of *Rebecca* the previous spring, though the publicity department was being revived to campaign for the Academy Awards. In the wake of the shattering success of *Gone with the Wind*, David was "faced with the problem of competing with himself," and "reading scripts like mad," reported Louella Parsons in the *Los Angeles Examiner*.[56] "He has asked Alfred Hitchcock to try and clear the rights to 'The Lodger,' Mrs. Belloc Lowndes' famous mystery story which Hitchcock made 12 years ago in London." Selznick had in mind Joan Fontaine and Charles Boyer for the leads.

Things were rather more advanced than Parsons let on, and rather more involved, because the project was a source of friction between the Selznicks. Hitchcock and Myron had purchased the rights from Lowndes in the summer of 1940, shortly before Hitchcock directed a half-hour radio adaptation of the story as a pilot episode for CBS, broadcast on 22 July. *Rebecca* was on wide release in the United States at the time; in London, bracing itself for aerial bombardment, it was in its fourth week at the Gaumont cinema, as the Capitol had been renamed. There was interest in the Lowndes property. In May, Parsons had reported that Orson Welles, then preparing to shoot *Citizen Kane* at RKO, had "ordered a half dozen copies" of the novel with a view to filming it.[57] Hitchcock's radio version was narrated by and starred Herbert Marshall, whom he had recently directed in *Foreign Correspondent*, and used musical themes written for CBS by Bernard Herrmann—their first, unacknowledged, collaboration.[58]

David O. Selznick was only informed of all this later, and in a memo to Dan O'Shea, one of his executives, a week after the broadcast, wondered whether Hitchcock should be "added to the ranks of Leigh, Fontaine, etc. who are doing whatever they damn please without any control or discipline from us"—and even considered telling RKO that Hitchcock had been working "for himself on their time."[59] With this off his chest, however, Selznick called *The Lodger* "a very exciting piece of property" that might be "an ideal vehicle in which to introduce" Jean Gabin, "because of the very little dialogue required of the lead." Gabin, he thought, "would be very anxious indeed to get out of France right now, and that we might work out the type of deal that he refused in happier days." Selznick saw Fontaine as the likely female lead—or possibly Bergman, "although I believe an English girl is required."

Selznick asked O'Shea for a transcript of the radio broadcast, and later in 1940 asked whether it might be possible to have a print of Hitchcock's first version of *The Lodger* sent over from England—a request that would be repeated but never fulfilled.[60] At the end of October, Selznick's New York representative Kay Brown, who had brought both *Rebecca* and *Gone with the Wind* to the studio, told him that "THE LODGER is wonderful. Hitchcock should make it and it should be an easy picture to cast."[61] O'Shea was by now looking into the property's copyright status, evidently unconvinced that the rights had been Lowndes's to sell when Hitchcock and Myron bought them.

At the start of December 1940, Selznick wrote O'Shea a summary of a long conversation he had had with Hitchcock about the project. Both men were agreed on Fontaine, but for the male lead they now contemplated Boyer, just as Parsons would report, though as "the next best bet" after Laurence Olivier, who was committed to the war effort.[62] The casting of Boyer apparently suggested to Hitchcock a switch of location to New Orleans. Hitchcock was also "trying to sell us the idea of doing it in color, which he realizes would add to the cost." It still rankled with Selznick that Hitchcock had initiated the project without his knowledge, and he told O'Shea that "I don't deceive myself that any script done by Mrs. Hitchcock and Miss Harrison will be finished or will require much less work than if we started from scratch." Indeed, he described theirs as being an "illegal script," and wondered whether, if the film were not in the end made by Selznick International, he should prevent Hitchcock from making it elsewhere, "to stop him dead in his tricks [*sic*] on illegal activities of this kind."

Selznick had not seen the script, which does not seem to have survived—if there ever was one. The radio version may give some indication of what Hitchcock had in mind, however. Though necessarily compressed, its plot cleaves closer to the novel than had the film. As in the novel, the action is largely confined to the Buntings' house; Mrs. Bunting's financial rationale for not alerting anyone to her suspicions is explicit; Daisy is absent till halfway through; and there is no love triangle—and so no dress. Above all, the Lodger—Mr. Sleuth—is a "woman-hating teetotal fanatic," in Lowndes's words, prone to quoting scripture; as is the killer, though the final revelation of whether they are one and the same never arrives. Instead, the story collapses, with director Hitchcock, played by an actor, coming on to ask the actors how they think it ought to end, and refusing to give a definitive answer himself. Until that point, however, the radio

Hitchcock with Joan Harrison in Culver City. Photo by Peter Stackpole/The LIFE
Picture Collection via Getty Images.

play is a striking example of subjective suspense, being told, far more
strictly so than the film, from Mrs. Bunting's point of view—often literally
from her point of hearing, using sounds real and imagined. There is an
unmistakable reference to the famous "knife" scene from *Blackmail*. The
adaptation was not credited on air; in the press it was attributed to a Joan
Morrison. It seems abundantly more likely that the writer responsible was
Joan Harrison, who at the time it was broadcast was about to begin work
on *Suspicion*, also told from a single point of view, that of a murderer's
wife, played by Joan Fontaine.

In mid-January 1941, immediately after Parsons's report appeared, Selznick told O'Shea that he was "in a terrible state of confusion" over the project.[63] Hitchcock and Myron were, he said, "insistent that we give them a
decision," but they had not given him anything concrete to make a decision
about. He had heard "the records" of the radio version, "but I understand

that these are only partially Hitch's ideas, and do not really represent the picture, especially since the radio show had no finish." Selznick was "getting somewhat cold on the whole idea because of my feeling that we could utilize Hitch to much better advantage on a more topical subject."

In February 1941, early in the production of *Suspicion*, days before the Academy Awards ceremony at which *Rebecca* won best picture for Selznick, the *Los Angeles Times* provided more details of Hitchcock's plans. "Two of our finest directors," wrote Philip K. Scheuer, "expressed themselves in almost identical terms on the subject of color last week."[64] One was Mamoulian, the other was Hitchcock, "who dreams of remaking his first movie, Mrs. Belloc-Lowndes' 'The Lodger,' as his first Technicolor effort." Scheuer quoted Hitchcock describing the very same "red hat" idea that C. A. Lejeune had quoted in 1935, then wrote that for *The Lodger* he wanted to "frighten people to death with his colors. He'd start out with black and white (in effect), gradually introduce a yellow London fog, and then spring dripping red blood and other violent manifestations of the spectrum."[65] This too echoed what Hitchcock had said in the 1930s. "'Think what you could do with complexions,' he beamed," to Scheuer. "'Florid-faced doctor and chalk-white patient, for instance! The possibilities are endless.'"

Mr. and Mrs. Smith, the first of Hitchcock's American films to be set in the United States, had not been a critical success. In July 1941, Parsons wrote that she was "glad that Alfred Hitchcock is going to make a mystery story and leave screwy comedy to other directors."[66] *The Lodger*, which she said would be made at RKO, would be "the first psychological film to be made in color." Like *Suspicion*, it would also have been a retreat to a studio-made England. But for all his willingness to discuss with journalists what he had in store, Hitchcock still would not deliver a script to Selznick, despite entreaties. In August 1941, Selznick told O'Shea to tell Hitchcock to "cut out the nonsense." His only chance was "to let us see a script on it, which we can't understand why he won't do if he has a script as I suspect he has—and as I suspect he and Miss Harrison are now working on on our time." By then the project was probably doomed, at least as a Hitchcock film. Hitchcock went to Universal to make *Saboteur*; finding an ending for *Suspicion* had been torturous, and *The Lodger* would have presented a similar problem. Selznick International remained dormant. Harrison went her own way.[67] Hitchcock would not work in color until he made *Rope*, in 1948.

At the end of 1942, Hitchcock sold his interest in the property to Selznick's company, Vanguard Films, and then Vanguard and Myron sold their two half-shares on to Twentieth Century-Fox. Fox's remake was virtually in production when the deal formally went through, in July 1943. Before making the sale, Selznick had two attorneys look into the rights question. "As for the previous motion picture plays and radio productions of the novel," wrote a third attorney, hired to look over the work of the first two, "the history seems to be a little hazy and there apparently is some question as to whether the plays mentioned in the copyright reports were even based upon the novel."[68] The task of making the history less hazy, "IN ORDER MAKE TITLE SATISFACTORY TO PURCHASER TWENTIETH CENTURY FOX," fell to Selznick's representative in London, Jenia Reissar, who was instructed to procure photostats of, among other documents, "CONTRACT WITH H A VACHELL UNDER WHICH PROPERTY WAS DRAMATIZED AND PRESENTED UNDER TITLE QUOTE WHO IS HE UNQUOTE AT HAYMARKET THEATRE LONDON IN DECEMBER NINETEENFIFTEEN" and "CONTRACT PURSUANT TO WHICH THE HITCHCOCK GAINSBOROUGH PICTURE RELEASED IN NINETEEN TWENTYSEVEN WAS MADE."[69]

Reissar reported her findings in May 1943, by which time the remake was already being cast: "BELLOC LOWNDES ORIGINAL LODGER CONTRACTS DESTROYED HAS NO EVIDENCE SUPPORT CLAIM RIGHTS HAD REVERTED TO HER WHEN SHE SOLD HITCHCOCK STOP GAINSBOROUGH CANT TRACE COPY THEIR CONTRACT BUT SAY FEELS CERTAIN PROPERTY REVERTED AUTHOR." One line of enquiry was stymied "AS LAWYERS OFFICE WAS BLITZED."[70] The trail had gone cold—and it remains so—but Fox was satisfied that it was safe to proceed. As late as March, when the project was first announced at the studio, it was still a "question of debate" whether Hitchcock would take charge, according to the *Los Angeles Times*, but it was not to be.[71] *The Lodger* was remade by Fox while Hitchcock was at work on *Lifeboat*, at the same studio, at the same time.

By then, however, Hitchcock had drawn on *The Lodger* for what he would often call his favorite among his own films, *Shadow of a Doubt*, which opened in January 1943. The similarities extend from plot outline to small details—such as the propensity of Joseph Cotten's character, Uncle Charlie, the "Merry Widow Murderer," to leave money lying around. As in *The Lodger*, the audience is primed to suspect him before any other character does. If Daisy seems to will the Lodger's arrival, out of an unvoiced dissatisfaction with her fiancé and family, Teresa Wright's character, also called Charlie, actually invites her uncle into the family home, out of a definite dissatisfaction at the "rut" she believes them to have fallen into. As in the novel and Hitchcock's radio version of *The Lodger*, only one member of the household suspects the visitor—young Charlie—and her point of view predominates. She protects her uncle partly out of love, partly to spare the family shame, much as Mrs. Bunting does in the novel and the radio version. As in the novel and the film, the father of the house is addicted to crime fiction but oblivious to the criminal in his midst. The detective with whom young Charlie more or less falls in love is as uninspiring a character as Joe. Uncle Charlie, meanwhile, is a nihilist rather than a zealot, but the effect is much the same; both are avowedly woman-hating killers. In these ways the first true "British" Hitchcock became the model for the first true "American" Hitchcock.

In June 1939, two months after the Hitchcocks' arrival in Los Angeles, Alma Reville wrote to Iris Barry, who was planning to mount a Hitchcock exhibition at the Museum of Modern Art and was in search of documents and photographs. Reville was unable to provide much help: "I'm afraid we have destroyed quite a lot of stuff," she told Barry.[72] Explaining her delayed reply, she wrote that "time simply flies here, I am sure they go by a different clock to the civilized world." She had spent a month trying to find a furnished house at a reasonable rent, and had had to make do with an "ultra modern apartment" in the Wilshire Palms complex, on a stretch of Wilshire Boulevard separated from Beverly Hills to the east by the Los Angeles Country Club. The building had been completed in the interval between the Hitchcocks' first visit to Los Angeles in 1938 and what would, in time, prove to be their permanent move there; but at this moment their future was uncertain and Reville was not enamored of the place. "One finds one is always doing things one doesn't really want to and seeing people one doesn't want to, and the things one wants to do one never does. In fact it is an entirely different life to any other, and we're not being particularly gay either."

A few years later, Hitchcock used the same word when he described traveling with Thornton Wilder to Santa Rosa, in northern California, to research the setting of *Shadow of a Doubt,* and then writing it "back in Hollywood and away from civilization."[73] In "Hitch: A Tale of Two Cities," Peter Wollen wrote that Hitchcock wanted "to combine a view of the world that was quintessentially English" with "the gloss, sophistication and technical polish of Hollywood. He wanted both London and Los Angeles."[74] Liberated from London's "merciless social scene to which he felt fundamentally unfitted by his class and his cultural background," Los Angeles "gave him licence to turn himself into something of a caricature without the shame he might have felt in London."[75] But if Hitchcock wanted Los Angeles, he wanted very little of it. In the 1960s, long after the Hitchcocks had settled in Bel Air, Paul Mayersberg asked him about his interests outside work: "House and Garden, I'd say. Home lover. A few paintings collected. We live a very suburban life here. We're in bed by nine o'clock every night."[76] Soon afterward he gave Penelope Gilliatt the impression "that his reason for liking Hollywood is that it leaves him alone."[77]

Hitchcock did not keep up the tramp stuff as he had hoped. Even as *Titanic* was being announced, Selznick International was coming around to the property Hitchcock himself wanted to adapt. *Rebecca,* with a largely British cast, was set in Cornwall, and shot in Culver City, but takes place in the mind of its heroine. Figuratively speaking, Hitchcock remained inside the car for forty years, scarcely exposing a foot of film in the city outside the studios. Some of his American films, like *Shadow of a Doubt,* involved extensive location work; others were shot exclusively inside the studio; but in either case, while Hitchcock spent the next four decades in Los Angeles, almost exactly half his life, the films he made there do not exhibit the remotest interest in the place. "Seeing the place" made no difference. In the studios and on the backlots, he would recreate Mount Rushmore, a Rio de Janeiro mansion, and Manderley, but not the city, or urban region, in which he lived. The director who had started out wanting to do a night scene in the center of London would film on the streets of San Francisco and New York and elsewhere, but not in the place he made his home.

Toward the end of Hitchcock's career, in May 1972, Truffaut interviewed him for French television, and asked which of his films he would remake if he could. Hitchcock's answer was *The Lodger.* He was in France for the

Cannes film festival launch of what would turn out to be his penultimate film, *Frenzy*. Remarking that this was his "first European movie in twenty years," Truffaut asked Hitchcock to comment on the difference between his work in Hollywood and his work in England.[78] "When I enter the studios," came the reply, "and the heavy doors close behind me, there is no difference. A coal mine is always a coal mine." But *Frenzy* had been shot substantially on location in central London, mostly around Covent Garden, and betrays Hitchcock's sensitivity to place—as well as his compulsion to repeat himself. The first scene unfolds on the banks of the Thames, albeit in daylight, opposite the spot where the first true Hitchcock had begun, nearly half a century earlier.

The scene begins with an aerial view of a crowd listening to a politician giving a speech outside County Hall, attended to also by reporters and police, and ends with a dead woman being sighted in the water. Hitchcock, in probably his most conspicuous cameo, appears in the crowd, a besuited caricature Englishman, whose image was familiar from hundreds of television appearances, but whose archetype was no longer much in evidence. "His air of unctuous gloom and his black bowler hat," wrote Raymond Durgnat, "are both as anachronistic as an Edwardian undertaker's man."[79] He might have wandered over from the set of *The Lodger*. Almost the first words the politician speaks are Wordsworth's—not "Composed Upon Westminster Bridge," though the bridge is in sight, but the line "Bliss was it in that dawn to be alive," taken from "French Revolution," but used here to evoke a bucolic vision of England before the Industrial Revolution. To general approval, he promises to restore to England's rivers their flora and fauna, clear the waters of pollution, reverse the ravages of the machine age. It is a vision that Hitchcock alone, a creature of the modern city, refuses to applaud.

Notes

ABBREVIATIONS

My guiding principle has been to quote from the original; however, many of Hitchcock's publications and utterances have been collected and made available to the general reader by Sidney Gottlieb, in books whose titles I have abbreviated as follows:

AHI   Sidney Gottlieb (ed.), *Alfred Hitchcock Interviews* (Jackson: University Press of Mississippi, 2003)

HoH 1   Sidney Gottlieb (ed.), *Hitchcock on Hitchcock* (Berkeley: University of California Press, 1995)

HoH 2   Sidney Gottlieb (ed.), *Hitchcock on Hitchcock*, vol. 2 (Oakland: University of California Press, 2015)

I have also abbreviated the names of archives and libraries:

BBC   BBC Archives

BDCM   Bill Douglas Cinema Museum

BFI   British Film Institute Special Collections

BIMI   Birkbeck Institute for the Moving Image Archive

BL   British Library, Western Manuscripts Collection

HRC   Harry Ransom Center

LOC   Library of Congress

MoMA   Museum of Modern Art Archives

Slade   Slade Film Department Archive, University College London

AUDIO RECORDINGS

Sections from Truffaut's famous interview with Hitchcock have appeared on numerous DVDs and Blu-ray discs, and more are available online. Large extracts were broadcast on French radio in the 1990s, in a series of twenty-five episodes, and these are available from a variety of sites. In the notes they are designated "Truffaut/Hitchcock interview," with the appropriate episode number.

CHAPTER 1. THE EMBANKMENT AT MIDNIGHT

1. *Kinematograph Weekly*, 4 March 1926, 52.

2. *Evening News*, 1 March 1926, 9.

3. *Illustrated Sunday Herald*, 28 February 1926, 16.

4. Alfred Hitchcock, "Life Among the Stars—3: One Scene That Made a Girl a Star," *News Chronicle*, 3 March 1937, 14. Repr. in *HoH 1*.

5. *Daily Mail*, 24 February 1926, 7.

6. "Alma in Wonderland," *Picturegoer*, December 1925, 48. Repr. in *Hitchcock Annual*, vol. 15, 2006–7.

7. Mrs. Alfred Hitchcock, as told to Martin Abramson, "My Husband Alfred Hitchcock Hates Suspense," *Coronet*, August 1964, 16.

8. *Sunday Express*, 14 February 1926, 10.

9. Cedric Belfrage, "Alfred the Great," *Picturegoer*, March 1926, 60.

10. *Motion Picture News*, 10 July 1920, 390.

11. *Motion Picture Studio*, 28 October 1922, 25.

12. Cecil B. DeMille, *The Autobiography of Cecil B. DeMille* (London: W. H. Allen, 1960), 123.

13. *Photoplay*, February 1922, 45.

14. Richard Meryman, *Mank: The Wit, World, and Life of Herman Mankiewicz* (New York: William Morrow, 1978), 124.

15. Will Irwin, *The House That Shadows Built* (Garden City, NY: Doubleday, Doran & Co., 1928), 277.

16. *Star*, 24 February 1926, 8.

17. François Truffaut, with Helen G. Scott, *Hitchcock* (New York: Simon and Schuster, 1967), 88.

18. Ibid., 89.

19. *New Yorker*, 27 March 1926, 32.

20. *Cinema News*, 8 July 1926, 3.

21. Peter Noble, *Ivor Novello: Man of the Theatre* (London: The Falcon Press, 1951), 114.

22. *Daily Mail*, 30 January 1926, 6.

23. Henry Kendall, *I Remember Romano's* (London: Macdonald, 1960), 87.

24. *Morning Post*, 14 April 1926, 9.

25. June, *The Glass Ladder* (London: Heinemann, 1960), 55.

26. *Daily Express*, 20 January 1926, 6.

27. *Daily Express*, 17 February 1926, 7.

28. June, *Glass Ladder*, 156.

29. Ivor Novello, "Why I Loathe My Looks," *Daily Sketch*, 2 March 1926, 7.

30. BIMI: Film Society prospectus, c. September 1925.

31. Truffaut/Hitchcock interview, ep. 8.

32. *Sphere*, 31 October 1925, vi.

33. *Daily Graphic*, 21 December 1925, 5.

34. *Westminster Gazette*, 21 December 1925, 9.

35. Mrs. Belloc Lowndes, *The Merry Wives of Westminster* (London: Macmillan, 1946), 92.

36. Mrs. Belloc Lowndes, "The Lodger," *McClure's*, January 1911, 262.

37. François Truffaut and Claude Chabrol, "Entretien avec Alfred Hitchcock," *Cahiers du cinéma*, no. 44, February 1955, 22. Repr. in *HoH* 2.

38. G. M. Young, *Victorian England: Portrait of an Age* (Oxford: Oxford University Press, 1936), 82.

39. Joseph Gollomb, *Scotland Yard* (London: Hutchinson, 1926), 60.

40. James Morris, *Farewell the Trumpets: An Imperial Retreat* (London: Faber and Faber, 1978), 68, 91.

41. *G. K.'s Weekly*, 30 January 1926, 503.

42. H. G. Wells, *The Outline of History: Being a Plain History of Life and Mankind* (London: Cassell, 1920), 578.

43. Arnold Hauser, *The Social History of Art*, vol. 2 (Routledge & Kegan Paul, 1951), 921.

44. Sigmund Freud, *Beyond the Pleasure Principle* (London: International Psycho-Analytical Press, 1922), 44.

45. Iris Barry, "We Enjoyed the War," *Scribner's Magazine*, November 1934, 283.

46. J. M. Keynes, *The Economic Consequences of Mr Churchill* (London: Hogarth Press, 1925), 24.

47. Vincent Sheean, *Personal History* (Garden City, NY: Doubleday, Doran, 1935), 80.

48. *Nation and Athenaeum*, 24 October 1925, 138.

49. *Spectator*, 5 December 1925, 1009.

50. *G. K.'s Weekly*, 24 October 1925, 31.

51. Hilaire Belloc, "On the Locarno Spirit," *G. K.'s Weekly*, 28 November 1925, 257.

52. Charles B. L. Tennyson, "Film Lessons from Germany," *Daily Mail*, 24 February 1926, 8.

53. *Daily Mail*, 22 January 1926, 9.

54. *Evening Standard*, 12 March 1926, 8.

55. *Daily Express*, 15 December 1925, 6.

56. *Illustrated Sunday Herald*, 17 January 1926, 19.

57. Cedric Belfrage, "Should British Films Be Subsidised?," *Weekly Westminster*, 23 January 1926, 287.

58. *Westminster Gazette*, 24 February 1926, 4.

59. *Daily Graphic*, 25 February 1926, 3.

60. Michael Balcon, *Michael Balcon Presents . . . A Lifetime of Films* (London: Hutchinson, 1969), 21.

61. Ernst Lubitsch, "Will the American Public Accept a Cinema Tragedy?," *New York World*, 7 March 1926, M4.

62. *Life*, 30 July 1925, 26.

63. Iris Barry, *Let's Go to the Pictures* (London: Chatto and Windus, 1926), 15.

64. Gilbert Seldes, *The Seven Lively Arts* (New York: Harper & Brothers, 1924), 336–8.

65. Barry, *Let's Go to the Pictures*, 247.

66. *Manchester Guardian*, 4 February 1926, 8.

67. *Evening Standard*, 8 February 1926, 6.

68. Iris Barry, "Three Films," *Adelphi*, March 1924, 926–27.

69. Ibid., 929.

70. Ibid., 928.

71. André Bazin, "Montage," in Antonio Petrucci (ed.), *Twenty Years of Cinema in Venice* (Rome: Edizioni dell'Ateneo, 1952), 363.

72. Ibid., 368.

73. Ibid., 370.

74. Ibid., 363.

75. Ibid., 377.

76. Truffaut, *Hitchcock*, 71.

77. Ibid., 50.

78. Alfred Hitchcock, "Director's Problems," *Listener*, 2 February 1938, 242. Repr. in *HoH 1*.

79. Seldes, *Seven Lively Arts*, 339.

80. *Manchester Guardian*, 21 March 1925, 7.

81. Sigmund Freud, "Psychogenic Visual Disturbance According to Psycho-Analytical Conceptions," in *Collected Papers*, vol. 2 (London: Hogarth Press and the Institute of Psycho-Analysis, 1924), 110.

82. *International Journal of Psycho-Analysis*, April 1925, 238.

83. Sigmund Freud, *Three Contributions to the Theory of Sex* (New York: Nervous and Mental Disease Publishing Co., 1920), 20.

84. Truffaut, *Hitchcock*, 167.

85. Freud, "Psychogenic Visual Disturbance," 112.

86. Geoffrey T. Hellman, "Alfred Hitchcock: England's Best and Biggest Director Goes to Hollywood," *Life*, 20 November 1939, 33.

87. Maxwell Anderson, *Off Broadway: Essays about the Theater* (New York: William Sloane, 1947), 70.

88. Truffaut, *Hitchcock*, 90.

89. *Illustrated Sunday Herald*, 28 February 1926, 16.

90. Hitchcock, "One Scene That Made a Girl a Star," 14.

91. Truffaut, *Hitchcock*, 30.

CHAPTER 2. THE REPUTATION AND THE MYTH

1. Eric Rohmer and Claude Chabrol, *Hitchcock* (Paris: Éditions Universitaires, 1957), 15.

2. BIMI: Film Society program notes, 8 February 1931.

3. *Cinema News*, 11 February 1931, 1.

4. *Yorkshire Post*, 10 February 1931, 6.

5. *Observer*, 1 March 1931, 12.

6. Slade: "T. D. Inaugural Lecture," January 1969.

7. Ernest Lindgren, "Nostalgia," *Sight and Sound*, Autumn 1940, 49–50.

8. "T. D. Inaugural Lecture."

9. Paul Rotha, *The Film Till Now: A Survey of the Cinema* (London: Jonathan Cape, 1930), 311, 31, 85.

10. Ibid., 33, 230.

11. Ibid., 232.

12. Ivor Montagu, "Not 'Highbrows': A Defence of the Film Society," *Kinematograph Weekly*, 15 October 1925, 69.

13. *London Mercury*, October 1932, 562.

14. *Evening Standard*, 8 December 1934, 8.

15. *Observer*, 9 June 1935, 10.

16. *Observer*, 1 March 1931, 12.

17. *Listener*, 7 October 1936, 675.

18. BDCM: Palace Theatre program, 16 October 1938.

19. Marie Seton, "Silent Shadows," *Sight and Sound*, Spring 1938, 32.

20. Email correspondence with Bryony Dixon, BFI Curator of Silent Film, 27 October 2020.

21. "Early Screen Masterpieces Discovered in London Cellar," *World Film News*, June 1936, 8.

22. *Kinematograph Year Book 1939* (London: Kinematograph Publications, 1939), 389.

23. *New Republic*, 22 July 1940, 118.

24. Janet White, "Picture Parade," *Brooklyn Daily Eagle*, 30 August 1937, 9.

25. B. R. Crisler, "Hitchcock: Master Melodramatist," *New York Times*, 21 June 1938, X3.

26. Katharine Roberts, "Mystery Man," *Collier's*, 5 August 1939, 22.

27. *News Chronicle*, 12 February 1944, 2.

28. *New Republic*, 24 January 1944, 116.

29. *Sunday Times*, 23 April 1944, 2.

30. *Sunday Times*, 14 April 1946, 2.

31. BDCM: *Fifty Years of Cinema: A Retrospect, with Twenty Illustrations, of the First Season, 1945-46, of the New London Film Society* (London: New London Film Society, 1946), 4.

32. *Sunday Times*, 14 April 1946, 2.

33. MoMA: Department of Film Archive, A-49: Letter from Vaughan to Barry, 26 June 1945.

34. Denis Forman, "The Work of the British Film Institute," in Roger Manvell (ed.), *The Year's Work in the Film, 1949* (London: Longmans, Green, 1950), 75.

35. *Sunday Times*, 2 November 1947, 2.

36. Lindsay Anderson, "Alfred Hitchcock," *Sequence*, no. 9, Autumn 1949, 117, 119. Repr. in *Never Apologise: The Collected Writings* (London: Plexus, 2004).

37. Ibid., 115.

38. *Sight and Sound*, Autumn 1949, 5.

39. *Monthly Film Bulletin*, 30 November 1949, 189.

40. BFI: BFI Special Collection, Box 87: Lindsay Anderson, "Some Notes on The Lodger."

41. Paul Willetts (ed.), *Julian Maclaren-Ross: Selected Letters* (London: Black Spring Press, 2008), 77.

42. Email correspondence with Paul Willetts, 2 August 2006.

43. J. Maclaren-Ross, "The World of Alfred Hitchcock," *New Writing and Daylight*, no. 7, 1946, 134-35. Repr. in *Bitten by the Tarantula and other writing* (London: Black Spring Press, 2005).

44. Ibid., 135.

45. Ruth Partington, "A 'Travelling' in Paris," *Sequence*, no. 9, Autumn 1949, 126.

46. *Sequence*, no. 13, New Year 1951, 47.

47. Robert E. Kapsis, *Hitchcock: The Making of a Reputation* (Chicago: University of Chicago Press, 1992), 1-2, 156-57.

48. François Truffaut, "Un trousseau de fausses clés," *Cahiers du cinéma*, no. 39, October 1954, 50.

49. Rohmer and Chabrol, *Hitchcock*, 1.

50. Anderson, "Alfred Hitchcock," 115; Rohmer and Chabrol, *Hitchcock*, 16.

51. Rohmer and Chabrol, *Hitchcock*, 64.

52. Kapsis, *Hitchcock*, 244.

53. *Variety*, 3 August 1927, 3.

54. *Daily Mail*, 27 June 1929, 17.

55. *Los Angeles Times*, 9 April 1939, III, 3.

56. *Los Angeles Times*, 27 April 1943, I, 14.

57. Truffaut/Hitchcock interview, ep. 2.

58. Anderson, "Alfred Hitchcock," 115.

59. H. D. Wilson, "Hitchcock in Hollywood: An Interim Report: 1939–46," *Film Miscellany*, Winter 1946–57, 36–41

60. *Listener*, 10 July 1947, 67.

61. Peter Noble, *An Index to the Work of Alfred Hitchcock*, Special Supplement to *Sight and Sound*, no. 18, May 1949, 8.

62. Rotha, *The Film Till Now*, 227.

63. V. F. Perkins, "Fifty Famous Films 1915–45," *Oxford Opinion*, no. 38, 30 April 1960, 37.

64. Rachael Low, *The History of the British Film, 1918–1929* (London: George Allen & Unwin, 1971), 304.

65. Ibid., 217.

66. Ivor Montagu, *The Youngest Son: Autobiographical Sketches* (London: Lawrence and Wishart, 1970), 348.

67. Ibid., 350.

68. Ivor Montagu, "Working with Hitchcock," *Sight and Sound*, Summer 1980, 190.

69. Donald Spoto, *The Life of Alfred Hitchcock: The Dark Side of Genius:* (London: Collins, 1983), 88.

70. Peter Wollen, "The Last New Wave: Modernism in the British Films of the Thatcher Era," in Lester Friedman (ed.), *British Cinema and Thatcherism: Fires Were Started* (London: UCL Press, 1993), 38–39.

71. Ibid., 39.

72. Peter Wollen, "Hitch: A Tale of Two Cities (London and Los Angeles)," in *Paris Hollywood: Writings on Film* (London: Verso, 2002), 71, 67.

73. Richard Allen, "*The Lodger* and the Origins of Hitchcock's Aesthetic," *Hitchcock Annual*, vol. 10, 2001–2, 52.

74. Ibid., 54.

75. Tom Ryall, *Alfred Hitchcock and the British Cinema* (London: Croom Helm, 1986), 26.

76. Allen, "*The Lodger*," 55.

77. Charles Barr, *English Hitchcock* (Moffat, UK: Cameron and Hollis, 1999), 31.

78. Wollen, "Hitch: A Tale of Two Cities," 66.

79. Wollen, "The Last New Wave," 39.

80. Alan Young and Michael Schmidt, "Conversation with Edgell Rickword," *Poetry Nation*, no. 1, 1973, 81.

81. Barr, *English Hitchcock*, 14.

82. François Truffaut, with Helen G. Scott, *Hitchcock* (New York: Simon & Schuster, 1967), 96.

83. Arthur Knight, "Conversation with Alfred Hitchcock," *Oui*, February 1973, 82. Repr. in *AHI*.

84. Gavin Lambert, "A Last Look Round," *Sequence*, no. 14, New Year 1952, 4-5.

85. J. Maclaren-Ross, "A Totem of the 1920's," *Encounter*, March 1954, 76. Repr. in *Bitten by the Tarantula*.

86. J. Maclaren-Ross [unsigned], "Out of the Ordinary: The Novel of Pursuit and Suspense," *Times Literary Supplement*, Detective Fiction section, 25 February 1955, vi. Reprinted in *Bitten by the Tarantula*.

87. J. Maclaren-Ross [unsigned], "The Hunted and the Heather," *Times Literary Supplement*, 1 June 1956, 327. Reprinted in *Bitten by the Tarantula*.

CHAPTER 3. NO OLD MASTERS

1. *Star*, 7 December 1915, 2.

2. *Daily News*, 10 December 1915, 2.

3. *Pall Mall Gazette*, 10 December 1915, 5.

4. Alfred Hitchcock, "An Autocrat of the Film Studio," *Cassell's Magazine*, January 1928, 30. Repr. in *HoH 2*.

5. J. H. Graham-Cutts, "There Is a High-Class Film Public!," *Cinema News*, 25 November 1915, 13.

6. Joan Weston Edwards, "Making Good in the Film Trade," *Home Notes*, 26 February 1927, 531.

7. *Bioscope*, 4 June 1914, 1004.

8. *Daily Mail*, 5 April 1927, 9.

9. *Kinematograph and Lantern Weekly*, 2 December 1915, 93.

10. *Picture Palace News*, 6 December 1915, 117.

11. *Eastern Mercury*, 7 December 1915, 1.

12. *Eastern Mercury*, 21 December 1915, 2.

13. *Picturegoer*, 7 August 1915, 348.

14. *Evening News*, 18 August 1915, 6.

15. *Evening News*, 13 August 1915, 5.

16. *Kinematograph and Lantern Weekly*, 29 April 1915, supp., xxi.

17. *Cinema News*, 23 September 1915, 61.

18. Richard Koszarski, *The Rivals of D. W. Griffith: Alternative Auteurs, 1913-1918* (Minneapolis, MN: Walker Art Center, 1976), 43-44.

19. *Cinema News*, 16 September 1915, 27.

20. Hitchcock, "Autocrat of the Film Studio," 28.

21. *Cinema News*, 21 October 1915, supp., vii. The words were in fact those of his brother William, taken from *Moving Picture World*.

22. *Cinema News*, 15 July 1915, 62.

23. Eliot Stannard, "What's in a Name?," *Kinematograph and Lantern Weekly*, 24 June 1915, 78.

24. Alfred Hitchcock, "Lecture at Columbia University," in Sidney Gottlieb (ed.), *Hitchcock on Hitchcock* (Berkeley: University of California Press, 1995), 272.

25. Alfred Hitchcock, "Core of the Movie—The Chase," *New York Times Magazine*, 29 October 1950, 22–23, 44–46. Repr. in *HoH 1*.

26. Charles Barr, *English Hitchcock* (Moffat, UK: Cameron and Hollis, 1999), 15.

27. Alfred Hitchcock, "Pourquoi j'ai peur la nuit," *Arts*, 1 June 1960, 1, 7. Repr. in *HoH 1*.

28. John Buchan, "Introduction," in Edgar Allan Poe, *Tales of Mystery and Imagination* (London: Thomas Nelson and Sons, n.d.), 5–7.

29. *Weekly Dispatch*, 12 September 1915, 7.

30. Alfred Hitchcock, "Columbus of the Screen," *Film Weekly*, 21 February 1931, 9. Repr. in *HoH 2*.

31. Charles Baudelaire, "Edgar Allan Poe: His Life and Works," trans. H. Curwen, in *Poe's Choice Works* (London: Chatto and Windus, 1902), 2–3.

32. *Wid's Daily*, 16 May 1919, 2; *Wid's Daily*, 17 May 1919, 1.

33. Adolph Zukor, *The Public Is Never Wrong* (London: Cassell, 1954), 171.

34. Terry Ramsaye, "'Jaydee': The Story of the Spectacular Career of J. D. Williams," *Motion Picture Herald*, 1 September 1934, 13.

35. *Wid's Daily*, 1 July 1919, 2.

36. *Wid's Daily*, 3 July 1919, 1.

37. Rodney Ackland, "The Bubble-Reputation," *Sight and Sound*, Summer 1943, 8.

38. Truffaut/Hitchcock interview, ep. 20.

39. Rudy Behlmer (ed.), *Memo from David O. Selznick* (New York: Viking Press, 1972), 283.

40. Paul Mayersberg, *Hollywood the Haunted House* (London: Allen Lane The Penguin Press, 1967), 35–6.

41. *Daily Mail*, 8 July 1919, 3.

42. Peter Bogdanovich, *Who the Devil Made It* (New York: Alfred A. Knopf, 1997), 507.

43. Truffaut/Hitchcock interview, ep. 8.

44. *Aquarius: Alfred the Great*, London Weekend Television, 5 August 1972.

45. Truffaut/Hitchcock interview, ep. 8.

46. Bogdanovich, *Who the Devil Made It*, 486

47. Truffaut/Hitchcock interview, ep. 8.

48. *Kinematograph and Lantern Weekly*, 10 July 1919, 118.

49. *Kinematograph and Lantern Weekly*, 24 July 1919, 114.

50. Elsie Codd, "Strolls Around the Studios," *Kinematograph Weekly*, 13 November 1919, 109.

51. Elsie Codd, "The Art of the Sub-Title," *Kinematograph Weekly*, 22 January 1920, supp., xxiii.

52. A. J. Hitchcock, "Titles—Artistic and Otherwise," *Motion Picture Studio*, 23 July 1921, 6. Repr. in *HoH 2*.

53. *Kinematograph Weekly*, 16 September 1920, 101.

54. Alfred Hitchcock, "My Ten Favorite Pictures," *New York Sun*, 15 March 1939, 33.

55. Alfred Hitchcock, "'Stodgy' British Pictures," *Film Weekly*, 14 December 1934, 14. Repr. in *HoH 1*.

56. John Russell Taylor, *The Rise and Fall of the Well-Made Play* (London: Methuen, 1967), 92, 76.

57. Ibid., 115.

58. *Moving Picture World*, 28 January 1922, 375.

59. *The Times*, 21 February 1922, supp., xiv.

60. Richard Schickel, *The Men Who Made the Movies* (New York: Atheneum, 1975), 302.

61. Alfred Hitchcock, "My Screen Memories—1: I Begin with a Nightmare," *Film Weekly*, 2 May 1936, 16. Repr. in *HoH 1*.

62. Charles Barr and Alain Kerzoncuf, *Hitchcock Lost and Found: The Forgotten Films* (Lexington: University Press of Kentucky, 2015), 28–29.

63. Alma Reville, "Cutting and Continuity," *Motion Picture Studio*, 13 January 1923, 10. Repr. in *Hitchcock Annual*, vol. 15, 2006–7.

64. Michael Balcon, "Henry Harris: Lighting Cameraman," *Film and Television Technician*, November 1971, 26.

65. Adrian Brunel, "Megaphone Moments III," *Motion Picture Studio*, 26 August 1922, 6.

66. Oliver Baldwin, "These People Make British Pictures, No. 1: Walter Mycroft," *Picturegoer*, 17 June 1939, 10.

67. Walter C. Mycroft, *The Time of My Life* (Lanham, MD: The Scarecrow Press, 2006), 30.

68. Ibid., 17.

69. *Evening Standard*, 5 March 1923, 3.

70. C. A. Lejeune, *Thank You for Having Me* (London: Hutchinson, 1964), 162.

71. *Manchester Guardian*, 31 March 1923, 7.

72. Lejeune, *Thank You for Having Me*, 92.

73. *Manchester Guardian*, 27 January 1923, 9.

74. *Daily Express*, 13 November 1923, 10.

75. *Cinema News*, 23 October 1923, 5.

76. Truffaut/Hitchcock interview, ep. 8.

77. Iris Barry, *Let's Go to the Pictures* (London: Chatto and Windus, 1926), 234.

78. *Manchester Guardian*, 9 February 1924, 9.

79. *Spectator*, 16 February 1924, 256.

80. *Manchester Guardian*, 25 February 1924, 5.

81. *Daily Herald*, 28 June 1923, 5.

82. Graham Cutts, "What Does the Public Want?," *Kinematograph Weekly*, 14 February 1924, 50–51.

83. *Spectator*, 15 March 1924, 434.

84. *Bioscope*, 20 March 1924, 37.

85. John Russell Taylor, *Hitch: The Life and Work of Alfred Hitchcock* (London: Faber and Faber, 1978), 57.

86. Truffaut/Hitchcock interview, ep. 1.

87. *Evening Standard*, 20 May 1924, 12.

88. *Evening Standard*, 19 August 1924, 12.

89. BFI: Adrian Brunel Special Collection, Box 112, Item 1: Letter from Balcon to Brunel, 17 November 1924.

90. Ibid., Box 112, Item 3: Letter from Balcon to Pommer, 28 February 1925.

91. Ibid., Box 145, Item 3: Note on Alfred Hitchcock.

92. Ibid., Box 112, Item 3: Letter from Balcon to Pommer, 12 February 1925.

93. Ibid., Box 112, Item 3: Letter from Balcon to Hitchcock, 17 March 1925.

94. Ibid., Box 112, Item 3: Letter from Balcon to Brunel, 2 April 1925.

95. *Evening Standard*, 2 June 1925, 12.

96. BFI: Adrian Brunel Special Collection, Box 112, Item 1: Undated letter from Hitchcock to Brunel.

97. Thomas Elsaesser, "Too Big and Too Close: Alfred Hitchcock and Fritz Lang," *Hitchcock Annual*, vol. 12, 2003–4, 3.

98. *Kinematograph Weekly*, 1 October 1925, 74.

99. *Kinematograph Weekly*, 22 October 1925, 44.

100. *Variety*, 21 October 1925, 2.

101. *Bioscope*, 19 November 1925, 33.

102. *Illustrated Sunday Herald*, 1 November 1925, 19.

CHAPTER 4. THE AUTOCRAT OF THE STUDIO

1. Eliot Stannard, "Artistic Frauds on the Picture Public," *Film Renter*, 5 June 1920, 6.

2. Eliot Stannard, "Scenario Writing as a Fine Art," *Motion Picture Studio*, 1 September 1923, 10.

3. Mrs. Belloc Lowndes, "The Novelist and the Film," *John o' London's Weekly*, 4 August 1923, 578.

4. Mrs. Belloc Lowndes, "The Novel and the Film," *The Times*, 21 February 1922, supp. xi.

5. *Cinema News*, 7 January 1926, 15.

6. BL: Society of Authors Archive, Add MS 56739: Letter from Lowndes to Thring, 23 May 1922.

7. Ibid., Letter from Lowndes to Denys Kilham Roberts, 13 July 1931.

8. BFI: Michael Balcon Special Collection, MEB-4-19: "'The Lodger' Detailed Cost of Production," c. June 1926.

9. BL: Society of Authors Archive, Add MS 56740: Undated statement of the *Chink in the Armour* case, c. 1936.

10. Eliot Stannard, *Writing Screen Plays* (London: Standard Art Book Co., n.d.), 25.

11. Gavin Lambert, *Mainly about Lindsay Anderson* (London: Faber and Faber, 2000), 35.

12. Eliot Stannard, "The Art of Kinematography No. 1—Symbolism," *Kinematograph and Lantern Weekly*, 23 May 1918, 76.

13. C. R. W. Nevinson, "My Ideal Cinema," *Bioscope*, 10 April 1924, 23.

14. *Evening Standard*, 28 October 1924, 12.

15. *Evening Standard*, 17 March 1925, 12.

16. *Spectator*, 28 March 1925, 13.

17. *Manchester Guardian*, 28 March 1925, 7.

18. Bob Thomas, "Alfred Hitchcock: The German Years," *Action* 8, no. 1, January–February 1973, 23–24. Repr. in *AHI*.

19. *Vogue*, Early April 1926, 52–53.

20. Renie Marrison, "Memory by Proxy," *Picturegoer*, October 1926, 29.

21. E. E. Barrett, "Ivor in Bloomsbury," *Picturegoer*, May 1926, 12.

22. *Daily Mail*, 22 March 1926, 6.

23. *Evening Standard*, 23 March 1926, 3.

24. Ivor Montagu, *The Youngest Son: Autobiographical Sketches* (London: Lawrence and Wishart, 1970), 268.

25. Richard Schickel, *The Men Who Made the Movies* (New York: Atheneum, 1975), 302.

26. François Truffaut, with Helen G. Scott, *Hitchcock* (New York: Simon and Schuster, 1967), 33.

27. *Manchester Guardian*, 27 November 1924, 14.

28. Ibid.

29. *Spectator*, 7 June 1924, 915.

30. Ibid., 916.

31. Truffaut, *Hitchcock*, 42.

32. C. F. Elwell, "De Forest Phonofilms or Talking Motion Pictures," *Journal of the Royal Society of Arts*, 12 December 1924, 91.

33. Vivian Van Damm, *Tonight and Every Night* (London: Stanley Paul, 1952), 68.

34. *Kinematograph Weekly*, 2 July 1925, 32.

35. *Evening Standard*, 7 July 1925, 12.

36. BIMI: Film Society program notes, 17 January 1926.

37. *Daily Mail*, 29 January 1926, 13.

38. *Daily Express*, 29 January 1926, 4.

39. *Bioscope*, 1 April 1926, 35.

40. *Manchester Guardian*, 6 December 1924, 9.

41. *Manchester Guardian*, 28 April 1923, 9.

42. Alfred Hitchcock, "An Autocrat of the Film Studio," *Cassell's Magazine*, January 1928, 28. Repr. in *HoH 2*.

43. *Manchester Guardian*, 9 March 1926, 14.

44. *Observer*, 14 July 1935, 12.

45. Margaret Burrows, "Colour—Seen through the Eyes of Alfred Hitchcock, Britain's Ace Director," *Film Pictorial*, 17 July 1937, 16.

46. Alfred Hitchcock, "Direction," in Charles Davy (ed.), *Footnotes to the Film* (London: Lovat Dickson, 1937), 7. Repr. in *HOH 1*.

47. *Daily Express*, 26 March 1926, 3.

48. *Evening Standard*, 30 March 1926, 3.

49. *Illustrated Sunday Herald*, 28 March 1926, 18.

50. *Daily Mail*, 24 March 1926, 7.

51. *Evening Standard*, 30 May 1927, 5.

52. *Daily Express*, 18 June 1926, 7.

53. *Kinematograph Weekly*, 20 November 1924, 41.

54. Van Damm, *Tonight and Every Night*, 63.

55. *Evening Standard*, 12 March 1926, 5.

56. *Sunday Express*, 11 April 1926, 10.

57. *Spectator*, 24 April 1926, 755.

58. *Evening News*, 12 April 1926, 9.

59. June, *The Glass Ladder* (London: Heinemann, 1960), 156.

60. *Daily Mail*, 15 April 1926, 8.

61. *Observer*, 18 April 1926, 5.

62. *Observer*, 2 May 1926, 22.

63. *Los Angeles Examiner*, 26 April 1926, 1.

64. *Kinematograph Weekly*, 22 April 1926, 56.

65. *Film Renter*, 1 May 1926, 61.

66. Walter Mycroft, *The Time of My Life* (Lanham, MD: The Scarecrow Press, 2006), 34.

67. J. M. Keynes, "Coal: A Suggestion," *Nation and Athenaeum*, 24 April 1926, 92.

68. J. M. Keynes, "To the *Chicago Daily News*, 6 May 1926," in Donald Moggridge (ed.), *The Collected Writings of John Maynard Keynes*, vol. 19: *Activities 1922–1929* (London: Macmillan, 1981), 530.

69. Mycroft, *Time of My Life*, 54.

70. Montagu, *Youngest Son*, 343.

CHAPTER 5. TO CATCH A THIEF

1. *Film Renter*, 10 July 1926, 8.

2. *Cinema News*, 2 September 1926, 18.

3. Michael Balcon, *Michael Balcon Presents . . . A Lifetime of Films* (London: Hutchinson, 1969), 23.

4. *Exhibitors Herald*, 29 May 1926, 161.

5. *Cinema News*, 20 May 1926, 33.

6. *Spectator*, 5 June 1926, 946.

7. *Daily Express*, 21 May 1926, 11.

8. *Daily Mail*, 22 May 1926, 9.

9. *Spectator*, 5 June 1926, 946.

10. *Morning Post*, 29 May 1926, 6.

11. *Observer*, 30 May 1926, 23.

12. Michael Balcon, "Tribute to Thalberg," *World Film News*, October 1936, 15.

13. Alfred Hitchcock, "In the Hall of Mogul Kings," *The Times*, 23 June 1969, Movies supp., I. Repr. in *HoH 1*.

14. Alfred Hitchcock, "Films We Could Make," *Evening News*, 16 November 1927, 13. Repr. in *HoH 1*.

15. *Morning Post*, 16 September 1926, 16.

16. *Daily Express*, 7 May 1925, 1

17. *Daily Express*, 26 January 1926, 8.

18. Budd Schulberg, *Moving Pictures: Memories of a Hollywood Prince* (New York: Stein and Day, 1981), 304–5.

19. *Los Angeles Examiner*, 23 May 1926, V7.

20. Ibid., V8.

21. Ibid.

22. *Film Daily*, 8 May 1923, 3.

23. Charles Lapworth, "Production—Or the Parish?," *Kinematograph Weekly*, 23 July 1925, 44.

24. Michael Balcon, "Will You, Sir William?," *Kinematograph Weekly*, 23 July 1925, 49.

25. *Film Daily*, 24 March 1926, 1.

26. H. L. Mencken, "The Movies," *American Mercury*, February 1927, 253.

27. *Evening News*, 26 April 1926, 9.

28. *Daily Mail*, 16 June 1926, 7.

29. *Cinema News*, 24 June 1926, 1.

30. Ibid., 10.

31. *Kinematograph Weekly*, 24 June 1926, 42.

32. *Kinematograph Weekly*, 1 July 1926, 25.

33. *Los Angeles Times*, 6 June 1926, II, 10.

34. Balcon, *Lifetime of Films*, 3.

35. Cedric Belfrage, "The Broadway Boulevardier," *Picturegoer*, October 1926, 62.

36. BFI: Adrian Brunel Special Collection, Box 86, Folder 2: "Personalia."

37. Balcon, "Will You, Sir William?," 49.

38. C. M. Woolf, "Where Is the Difficulty of Producing British Films?," *Film Renter*, 20 March 1926, 13.

39. *Daily Express*, 27 August 1926, 7.

40. *Kinematograph Weekly*, 27 August 1925, supp., x.

41. *Cinema News*, 20 May 1926, 33.

42. *Evening Standard*, 20 May 1926, 3.

43. *Evening Standard*, 1 June 1926, 3.

44. *Kinematograph Weekly*, 22 April 1926, 26.

45. Charles Lapworth, "About That 'Nucleus,'" *Kinematograph Weekly*, 8 July 1926, 26.

46. J. D. Williams, "A J. D. Williams Comment," *Kinematograph Weekly*, 22 July 1926, 28.

47. *Morning Post*, 29 May 1926, 12.

48. L'Estrange Fawcett, *Films: Facts and Forecasts* (London: Geoffrey Bles, 1927), 58–59.

49. Peter Bogdanovich, *Who the Devil Made It* (New York: Alfred A. Knopf, 1997), 489–90.

50. Balcon, *Lifetime of Films*, 26.

51. *Cinema News*, 20 May 1926, 1.

52. *Bioscope*, 20 May 1926, 54.

53. *Cinema News*, 3 June 1926, 21.

54. *Bioscope*, 10 June 1926, 47.

55. *Film Renter*, 22 May 1926, 41.

56. *Kinematograph Weekly*, 3 June 1926, supp., iv.

57. *Film Renter*, 19 June 1926, 31.

58. BFI: Michael Balcon Special Collection, MEB-4-19: "'The Lodger' Detailed Cost of Production," c. June 1926.

59. BFI: Ivor Montagu Special Collection, Item 40a: Letter from Brunel to Montagu, 20 July 1926.

60. Ibid.: Telegram from Montagu to Brunel, received 28 July 1926.

61. Ivor Montagu, *The Youngest Son: Autobiographical Sketches* (London: Lawrence and Wishart, 1970), 348.

62. Ivor Montagu, "Working with Hitchcock," *Sight and Sound*, Summer 1980, 189.

63. BFI: Adrian Brunel Special Collection, Box 112, Item 3: Letter from Brunel to Balcon, 11 November 1925.

64. Montagu, *Youngest Son*, 330.

65. *Illustrated Sunday Herald*, 21 March 1926, 16.

66. BFI: Ivor Montagu Special Collection, Item 43a: Letter from Balcon to Montagu, 10 February 1926.

67. *Observer*, 7 March 1926, 7.

68. BFI: Ivor Montagu Special Collection, Item 426a: Letter from MacPhail to Montagu, 27 April 1926.

69. *Observer*, 18 April 1926, 6.

70. BFI: Adrian Brunel Special Collection, Box 112, Item 4: Letter from Brunel to Cutts, 25 March 1926.

71. BFI: Adrian Brunel Special Collection, Box 111, Folder 1: Letter from Gainsborough to Brunel, 12 May 1926.

72. BFI: Ivor Montagu Special Collection, Item 43a: Letter from Balcon to Montagu, 6 August 1926.

73. *Evening Standard*, 9 August 1926, 8.

74. Montagu, *Youngest Son*, 350.

75. Montagu, "Working with Hitchcock," 190.

76. Ibid.

77. Montagu, *Youngest Son*, 350.

78. Norman Swallow, *Eisenstein: A Documentary Portrait* (London: George Allen & Unwin, 1976), 74.

79. BFI: Adrian Brunel Special Collection, Box 145, Item 3: Note on Alfred Hitchcock.

80. Adrian Brunel, *Filmcraft: The Art of Picture Production* (London: George Newnes, 1933), 210.

81. *Bioscope*, 12 August 1926, 23.

82. *Evening News*, 17 June 1926, 12.

83. *Daily Express*, 7 July 1926, 7.

84. *Daily Sketch*, 21 Jul 1926, 5.

85. *Kinematograph Weekly*, 12 August 1926, 62.

86. BFI: Adrian Brunel Special Collection: Note on Alfred Hitchcock.

87. Montagu, *Youngest Son*, 349.

88. BFI: Ivor Montagu Special Collection, Item 18: *The Lodger* title lists.

89. *Evening Standard*, 10 August 1926, 3.

90. E. McKnight Kauffer, *Posters* (New York: Museum of Modern Art, 1937), n.p.

91. Roger Fry, "Poster Designs and Mr. McKnight Kauffer," *Nation and Athenaeum*, 23 May 1925, 236–37.

92. BFI: Ivor Montagu Special Collection, Item 426a: Undated letter from MacPhail to Montagu.

93. BFI: Ivor Montagu Special Collection, Item 43a: Letter from Balcon to Montagu, 1 September 1926.

94. BFI: Ivor Montagu Special Collection, Item 426a: Letter from MacPhail to Montagu, 2 September 1926.

95. Montagu, *Youngest Son*, 225.

96. Bogdanovich, *Who The Devil Made It*, 502.

CHAPTER 6. THE FIRST TRUE HITCHCOCK

1. *Birmingham Gazette*, 4 March 1914, 10.

2. *Daily Mail*, 15 September 1926, 7.

3. Alfred Hitchcock, "Lecture at Columbia University," in Sidney Gottlieb (ed.), *Hitchcock on Hitchcock* (Berkeley: University of California Press, 1995), 273.

4. François Truffaut, with Helen G. Scott, *Hitchcock* (New York: Simon & Schuster, 1967), 32.

5. *Daily Mail*, 2 May 1928, 9.

6. Peter Bogdanovich, *The Cinema of Alfred Hitchcock* (New York: Museum of Modern Art Film Library, 1963), 46.

7. BFI: Ivor Montagu Special Collection, Item 18: Annotated title list for *The Lodger*.

8. BL: Lord Chamberlain's Play Collection, 1915/32: *Who Is He?* by Horace Annesley Vachell.

9. Mario Praz, *The Romantic Agony*, trans. Angus Davidson (London: Oxford University Press, 1933), 59.

10. *Manchester Guardian*, 15 December 1923, 7.

11. *Picture Show*, 19 June 1926, 9.

12. Willard Huntington Wright, "The Detective Novel," *Scribner's Magazine*, November 1926, 537.

13. Alfred Hitchcock, "Direction," in Charles Davy (ed.), *Footnotes to the Film* (London: Lovat Dickson, 1937), 13. Repr. in *HOH 1*.

14. Truffaut, *Hitchcock*, 52.

15. *Illustrated London News*, 19 August 1922, 270.

16. G. K. Chesterton, *The Defendant* (London: R. Brimley Johnson, 1902), 120.

17. Willard Huntington Wright, "The Detective Story," in *The Great Detective Stories: A Chronological Anthology* (New York: Charles Scribner's Sons, 1927), 26.

18. BL: Society of Authors Archive, Add MS 56740: Letter from Denys Kilham Roberts to Marie Belloc Lowndes, 12 July 1938.

19. *Illustrated London News*, 28 August 1920, 312.

20. "Falstaff in Manhattan," *New York Times*, 5 September 1937, X4.

21. *Bioscope*, 12 August 1926, 23.

22. *Evening Standard*, 31 August 1926, 12.

23. John Russell Taylor, *Hitch: The Life and Work of Alfred Hitchcock* (London: Faber and Faber, 1978), 73.

24. BFI: Ivor Montagu Special Collection, Item 426a: Letter from MacPhail to Montagu, 15 September 1926.

25. Truffaut/Hitchcock interview, ep. 2; Bogdanovich, *Cinema of Alfred Hitchcock*, 11.

CHAPTER 7. STORIES OF THE DAYS TO COME

1. *Kinematograph Weekly*, 12 August 1926, 47.

2. *Daily Mail*, 29 September 1926, 6.

3. *Observer*, 26 September 1926, 14.

4. *Cinema News*, 28 October 1926, 20.

5. *Evening Standard*, 5 October 1926, 5.

6. Louis Levy, "Big British Musical Revival," *Cinema News*, 4 November 1926, 62.

7. Stephen Watts, "Alfred Hitchcock on Music in Films," *Cinema Quarterly*, Winter 1933–34, 80. Repr. in *HoH 1*.

8. *Manchester Guardian*, 9 October 1926, 11.

9. *Film Renter*, 9 October 1926, 18.

10. *Evening Standard*, 5 October 1926, 5.

11. *Daily Mail*, 2 October 1926, 6.

12. *Film Daily*, 22 August 1926, 3.

13. *Exhibitors Herald*, 29 May 1926, 161.

14. *Bioscope*, 30 September 1926, 37.

15. *Cinema News*, 30 September 1926, 26.

16. J. Danvers Williams, "The Censor Wouldn't Pass It," *Film Weekly*, 5 November 1938, 6. Repr. in *HoH 1*.

17. *Kinematograph Weekly*, 23 September 1926, 63.

18. *Evening Standard*, 16 October 1926, 8.

19. *Kinematograph Weekly*, 21 October 1926, 63.

20. H. G. Wells, *Anticipations* (London: Chapman and Hall, 1902), 39–40.

21. Ibid., 49, 56.

22. Ibid., 61.

23. L'Estrange Fawcett, *Films: Facts and Forecasts* (London: Geoffrey Bles, 1927), 90.

24. Ibid., 91–92.

25. *Variety*, 3 November 1926, 7.

26. *Syracuse American*, 2 October 1926, S5.

27. *Variety*, 27 October 1926, 55.

28. Fawcett, *Films: Facts and Forecasts*, 98.

29. *Film Daily*, 31 October 1926, 11.

30. *Evening Standard*, 21 September 1926, 5.

31. *Evening Standard*, 27 October 1926, 11.

32. *Daily Mail*, 25 August 1926, 6.

33. *Los Angeles Times*, 14 November 1926, VI, 8.

34. Reyner Banham, *Los Angeles: The Architecture of Four Ecologies* (London: Allen Lane The Penguin Press, 1971), 87.

35. *Film Renter*, 11 December 1926, 9.

36. *Cinema News*, 9 December 1926, 3.

37. *Film Renter*, 11 December 1926, 9.

38. *Daily Mail*, 28 September 1926, 7.

39. *Daily Mail*, 22 October 1926, 10.

40. Max Beloff, *Imperial Sunset*, vol. 2: *Dream of Commonwealth, 1921–42* (Basingstoke: Macmillan, 1989), 101.

41. *Daily Mail*, 27 November 1926, 9.

42. *Cinema News*, 2 December 1926, 1.

43. *Daily Film Renter*, 10 January 1927, 1.

44. *Kinematograph Weekly*, 23 December 1926, 9.

45. Michael Balcon, "Re-Examining Our Production Methods," *Film Renter*, 1 January 1927, n.p.

46. *Illustrated Sunday Herald*, 19 December 1926, 10.

47. *Evening Standard*, 28 December 1926, 1.

48. *Daily Express*, 1 January 1926, 11.

49. *Evening Standard*, 23 November 1926, 12.

50. *Evening News*, 20 September 1926, 9.

51. BBC: Programme as Broadcast sheet, 25 January 1927.

52. Walter C. Mycroft, *The Time of My Life* (Lanham, MD: The Scarecrow Press, 2006), 35.

53. Bernard Herrmann, "Bernard Herrmann, Composer," in Evan William Cameron (ed.), *Sound and the Cinema: The Coming of Sound to American Film* (Pleasantville, NY: Redgrave Publishing Company, 1980), 121–22.

54. *Spectator*, 29 January 1927, 148.

55. *The Times*, 9 February 1927, 11.

56. *Daily Film Renter*, 27 January 1927, 1.

57. Glasgow *Evening Times*, 12 March 1927, 7.

58. *Midland Daily Telegraph*, 28 February 1927, 2.

59. *Manchester Guardian*, 5 March 1927, 11.

60. *New York Sun*, 12 March 1927, 8.

61. *New York Sun*, 19 March 1927, 8.

62. *Liverpool Echo*, 8 March 1927, 1.

63. *Evening Standard*, 1 March 1927, 10.

64. Miles Mander, "Who Made the First British Talkie?," *Film Weekly*, 13 May 1929, 7.

65. Alfred Hitchcock, "How a Talking Film Is Made," *Film Weekly*, 18 November 1929, 16. Repr. *HoH 2*.

66. *Film Daily*, 23 February 1927, 1.

67. *Observer*, 6 October 1940, 10.

68. *New York Evening Post*, 22 January 1927, V10.

69. *Variety*, 31 March 1926, 38.

70. Pauline Kael, "Raising Kane—I," *New Yorker*, 20 February 1970, 52.

71. Michael Balcon, *Michael Balcon Presents . . . A Lifetime of Films* (London: Hutchinson, 1969), 30.

72. Allen Eyles (ed.), "The Autobiographical Notes of Alfred Davis, Showman," *Picture House*, no. 30, 2005, 14.

73. John Russell Taylor, *The Rise and Fall of the Well-Made Play* (London: Methuen, 1967), 137.

74. *Manchester Guardian*, 27 March 1927, 12.

75. Mycroft, *Time of My Life*, 33.

76. *Daily Mail*, 24 January 1929, 16.

77. François Truffaut, with Helen G. Scott, *Hitchcock* (New York: Simon & Schuster, 1967), 58.

78. Donald Spoto, *The Life of Alfred Hitchcock: The Dark Side of Genius* (London: Collins, 1983), 392.

CHAPTER 8. WILSHIRE PALMS

1. David Thomson, *Showman: The Life of David O. Selznick* (London: André Deutsch, 1993), 193.

2. *Observer*, 17 November 1935, 13.

3. *New York Sun*, 6 November 1935, 32.

4. *Variety*, 4 April 1928, 43.

5. *New York Sun*, 27 October 1926, 19.

6. *Variety*, 13 July 1927, 20.

7. *Chicago Daily Tribune*, 9 November 1927, 39.

8. *Variety*, 6 June 1928, 8.

9. *New York Times*, 11 June 1928, 27.

10. Peter Bogdanovich, *Who the Devil Made It* (New York: Alfred A. Knopf, 1997), 486.

11. *New York Herald Tribune*, 11 June 1928, 10.

12. *Variety*, 13 June 1928, 12.

13. *New York Times*, 24 November 1929, X8.

14. Seymour Stern, "Hollywood Bulletin," *Experimental Cinema*, no. 2, June 1930, 13.

15. *Film Daily*, 7 December 1930, 1.

16. *Motion Picture Daily*, 28 May 1935, 4.

17. *Motion Picture Daily*, 1 June 1934, 13.

18. *Motion Picture Daily*, 4 August 1934, 1.

19. *Motion Picture Daily*, 26 October 1934, 1.

20. *Motion Picture Daily*, 8 November 1934, 4.

21. *Film Daily*, 16 February 1935, 1.

22. *Motion Picture Daily*, 3 April 1935, 12.

23. *Variety*, 3 April 1935, 17.

24. *Film Daily*, 4 April 1935, 11.

25. *Film Daily*, 13 April 1935, 3.

26. *Philadelphia Inquirer*, 13 May 1956, 31.

27. *Variety*, 15 May 1935, 8.

28. BFI: Michael Balcon Special Collection, MEB-1126: Letter from Arthur Lee to Mark Ostrer, 19 September 1935.

29. *New York Sun*, 19 October 1935, 7.

30. *New York Times*, 4 December 1935, 26.

31. *Motion Picture Herald*, 28 December 1935, 16.

32. *New York Times*, 22 December 1935, X7.

33. *Motion Picture Herald*, 28 December 1935, 16.

34. *New York Times*, 2 January 1936, 21.

35. François Truffaut, with Helen G. Scott, *Hitchcock* (New York: Simon & Schuster, 1967), 90.

36. BFI: Adrian Brunel Special Collection, Box 206: Letter from MacPhail to Brunel, 2 November 1936.

37. *New York Times*, 28 March 1937, X3.

38. *Los Angeles Times*, 27 March 1937, I, 10.

39. *Variety*, 25 August 1937, 4.

40. *New York Sun*, 6 November 1935, 32.

41. *New York Sun*, 1 September 1937, 26.

42. *New York Sun*, 15 June 1938, 26.

43. Alfred Hitchcock, "The Men Behind the Stars—3: I Met These Stars in Hollywood," *Evening News*, 29 July 1938, 4. Repr. in *Hitchcock Annual*, vol. 22, 2018.

44. Alfred Hitchcock, "The Men Behind the Stars—1: Hollywood's Big Uncles," *Evening News*, 27 July 1938, 2. Repr. in *Hitchcock Annual*, vol. 22, 2018.

45. Hitchcock, "I Met These Stars in Hollywood," 4.

46. *Los Angeles Times*, 12 July 1938, B15.

47. *Los Angeles Examiner*, 7 July 1938, 11.

48. Alfred Hitchcock, "In the Hall of Mogul Kings," *The Times*, 23 June 1969, Movies supp., I. Repr. in *HoH 1*.

49. Hitchcock, "Hollywood's Big Uncles," 2.

50. *Los Angeles Examiner*, 25 July 1938, 9.

51. *New York Times*, 25 July 1938, 18; *Film Daily*, 6 August 1938, 3.

52. Thomson, *Showman*, 274.

53. Hitchcock, "I Met These Stars in Hollywood," 4.

54. Cedric Belfrage, *Promised Land* (London: Victor Gollancz, 1938), 157.

55. Ibid., 206.

56. *Los Angeles Examiner*, 7 January 1941, 11.

57. *Los Angeles Examiner*, 13 May 1940, 11.

58. LOC: CBS Radio Scripts, Box 43: *The Lodger* as Broadcast.

59. HRC: David O. Selznick Collection, Legal series, Box 926, Folder 8: Memo from Selznick to O'Shea, 31 July 1940. All subsequent references are from the same folder.

60. HRC: Memo from Selznick to O'Shea, 10 October 1940.

61. HRC: Memo from Kay Brown to Selznick, 30 October 1940.

62. HRC: Memo from Selznick to O'Shea, 4 December 1940.

63. HRC: Memo from Selznick to O'Shea and Val Lewton, 13 January 1941.

64. *Los Angeles Times*, 23 February 1941, III, 3.

65. *Los Angeles Times*, 2 March 1941, III, 3.

66. *Los Angeles Times*, 21 July 1941, 11.

67. Christina Lane, *Phantom Lady: Hollywood Producer Joan Harrison, The Forgotten Woman Behind Hitchcock* (Chicago: Chicago Review Press, 2020), 127.

68. HRC: Letter from Donald A. Dewar to Robert C. McCann, 17 March 1943.

69. HRC: Cable from O'Shea to Reissar, 1 April 1943.

70. HRC: Cable from Reissar to O'Shea, 3 May 1943.

71. *Los Angeles Times*, 2 March 1943, II, 9.

72. MoMA: Department of Film Archive, A-01: Letter from Reville to Barry, 24 June 1939.

73. Harry Alan Towers and Leslie Mitchell, *The March of the Movies* (London: Sampson Low, Marston, 1947), 34.

74. Peter Wollen, "Hitch: A Tale of Two Cities (London and Los Angeles)," in *Paris Hollywood: Writings on Film* (London: Verso, 2002), 69.

75. Ibid., 67, 72.

76. Paul Mayersberg, *Hollywood: The Haunted House* (London: Allen Lane The Penguin Press, 1967), 183.

77. Penelope Gilliatt, "The London Hitch," *New Yorker*, 11 September 1971, 91.

78. François Truffaut, with the collaboration of Helen G. Scott, *Hitchcock*, rev. ed. (New York: Simon & Schuster Paperbacks, 1984), 338.

79. Raymond Durgnat, *The Strange Case of Alfred Hitchcock* (London: Faber and Faber, 1974), 396.

Bibliography

Allen, Richard. "*The Lodger* and the Origins of Hitchcock's Aesthetic." *Hitchcock Annual* 10 (2001–2): 38–78.

Anderson, Lindsay. *Never Apologise: The Collected Writings*. London: Plexus, 2004.

Balcon, Michael. *Michael Balcon Presents . . . A Lifetime of Films*. London: Hutchinson, 1969.

Barr, Charles. "Before *Blackmail*: Silent British Cinema." In *The British Cinema Book*, edited by Robert Murphy, 5–16. London: British Film Institute, 1997.

———. *English Hitchcock*. Moffat, UK: Cameron and Hollis, 1999.

———. "Hitchcock and Early Filmmakers." In *A Companion to Alfred Hitchcock*, edited by Thomas Leitch and Leland Poague, 48–66. Chichester, UK: Wiley-Blackwell, 2011.

———. "Writing Screen Plays: Stannard and Hitchcock." In *Young and Innocent? The Cinema in Britain 1896*–1930, edited by Andrew Higson, 227–41. Exeter, UK: University of Exeter Press, 2002.

Barr, Charles, and Alain Kerzoncuf. *Hitchcock Lost and Found: The Forgotten Films*. Lexington: University Press of Kentucky, 2015.

Barry, Iris. *Let's Go to the Pictures*. London: Chatto and Windus, 1926.

Bogdanovich, Peter. *The Cinema of Alfred Hitchcock*. New York: Museum of Modern Art Film Library, 1963.

———. *Who the Devil Made It*. New York: Alfred A. Knopf, 1997.

Bordwell, David. "Alfred Hitchcock's *Notorious*." *Film Heritage* 4, no. 3 (Spring 1969): 6–10, 22.

Bordwell, David, Janet Staiger, and Kristin Thompson. *The Classical Hollywood Cinema: Film Style and Mode of Production to 1960*. London: Routledge & Kegan Paul, 1985.

Brunel, Adrian. *Nice Work: The Story of Thirty Years in British Film Production*. London: Forbes Robertson, 1949.

Burrows, Jon. *The British Cinema Boom, 1909–1914: A Commercial History*. London: Palgrave Macmillan, 2017.

Campbell, Russell. *Codename Intelligentsia: The Life and Times of the Honourable Ivor Montagu, Filmmaker, Communist, Spy*. Stroud, UK: The History Press, 2018.

Chapman, Gary. *London's Hollywood: The Gainsborough Studio in the Silent Years*. Edditt Publishing, 2014.

Condell, Caitlin, and Emily M. Orr. *E. McKnight Kauffer: The Artist in Advertising*. New York: Rizzoli Electa and Cooper Hewitt, 2020.

Dickinson, Margaret, and Sarah Street. *Cinema and State: The Film Industry and the Government, 1927–84*. London: British Film Institute, 1985.

Durgnat, Raymond. "The Business of Fear." *Hitchcock*. Special supplement to *Sight and Sound* (August 1999): 2–11.

———. *The Strange Case of Alfred Hitchcock*. London: Faber and Faber, 1974.

Gomery, Douglas. *Shared Pleasures: A History of Movie Presentation in the United States*. London: British Film Institute, 1992.

Gottlieb, Sidney (ed.). *Alfred Hitchcock Interviews*. Jackson: University Press of Mississippi, 2003.

———, (ed.). *Hitchcock on Hitchcock*. Vol. 1. Berkeley: University of California Press, 1995.

———, (ed.). *Hitchcock on Hitchcock*. Vol. 2. Oakland: University of California Press, 2015.

Herrmann, Bernard. "Bernard Herrmann, Composer." In *Sound and the Cinema: The Coming of Sound to American Film*, edited by Evan William Cameron, 117–35. Pleasantville, NY: Redgrave Publishing Company, 1980.

Hitchcock, Alfred. "The Men Behind the Stars." *Hitchcock Annual* 22 (2018): 82–96.

Hitchcock O'Connell, Pat, and Laurent Bouzereau. *Alma Hitchcock: The Woman Behind the Man*. New York: Berkley Books, 2003.

June. *The Glass Ladder*. London: Heinemann, 1960.

Kapsis, Robert E. *Hitchcock: The Making of a Reputation*. Chicago: University of Chicago Press, 1992.

Koszarski, Richard. *The Rivals of D. W. Griffith: Alternative Auteurs, 1913–1918*. Minneapolis, MN: Walker Art Center, 1976.

Kreimeier, Klaus. *The Ufa Story: A History of Germany's Greatest Film Company, 1918–1945*. Translated by Robert and Rita Kimber. New York: Hill and Wang, 1996.

Lambert, Gavin. *The Dangerous Edge*. London: Barrie & Jenkins, 1975.

———. *Mainly about Lindsay Anderson*. London: Faber and Faber, 2000.

Lane, Christina. *Phantom Lady: Hollywood Producer Joan Harrison, The Forgotten Woman behind Hitchcock*. Chicago: Chicago Review Press, 2020.

Lejeune, C. A. *Thank You for Having Me*. London: Hutchinson, 1964.

Low, Rachael. *The History of the British Film, 1918–1929*. London: George Allen & Unwin, 1971.

Lowndes, Mrs. Belloc. *The Lodger*. London: Methuen, 1913.

Maclaren-Ross, Julian, *Bitten by the Tarantula and Other Writing*. London: Black Spring Press, 2005.

McBride, Joseph. "Alfred Hitchcock's *Mary Rose*: An Old Master's Unheard *Cri de Coeur*." *Cineaste* 26, no. 2 (March 2001): 24–28.

McGilligan, Patrick. *Alfred Hitchcock: A Life in Darkness and Light*. Chichester, UK: Wiley, 2003.

Miller, Henry K. "Nobody Walks: Hitchcock's First Impressions of Hollywood." *Hitchcock Annual* 22 (2018): 74–81.

———. "Papa du Cinema." *Sight and Sound* (March 2016): 36–41.

———. "The Shaping of Alfred Hitchcock." In *39 Steps to the Genius of Hitchcock*, edited by James Bell, 10–15. London: British Film Institute, 2012.

———. "Sympathetic Guidance: Hitchcock and C. A. Lejeune." *Hitchcock Annual* 20 (2015): 33–64.

Montagu, Ivor. "Birmingham Sparrow: In Memoriam, Iris Barry, 1896–1969." *Sight and Sound* (Spring 1970): 106–8.

———. "Michael Balcon, 1896–1977." *Sight and Sound* (Winter 1977–78): 9–11.

———. "Old Man's Mumble: Reflections on a Semi-Centenary." *Sight and Sound* (Autumn 1975): 220–24, 247.

———. *With Eisenstein in Hollywood*. Berlin: Seven Seas, 1968.

———. "Working With Hitchcock." *Sight and Sound* (Summer 1980): 189–93.

———. *The Youngest Son: Autobiographical Sketches*. London: Lawrence and Wishart, 1970.

Moorehead, Caroline. *Sidney Bernstein: A Biography*. London: Jonathan Cape, 1984.

Morris, Nathalie. "The Early Career of Alma Reville." *Hitchcock Annual* 15 (2006–7): 1–31.

Mycroft, Walter C. *The Time of My Life*. Lanham, MD: The Scarecrow Press, 2006.

Noble, Peter. *An Index to the Work of Alfred Hitchcock*, Special Supplement to *Sight and Sound*, no. 18 (May 1949).

———. *Ivor Novello: Man of the Theatre*. London: The Falcon Press, 1951.

Reville, Alma. "Cutting and Continuity." *Hitchcock Annual* 15 (2006–7): 32–34.

Rothman, William. *Hitchcock: The Murderous Gaze*. Cambridge, MA: Harvard University Press, 1982.

Schickel, Richard. *The Men Who Made the Movies*. New York: Atheneum, 1975.

Sitton, Robert. *Lady in the Dark: Iris Barry and the Art of Film*. New York: Columbia University Press, 2014.

Sloan, Jane E. *Alfred Hitchcock: A Filmography and Bibliography*. Berkeley: University of California Press, 1995.

Spoto, Donald. *The Life of Alfred Hitchcock: The Dark Side of Genius*. London: Collins, 1983.

Taylor, John Russell, *Hitch: The Life and Work of Alfred Hitchcock*. London: Faber and Faber, 1978.

Thomson, David. *Showman: The Life of David O. Selznick*. London: André Deutsch, 1993.

Thompson, Kristin. *Exporting Entertainment: America in the World Film Market, 1907–1934*. London: British Film Institute, 1985.

Truffaut, François, with Helen G. Scott. *Hitchcock*. 1967; rev. ed. New York: Simon & Schuster, 1984.

Usborne, Richard. *Clubland Heroes: A Nostalgic Study of Some Recurrent Characters in the Romantic Fiction of Dornford Yates, John Buchan and Sapper*. London: Constable, 1953.

Vest, James M. *Hitchcock and France: The Forging of an Auteur*. Westport, CT: Praeger, 2003.

Williams, Michael. *Ivor Novello: Screen Idol*. London: British Film Institute, 2003.

Wilson, H. D. "Hitchcock in Hollywood: An Interim Report: 1939–46." *Film Miscellany* (Winter 1946–47): 36–41.

Wollen, Peter. "Hitch: A Tale of Two Cities (London and Los Angeles)." In *Paris Hollywood: Writings on Film*. London: Verso, 2002.

———. "Hitchcock's Vision." *Cinema* (Cambridge, UK), no. 3 (June 1969): 2–4.

———. "The Last New Wave: Modernism in the British Films of the Thatcher Era." In *British Cinema and Thatcherism: Fires Were Started*, edited by Lester Friedman, 35–51. London: UCL Press, 1993.

———. "*Rope*: Three Hypotheses." In *Alfred Hitchcock: Centenary Essays*, edited by Richard Allen and S. Ishi-Gonzales, 75–85. London: British Film Institute, 1999.

Wollen, Peter, Alan Lovell, and Sam Rohdie. "Ivor Montagu." *Screen* 13, no. 3 (1972): 71–113.

Index

Ackland, Rodney, 32, 61–62
Ainley, Henry, 49, 52, 156
Allen, Richard, 43–44
Anderson, Lindsay, 33–34, 37, 40
Anderson, Maxwell, 23, 176
Astaire, Fred, 97, 180
Atkinson, G. A., 3, 16, 71, 93, 104–5, 113
Ault, Marie, 84

Balcon, Michael, 6, 17, 42, 68–69, 71–75, 78,
    102–4, 105, 108–14, 116, 119–24, 128, 130,
    167, 168–69, 173, 177, 179, 187–88, 190
Barnato, "Babe," 112, 125
Barnato, Barney, 111–12, 172
Barnato, Leah, 111–12
Barr, Charles, 44–45, 57, 67, 78, 139
Barrie, J. M., 7, 45, 65–66
Barry, Iris, 2–3, 7, 9, 13, 18–20, 19*fig.*, 22, 32,
    39, 41, 43, 52–53, 56, 71–72, 83, 85, 88, 89,
    92, 93–94, 97, 104, 127, 130, 131, 157–58,
    159, 165, 167, 172, 179, 199
Bass, Saul, 127
Bazin, André, 20–21, 61, 107
BBC, xii*map*, 11, 97, 171
Belfrage, Cedric, 3–4, 6, 17, 86, 111, 123, 157;
    Promised Land, 193
Belloc, Hilaire, 14, 56, 57, 162

Bennett, Charles, 192
Bergman, Ingrid, 191, 194
Bernstein, Sidney, 68, 75, 159, 178
Big Parade, The, 104–6, 124, 125, 164, 172, 176
Blackwell, Carlyle, 110–12, 114, 116–17, 126
Bogdanovich, Peter, 64, 67, 92, 116, 128, 131,
    156
British Film Institute, 28–30, 31–34, 44
British International Pictures, 103, 114–15,
    161, 164–65, 166–69, 178–79, 181, 185
British National Pictures. *See* British Interna-
    tional Pictures
Brunel, Adrian, 40, 43, 69, 72, 74–76, 92, 112,
    119–25, 189
Buchan, John, 46–47, 57–58, 71; *Hunting-
    tower*, 114, 118, 161

Cahiers du cinéma, 20, 36–37
Caine, Hall, 52, 65, 108
Capitol cinema, xii*map*, 5, 83, 92–94, 94*fig.*,
    121, 131, 157–59, 169, 172, 177, 194
Carroll, Madeleine, 175, 186
Chabrol, Claude, 9, 25–26, 37
Chaplin, Charlie, 29, 52, 60, 76, 108, 127, 183
Chesterton, G. K., 11–12, 14, 45, 46, 56, 148–49
Christie, Agatha, 147
Churchill, Winston, 13, 99

Cinematograph Films Act 1927. *See* Quota Act
Cobham, Alan, 13, 161
Codd, Elsie, 64–65, 67
Collier, Constance, 6, 72, 125
color, introduction of, 87, 90–91, 93, 172
Compson, Betty, 68, 72
Cooke, Alistair, 28–29, 30
Corelli, Marie, 79; *The Sorrows of Satan*, 62–64, 164
Coward, Noël, 7, 178
Cox, Anthony Berkeley, 147, 149
Creelman, Eileen, 181, 187–91
Cunliffe-Lister, Molly, 100, 177
Cunliffe-Lister, Philip, 16, 100, 167, 173
Cutts, Graham, 6, 51–52, 67–69, 72–76, 102–3, 108, 110, 116, 123, 129–30; *The Blackguard*, 73–76, 86, 102; *Flames of Passion*, 67, 90; *The Passionate Adventure*, 72, 73, 76, 102; *The Prude's Fall*, 74–76, 86, 102, 159; *The Rat*, 6, 17, 72, 75, 102, 104, 159–60; *The Sea Urchin*, 102, 109, 121–22; *The Triumph of the Rat*, 118, 125, 160; *Woman to Woman*, 68, 70–71, 72, 73

Dane, Clemence, 46, 148
Dansey Yard, xii*map*, 69, 74, 76, 119–25, 122*fig.*
Davis family, 52–53, 68, 71, 73, 105, 169, 171, 177–78
Davy, Charles, 26, 27, 29
De Forest Phonofilm, 87–90, 98–99, 157–59, 169, 175–76
DeMille, Cecil B., 4, 55, 65, 66; *The Unafraid*, 52; *The Volga Boatman*, 93
De Palma, Brian, 38*fig.*
Dickinson, Thorold, 26, 27, 29
di Ventimiglia, Gaetano, 86
Dostoyevsky, Fyodor, 8–9
Doyle, Arthur Conan, 11, 46, 70; Sherlock Holmes, 148–49, 181

Eisenstein, Sergei, 43–44, 124–25; *Battleship Potemkin*, 183
Eliot, T. S., ix, 43, 45, 46
Elvey, Maurice, 55, 64; *The Lodger* (1932), 27; *Mademoiselle from Armentières*, 160, 164
Elwell, Cyril, 87–88, 99, 157–58
Entr'acte, 89

Fairbanks, Douglas, 60; *The Black Pirate*, 90–91
Famous Players-Lasky. *See* Paramount
Farber, Manny, 31

Fawcett, L'Estrange, 106, 115, 163–64
Ferguson, Otis, 30–31, 189
Film Society, 8–9, 18, 25–26, 27, 28, 31, 41, 42–44, 69, 73–76, 83, 89, 92, 106, 121, 127, 184
First National, 60, 93, 102–4, 107–8, 172
Fontaine, Joan, 194–95, 196
Ford, John, 189; *3 Bad Men*, 157; *The Informer*, 189; *The Iron Horse*, 93; *The World Moves On*, 186
Fox Films, 54, 61, 99, 104, 107–8, 176, 186–87, 198
Freud, Sigmund, 12–13, 21–22
Fry, Roger, 126–27

Gainsborough Pictures, 6–8, 17, 72–75
Galsworthy, John, 26, 28, 45, 46, 57, 66, 67
Garbo, Greta, 5, 29, 107, 157, 172, 180, 189
Gaumont-British Picture Corporation, 53, 72–73, 113, 177–79, 181, 185–87, 189–90
Gaumont Film Company. *See* Gaumont-British Picture Corporation
General Strike, 100–101, 161
Gershwin, George, 97–98, 171, 172
Gish, Dorothy, 103, 164, 166
Godard, Jean-Luc, 36*fig.*
Graham-Cutts, Jack. *See* Cutts, Graham
Greenwood, Edwin, 69, 78, 92, 119
Grierson, John, 175, 183
Griffith, D. W., 56–57, 60, 105, 129, 164, 174; *The Avenging Conscience*, 59; *Broken Blossoms*, 10, 65; *The White Rose*, 172

Hall-Davies, Lillian, 175
Harman, A. Jympson, 1, 95–96
Harrison, Frederick, 49, 80
Harrison, Joan, 173, 190, 195–97, 196*fig.*
Hays, Will, 109
Hecht, Ben, 176–77, 189
Herrmann, Bernard, 98, 172, 194
Hitchcock, Alfred: apprenticeship at Famous Players-Lasky, ix, 3–4, 62–67, 180–81; attempt to remake *The Lodger*, ix, 193–98; career at British International Pictures, 114, 118, 165, 166, 178–79; career at Gainsborough, 6, 67–68; career at Gaumont-British, 179, 189–90; engagement and marriage, 3, 166; first visit to United States, 30, 149, 189–90; images of, 2*fig.*, 96*fig.*, 196*fig.*; move to Hollywood, ix, 22–23, 39, 56, 199–200; production of *The Lodger*, 1–3, 23–24, 39–40, 77, 83–86, 95–96, 99, 115–28; rehiring by

Gainsborough, 166, 168–69; second visit to United States, ix, 30, 190–93; "Ten Favorite Pictures," 66, 71, 94, 127; time in Germany, 73, 75–77; views on aesthetics, 21–22, 46, 51, 56–57, 62, 86–87, 88, 91, 130, 134, 148–50, 160–61, 171–72, 181; youth, ix, 3, 10, 50–51, 58–59, 64

Hitchcock, Alfred, films: *Blackmail*, 26, 29, 32, 175, 176, 184–85, 196; *Champagne*, 131; *Downhill*, 29, 125, 168, 175; *Easy Virtue*, 178; *The Farmer's Wife*, 7, 181; *Foreign Correspondent*, 14, 32, 194; *Frenzy*, 201; *I Confess*, 37; *Jamaica Inn*, 57, 78, 190; *Juno and the Paycock*, 7; *The Lady Vanishes*, 21, 29, 149, 154; *Lifeboat*, 31, 39, 108, 198; *The Man Who Knew Too Much*, 23, 28, 30, 47, 179, 180, 187–88; *The Manxman*, 52; *The Mountain Eagle*, 3, 42, 76–77, 102, 109, 155, 159–60; *Mr. and Mrs. Smith*, 193, 197; *Murder*, 26, 28, 139, 148, 185; *North by Northwest*, 179; *Notorious*, 151; *Number Seventeen*, 27, 32; *Number Thirteen*, 67, 121; *The Pleasure Garden*, 3, 42, 75–76, 78, 91–94, 102, 123, 141, 159–60, 164–65, 172; *Psycho*, 133, 139, 141, 150; *Rear Window*, 23, 62, 140, 141–43, 151, 154; *Rebecca*, 23, 37, 57, 58, 62, 63, 105, 137, 139, 154, 194, 200; *Rich and Strange*, 7; *The Ring*, 26, 178; *Rope*, 123, 139, 197; *Sabotage*, 10–11, 50–51, 139; *Saboteur*, 190, 197; *Secret Agent*, 181, 189; *Shadow of a Doubt*, 35, 198–99, 200; *The Skin Game*, 26, 28, 32, 185; *Spellbound*, 154; *Stage Fright*, 139, 158; *Strangers on a Train*, 139, 145; *Suspicion*, 149–50, 196–97; *The 39 Steps*, 23, 28, 138, 180, 186–89; *Under Capricorn*, 37, 158; *Vertigo*, 58, 137, 141, 142*fig.*, 151, 154, 155*fig.*; *Waltzes from Vienna*, 187; *Young and Innocent*, 91

Hopper, Hedda, 39, 191–92
Hugenberg, Alfred, 15, 178

Iles, Francis. *See* Cox, Anthony Berkeley
Ingram, Rex, 71, 77, 106–7, 119, 178; *The Magician*, 163, 172; *Scaramouche*, 141

June (Tripp), 7–8, 81, 85, 95–96, 96*fig.*, 112, 125, 146*fig.*

Kauffer, E. McKnight, 40, 126–27, 169–71
Kaufman, Al, 5, 61, 63
Keaton, Buster, 169, 172

Keen, Malcolm, 96*fig.*, 155, 169
Kent, Sidney, 16, 186
Keynes, John Maynard, 8, 13, 99–100, 109

Laemmle, Carl, 16, 54
Lambert, Gavin, 32–34, 40, 46, 81
Lang, Fritz, 31–32, 47; *Destiny*, 32, 71–72, 73, 141; *Dr. Mabuse*, 47, 70, 73; *M*, 32, 187; *Metropolis*, 17, 161, 168, 169
Lapworth, Charles, 108–10, 115, 126, 127
Lasky, Jesse, 4, 55
Lee, Arthur A., 102, 104, 159–60, 181, 184, 186, 188
Lejeune, C. A., 18, 21, 26, 27, 28, 70, 71–72, 83, 87–88, 90–91, 141, 158–59, 174, 176, 180–81, 197
Leni, Paul, 18, 127; *Waxworks*, 76–77
Levy, Louis, 158, 171
Levy, Sol, 129–30, 159, 173, 175
L'Herbier, Marcel, 92
Lime Grove. *See* Shepherd's Bush studio
Lindgren, Ernest, 26–30, 32
Lloyd, Harold, viii, 68, 74, 112, 124
Lodger, The (1944), 31, 198
Loew, Marcus, 60, 108, 110
Lombard, Carole, 191–92, 193
Low, Rachael, 41–42
Lowndes, Marie Belloc, 9, 11, 46, 49, 56, 57, 71, 79–81, 85, 148–49, 154, 174, 194–95, 198. *See also* Vachell, Horace Annesley
Lubitsch, Ernest, 5, 17, 18, 69–70, 75, 159, 165; *The Shop Around the Corner*, 192

Maclaren-Ross, Julian, 34–35, 47–48, 139
MacPhail, Angus, 97–98, 123, 127–28, 155, 179, 189–90
Mamoulian, Rouben, 91, 191, 197
Mander, Miles, 27, 75–76, 169, 175–76
Mankiewicz, Herman, 4–5, 18, 172, 176
Marble Arch Pavilion, xii*map*, 52–53, 71, 73, 169–71, 170*fig.*, 177
Marsh, Mae, 6, 67, 72, 104
Maxwell, John, 168, 173, 178–79, 190
Mayersberg, Paul, 62, 200
Metro. *See* MGM
Metro-Goldwyn-Mayer. *See* MGM
Meynell, Francis, 127, 152
MGM, 4, 5, 16, 53, 60, 68, 71, 77, 93, 104–7, 108, 172, 178, 180, 190, 191
Mindlin, Michael, 182–85
Montagu, Ivor, vii–viii, 27, 40–45, 69, 75, 91, 92, 97, 100–101, 105, 106, 119–28, 131, 133, 140, 143, 155, 179, 188, 190

Murnau, F. W., 73; *The Last Laugh*, 73, 83, 85, 93, 168; *Phantom*, 73, 131; *Sunrise*, 165
Museum of Modern Art, 32, 37, 41, 56, 130, 199
Mycroft, Walter, 2, 9, 17, 24, 69–70, 73, 74, 75–77, 82–83, 85–87, 89, 92, 99, 100–101, 114, 121, 124, 126, 152, 158, 159, 161, 164–65, 169–71, 171–72, 175, 178–79

Naldi, Nita, 76–77
Nevinson, C. R. W., 64, 82
New Gallery cinema, xii*map*, 8, 16, 17, 23, 52, 70, 94, 106, 112, 172
Noble, Peter, 40–41
Novello, Ivor, 6–9, 27, 40, 69, 72, 79, 81, 84, 85, 95, 97, 116, 125, 136*fig.*, 139, 146*fig.*, 153*fig.*, 156, 168, 174

Ostrer family, 72, 177, 186, 188

Paramount, 4–5, 16, 17, 23, 52, 53, 54, 55, 59–61, 62–67, 93, 103, 104, 107–8, 111, 112, 164, 166–67, 173, 177, 178, 191
Parsons, Louella O., 107, 164, 191–92, 194–97
Pickford, Mary, ix, 60, 165
Picture of Dorian Gray, The, 137
Pinero, Arthur Wing, 63, 66
Plaza cinema, xii*map*, 5–6, 17, 23, 52, 93, 103, 112, 172
Poe, Edgar Allan, 58–59, 73, 83, 137, 147, 152–54
Pommer, Erich, 17, 73–74, 172, 190
Poole Street studio, xii*map*, 4, 6, 17, 62–68, 63*fig.*, 72, 74–75, 79, 83–86, 95–96, 103, 112, 125, 175, 183
Powell, Dilys, 31–32
Praz, Mario, 139

Quota Act, 16, 17, 71, 100, 104, 109, 113–14, 115, 121, 167–68, 177–78

Renoir, Jean, 20
Reville, Alma, vii–viii, 3, 6, 8, 32, 52, 64, 65, 67, 68–70, 73–74, 75, 84, 115, 123, 125, 128, 132, 166, 173, 174, 175, 190, 191, 195, 199
Rhodes, Cecil, 13, 111
RKO, 176, 180, 187, 193–94, 197
Robertson, John S., 65–66, 76–77
Rohmer, Eric, 25–26, 36, 37
Rotha, Paul, 26–27, 41
Rózsa, Miklós, 98
Ruttmann, Walter, 76; *Berlin: Symphony of a Great City*, 131, 183

Saville, Victor, 68–69, 72, 130, 160; *I Was a Spy*, 186
Sayers, Dorothy, 147–48
Schickel, Richard, 38, 67, 86–87
Schlesinger, I. W., 115, 166, 167, 178
Seldes, Gilbert, 18, 21
Selznick, David O., 62, 65, 180, 191–92, 193–98
Selznick, Lewis J., 54, 71–73
Selznick, Myron, 66, 72, 102, 191–93, 193–96, 198
Seton, Marie, 29
Shaw, G. B., 8, 45, 65, 169; *Pygmalion*, 154
Shepherd's Bush Pavilion, 73, 74, 93, 158, 173, 177
Shepherd's Bush studio, 53, 177, 181
Sherwood, Robert E., 17–18, 23, 176, 189
Sjöström, Victor, 5, 108
sound, introduction of, 86–90, 97–99, 157–59, 169, 175–77
Spoto, Donald, viii, 42
Stannard, Eliot, 55–56, 67, 69, 78–81, 82*fig.*
Stevenson, R. S., 47; *Strange Case of Dr. Jekyll and Mr. Hyde*, 77, 137
Stiller, Mauritz, 5, 107, 172
Street, The, 86, 135

Taylor, John Russell, 42, 64, 66, 73, 152, 178
television, development of, 161–62
Thalberg, Irving, 105–7, 192
Tiomkin, Dimitri, 98
Tivoli cinema, xii*map*, 25, 71, 72, 74, 82, 89, 90, 91, 93, 97–98, 104–5, 106, 172
Tourneur, Maurice, 55, 71, 107, 172; *The Wishing Ring*, 53
Trilby, 145, 154
Truffaut, François, 5–6, 8, 9, 20–21, 22, 23, 25, 36–37, 38–40, 46, 58, 62, 63–64, 71, 73, 87, 88, 116, 128, 130, 132, 148, 156, 189, 200–201
Twentieth Century-Fox. *See* Fox Films

Ufa, 16–17, 73, 168, 178
Universal, 16, 51, 54, 93, 108, 197
Usborne, Richard, 47

Vachell, Horace Annesley, 49, 80, 198; *Who is He?*, 49, 51, 55, 56, 67, 77, 80–81, 132, 156, 198
Valentino, Rudolph, 5, 77, 103, 160
Van Damm, Vivian, 88, 93, 157–58, 169
Vaudeville, 94–95, 168
Vaughan, Olwen, 28, 31–32

W. & F., xii*map*, 40–42, 68, 72, 73–75, 92, 93,
    103, 110, 112–13, 115–19, 117*fig.*, 128, 169–
    70, 177
Warner Brothers, 5, 72, 98, 108, 112–13, 158, 176
Warning Shadows, 82–83
Waxman, Franz, 98
Wells, H. G., 8, 12, 45, 50, 79, 161–63
What Price Glory, 108, 165, 176
Whiteman, Paul, 97–98, 103, 104
Wiene, Robert, 8; *The Cabinet of Dr. Caligari*,
    8, 20, 21, 73, 83, 141, 171; *Crime and Pun-
    ishment*, 8–9; *Rosenkavalier*, 97

Wilcox, Herbert, 67–68, 103, 130, 164–65,
    166
Williams, J. D., 60, 103, 115, 161, 164–65, 166,
    181, 184, 186
Wilson, Harry, 40, 74
Winnington, Richard, 31
Woolf, C. M., vii, 40, 68, 110, 112–14, 116, 177
Wollen, Peter, viii–ix, 42–43, 44, 45, 200
Wordsworth, William, 1, 201
Wright, Willard Huntington, 147–48

Zukor, Adolph, 4, 5, 54, 60, 191

Founded in 1893,
UNIVERSITY OF CALIFORNIA PRESS
publishes bold, progressive books and journals
on topics in the arts, humanities, social sciences,
and natural sciences—with a focus on social
justice issues—that inspire thought and action
among readers worldwide.

The UC PRESS FOUNDATION
raises funds to uphold the press's vital role
as an independent, nonprofit publisher, and
receives philanthropic support from a wide
range of individuals and institutions—and from
committed readers like you. To learn more, visit
ucpress.edu/supportus.